Practical Mobile Forensics
Fourth Edition

Forensically investigate and analyze iOS, Android, and
Windows 10 devices

Rohit Tamma
Oleg Skulkin
Heather Mahalik
Satish Bommisetty

BIRMINGHAM - MUMBAI

Practical Mobile Forensics
Fourth Edition

Copyright © 2020 Packt Publishing

Commissioning Editor: Vijin Boricha
Acquisition Editor: Rohit Rajkumar
Content Development Editor: Ronn Kurien
Senior Editor: Rahul Dsouza
Technical Editor: Dinesh Pawar
Copy Editor: Safis Editing
Project Coordinator: Vaidehi Sawant
Proofreader: Safis Editing
Indexer: Rekha Nair
Production Designer: Deepika Naik

First published: July 2014
Second edition: May 2016
Third edition: January 2018
Fourth edition: April 2020

Production reference: 1090420

Published by Packt Publishing Ltd.
Livery Place
35 Livery Street
Birmingham
B3 2PB, UK.

ISBN 978-1-83864-752-0

www.packt.com

Contributors

About the authors

Rohit Tamma is a senior program manager currently working with Microsoft. With over 10 years of experience in the field of security, his background spans management and technical consulting roles in the areas of application and cloud security, mobile security, penetration testing, and secure coding. Rohit has also co-authored *Learning Android Forensics, from Packt*, which explain various ways to perform forensics on mobile platforms. You can contact him on Twitter at @RohitTamma.

I want to sincerely thank Satish Bommisetty, my ex-colleague and mentor, who inspired me early in my career and supported me throughout the journey of this book. I also want to thank the Packt team for their continued support and help in taking this book to the fourth edition. And finally, this book is for my parents, to whom I owe everything.

Oleg Skulkin is a senior digital forensic analyst at Group-IB, one of the global leaders in preventing and investigating high-tech crimes and online fraud. He holds a number of certifications, including GCFA, GCTI, and MCFE. Oleg has also co-authored *Windows Forensics Cookbook*, and *Learning Android Forensics, both from Packt*, as well as many blog posts and articles on digital forensics, incident response, and threat hunting that you can find online. You can contact him on Twitter at @oskulkin.

I would like to thank my family and the Group-IB Digital Forensics and Incident Response Team for their love and support, as well as the Packt team and my co-authors for making this book possible.

Packt>

Packt.com

Subscribe to our online digital library for full access to
as industry leading tools to help you plan your personal
career. For more information, please visit our website.

Why subscribe?

- Spend less time learning and more time coding with practi
from over 4,000 industry professionals

- Improve your learning with Skill Plans built especially for you

- Get a free eBook or video every month

- Fully searchable for easy access to vital information

- Copy and paste, print, and bookmark content

Did you know that Packt offers eBook versions of every book published, with PDF and
ePub files available? You can upgrade to the eBook version at www.packt.com and as a print
book customer, you are entitled to a discount on the eBook copy. Get in touch with us at
customercare@packtpub.com for more details.

At www.packt.com, you can also read a collection of free technical articles, sign up for a
range of free newsletters, and receive exclusive discounts and offers on Packt books and
eBooks.

Abou

Rohit Ta
years of
technic
penetr
Foren
You

Heather Mahalik is the senior director of digital intelligence at Cellebrite. She is a senior instructor and author for the SANS Institute, and she is also the course lead for the FOR585 Smartphone Forensic Analysis In-Depth course. With 18 years of experience in digital forensics, she continues to thrive on smartphone investigations, digital forensics, forensic course development and instruction, and research on application analysis and smartphone forensics.

Satish Bommisetty is a security architect currently working with JDA. His primary areas of interest include web and mobile application security, cloud security, and iOS forensics. He has presented at security conferences, such as ClubHACK and C0C0n. Satish is one of the top bug bounty hunters and is listed in the halls of fame of Google, Facebook, PayPal, Microsoft, Yahoo, Salesforce, and more, for identifying and reporting their security vulnerabilities. You can reach him on Twitter at @satishb3.

About the reviewers

Igor Mikhaylov has been working as a forensic examiner for 22 years. During this time, he has attended a lot of seminars and training classes by top digital forensic companies (such as Guidance Software, AccessData, and Cellebrite) and forensic departments of government organizations of the Russian Federation. He has experience and skills in computer forensics, incident response, cell phone forensics, chip-off forensics, malware forensics, data recovery, digital image analysis, video forensics, and big data. He has written three tutorials on cell phone forensics and incident response for Russian forensic examiners.

Detective Chad Prda has served in law enforcement for over 16 years. Throughout his distinguished career he has obtained several certifications, including Advanced Peace Officer, Advanced Interview and Interrogation, and Expert in Mobile Forensics. Detective Prda served on S.W.A.T. for 8 years as a firearms instructor and a lead marksman (sniper).

He later moved into criminal investigations, specializing in social media investigations, mobile forensics, and cellular mapping, as well as testifying in several criminal cases as an expert witness and studying at the United States Secret Service National Computer Forensics Institute.

Packt is searching for authors like you

If you're interested in becoming an author for Packt, please visit authors.packtpub.com and apply today. We have worked with thousands of developers and tech professionals, just like you, to help them share their insight with the global tech community. You can make a general application, apply for a specific hot topic that we are recruiting an author for, or submit your own idea.

Table of Contents

Preface

Mobile phone forensics is the science of retrieving data from a mobile phone under forensically sound conditions. This is the fourth edition of our successful *Practical Mobile Forensics* book that delves into the concepts of mobile forensics and its importance in today's world.

This book focuses on teaching you the latest forensic techniques in the investigation of mobile devices across various mobile platforms. You will learn forensic techniques on multiple OS versions, including iOS 12, iOS 13, Android 9, Android 10, and Windows 10. You will delve into the latest open source and commercial mobile forensic tools, enabling you to analyze and retrieve data effectively. You will learn how to inspect the device, retrieve data from the cloud, and successfully document reports of your investigations. You will explore reverse engineering of applications and ways to identify malware. You will also come across parsing popular third-party applications such as Facebook and WhatsApp.

By the end of this book, you will have mastered various mobile forensic techniques to analyze and extract data from mobile devices with the help of open source solutions.

Who this book is for

This book is intended for forensic examiners with little or only basic experience in mobile forensics or open source solutions for mobile forensics. This book will also be useful for computer security professionals, researchers, and anyone seeking a deeper understanding of mobile internals. Some understanding of digital forensics practices would be helpful.

What this book covers

Chapter 1, *Introduction to Mobile Forensics*, introduces you to the concepts of mobile forensics, its core values, and the challenges involved. This chapter also provides an overview of the practical approaches and best practices involved in performing mobile forensics.

Chapter 2, *Understanding the Internals of iOS Devices*, provides an insight into iOS forensics. You will learn about the filesystem layout, security features, and the way files are stored on an iOS device.

Chapter 3, *Data Acquisition from iOS Devices*, discusses tools that will help you obtain data from iOS devices to later examine forensically. Not all tools are created equal, so it's important to understand the best tools to get the job done properly.

Chapter 4, *Data Acquisition from iOS Backups*, discusses iOS device backup files in detail, including user, forensic, encrypted, and iCloud backup files, and the methods to conduct your forensic examination.

Chapter 5, *iOS Data Analysis and Recovery*, goes further into forensic investigation by showing the examiner how to analyze the data recovered from the backup files. Areas containing data of potential evidentiary value will be explained in detail.

Chapter 6, *iOS Forensic Tools*, for familiarity purposes, walks you through the use of a number of commercial tools, such as Elcomsoft iOS Forensic Toolkit, Cellebrite (UFED4PC, Touch, and Physical Analyzer), BlackLight, Oxygen Forensic Detective, AccessData MPE+, EnCase, Belkasoft Evidence Center, MSAB XRY, and many more, which are available for forensic acquisition and the analysis of iOS devices. This chapter provides details of the processes required to perform acquisitions and analysis of iOS devices.

Chapter 7, *Understanding Android*, introduces the fundamentals of the Android platform, its built-in security features, and its filesystem. This chapter establishes the basic forensic knowledge that will be helpful in the next chapters.

Chapter 8, *Android Forensic Setup and Pre-Data Extraction Techniques*, tells you what to consider when setting up a digital forensic examination environment. Step-by-step information about rooting an Android device and bypassing the screen lock feature is provided in this chapter.

Chapter 9, *Android Data Extraction Techniques*, helps you to identify the sensitive locations on an Android device and explains various logical and physical techniques that can be applied to the device in order to extract the necessary information.

Chapter 10, *Android Data Analysis and Recovery*, explains how to extract relevant data, such as call logs, text messages, and browsing history from an image file. We will also cover data recovery techniques, with which we can recover data that's been deleted from a device.

Chapter 11, *Android App Analysis, Malware, and Reverse Engineering*, explains that while the data extraction and data recovery techniques discussed in earlier chapters provide access to valuable data, app analysis in this chapter helps us to acquire information about the specifics of an application, such as preferences and permissions.

Chapter 12, *Windows Phone Forensics*, discusses Windows Phones, which do not occupy much of the mobile market space. Therefore, most forensic practitioners are unfamiliar with the data formats, embedded databases, and other artifacts that exist on the device. This chapter provides an overview of Windows Phone forensics, describing various methods of acquiring and examining data on Windows mobile devices.

Chapter 13, *Parsing Third-Party Application Files*, introduces you to the various applications seen on Android devices, iOS devices, and Windows Phones. Each application will vary due to versions and devices, but their underlying structures are similar. We will look at how the data is stored and why preference files are important to your investigation.

To get the most out of this book

Ensure that you have a test mobile device on which you can experiment with the techniques explained in the book. Do not try these techniques on your personal phone.

Some of the techniques explained in the book, such as rooting a device, are specific to the brand and the OS running on the device. Ensure that you research and gather sufficient information before trying these techniques.

If you are using the digital version of this book, we advise you to type the commands yourself. Doing so will help you avoid any potential errors related to the copying and pasting of code.

Download the color images

We also provide a PDF file that has color images of the screenshots/diagrams used in this book. You can download it here: http://www.packtpub.com/sites/default/files/downloads/9781838647520_ColorImages.pdf

Conventions used

There are a number of text conventions used throughout this book.

CodeInText: Indicates code words in text, database table names, folder names, filenames, file extensions, pathnames, dummy URLs, user input, and Twitter handles. Here is an example: "Mount the downloaded WebStorm-10*.dmg disk image file as another disk in your system."

A block of code is set as follows:

```
html, body, #map {
 height: 100%;
 margin: 0;
 padding: 0
}
```

When we wish to draw your attention to a particular part of a code block, the relevant lines or items are set in bold:

```
[default]
exten => s,1,Dial(Zap/1|30)
exten => s,2,Voicemail(u100)
exten => s,102,Voicemail(b100)
exten => i,1,Voicemail(s0)
```

Any command-line input or output is written as follows:

```
$ mkdir css
$ cd css
```

Bold: Indicates a new term, an important word, or words that you see on screen. For example, words in menus or dialog boxes appear in the text like this. Here is an example: "Select **System info** from the **Administration** panel."

 Warnings or important notes appear like this.

 Tips and tricks appear like this.

Disclaimer

The information within this book is intended to be used only in an ethical manner. Do not use any information from the book if you do not have written permission from the owner of the equipment. If you perform illegal actions, you are likely to be arrested and prosecuted to the full extent of the law. Packt Publishing does not take any responsibility if you misuse any of the information contained within the book. The information herein must only be used while testing environments with proper written authorization from the appropriate persons responsible.

Get in touch

Feedback from our readers is always welcome.

General feedback: If you have questions about any aspect of this book, mention the book title in the subject of your message and email us at customercare@packtpub.com.

Errata: Although we have taken every care to ensure the accuracy of our content, mistakes do happen. If you have found a mistake in this book, we would be grateful if you would report this to us. Please visit www.packtpub.com/support/errata, selecting your book, clicking on the Errata Submission Form link, and entering the details.

Piracy: If you come across any illegal copies of our works in any form on the internet, we would be grateful if you would provide us with the location address or website name. Please contact us at copyright@packt.com with a link to the material.

If you are interested in becoming an author: If there is a topic that you have expertise in and you are interested in, either writing or contributing to a book, please visit authors.packtpub.com.

Reviews

Please leave a review. Once you have read and used this book, why not leave a review on the site that you purchased it from? Potential readers can then see and use your unbiased opinion to make purchase decisions, we at Packt can understand what you think about our products, and our authors can see your feedback on their book. Thank you!

For more information about Packt, please visit packt.com.

Introduction to Mobile Forensics

There is no doubt that mobile devices have become part of our lives and have revolutionized the way we do most of our activities. As a result, a mobile device is now a huge repository that holds sensitive and personal information about its owner. This has, in turn, led to the rise of mobile device forensics, a branch of digital forensics that deals with retrieving data from a mobile device. This book will help you understand forensic techniques on three main platforms—Android, iOS, and Windows. We will go through various methods that can be used to collect evidence from different mobile devices.

In this chapter, we will cover the following topics:

- The need for mobile forensics
- Understanding mobile forensics
- Challenges in mobile forensics
- The mobile phone evidence extraction process
- Practical mobile forensic approaches
- Potential evidence stored on mobile phones
- Examination and analysis
- Rules of evidence
- Good forensic practices

The need for mobile forensics

According to Statista reports (`statista.com`), the number of mobile phone users in the world is expected to pass 5 billion by 2020. The world is witnessing technology and user migration from desktops to mobile phones. Most of the growth in the mobile market can be attributed to the continued demand for smartphones.

According to an Ericsson report, global mobile data traffic will reach 71 exabytes per month by 2022, from 8.8 exabytes in 2017, a compound annual growth rate of 42 percent. Smartphones of today, such as Apple's iPhone and the Samsung Galaxy series, are compact forms of computers with high performance, huge storage, and enhanced functionality. Mobile phones are the most personal electronic device that a user accesses. They are used to perform simple communication tasks, such as calling and texting, while still providing support for internet browsing, email, taking photos and videos, creating and storing documents, identifying locations with GPS services, and managing business tasks.

As new features and applications are incorporated into mobile phones, the amount of information stored on devices is continuously growing.

Mobile phones have become portable data carriers, keeping track of all your movements. With the increasing prevalence of mobile phones in people's daily lives and in crime, data acquired from phones has become an invaluable source of evidence for investigations relating to criminal, civil, and even high-profile cases. It is rare to conduct a digital forensic investigation that does not include a phone. Mobile device call logs and GPS data were used to help solve the attempted bombing in Times Square, New York, in 2010.

 The details of the case can be found at `https://www.forensicon.com/forensics-blotter/cell-phone-email-forensics-investigation-cracks-nyc-times-square-car-bombing-case/`.

The science behind recovering digital evidence from mobile phones is called mobile forensics, and we will be looking into it in the next section. Digital evidence is defined as information and data that is stored on, received by, or transmitted by an electronic device that is used for investigations. Digital evidence encompasses any and all digital data that can be used as evidence in a case.

Understanding mobile forensics

Digital forensics is a branch of forensic science focusing on the recovery and investigation of raw data residing in electronic or digital devices. The goal of the process is to extract and recover any information from a digital device without altering the data present on the device. Over the years, digital forensics has grown along with the rapid growth of computers and various other digital devices. There are various branches of digital forensics based on the type of digital device involved, such as computer forensics, network forensics, and mobile forensics.

Mobile forensics is a branch of digital forensics that deals with the acquisition and recovery of evidence from mobile devices. Forensically sound is a term used extensively in the digital forensics community to qualify and justify the use of a particular forensic technology or methodology. One of the core principles that drive sound forensic examination is that the original evidence must not be altered in any form. This is extremely difficult with mobile devices. Some forensic tools require a communication vector with the mobile device, and thus standard write protection will not work during forensic acquisition.

Other forensic acquisition methods may involve detaching a chip or installing a custom bootloader on the mobile device prior to extracting data for forensic examination. In cases where examination or data acquisition is not possible without changing the configuration of the device, the procedure and the changes must be carefully tested and documented for later reference. Following proper methodology and guidelines is crucial in examining mobile devices as doing so yields the most valuable data. As with any evidence gathering, not following the proper procedure during the examination can result in loss or damage of evidence or render it inadmissible in court.

The mobile forensics process is broken down into three main categories—*seizure*, *acquisition*, and *examination/analysis*. Forensic examiners face some challenges while seizing the mobile device as a source of evidence. At the crime scene, if the mobile device is found switched off, you as the examiner should place the device in a Faraday bag to prevent changes should the device automatically power on. Faraday bags are specifically designed to isolate a phone from a network.

If the phone is found switched on, switching it off has a lot of concerns attached to it. If the phone is locked by a PIN or password, or encrypted, you will be required to bypass the lock or determine the PIN to access the device. Mobile phones are networked devices and can send and receive data through different sources, such as telecommunication systems, Wi-Fi access points, and Bluetooth. So, if the phone is in a running state, a criminal could securely erase the data stored on the phone by executing a remote wipe command. When a phone is switched on, it should be placed in a Faraday bag. If possible, prior to placing a mobile device in a Faraday bag, you should disconnect it from the network to protect the evidence by enabling flight mode and disabling all network connections (Wi-Fi, GPS, hotspots, and so on). This will also preserve the battery, which will drain while in a Faraday bag, and protect against leaks in the Faraday bag. Once the mobile device is seized properly, the examiner may need several forensic tools to acquire and analyze the data stored on the phone.

Mobile device forensic acquisition can be performed using multiple methods, which will be defined later. Each of these methods affects the amount of analysis required, which will be discussed in greater detail in the upcoming chapters. Should one method fail, another must be attempted. Multiple attempts and tools may be necessary in order to acquire the maximum amount of data from the mobile device.

Mobile phones are dynamic systems that present a lot of challenges for us in extracting and analyzing digital evidence. The rapid increase in the number of different kinds of mobile phones from different manufacturers makes it difficult to develop a single process or tool to examine all types of devices. Mobile phones are continuously evolving as existing technologies progress and new technologies are introduced. Furthermore, each mobile is designed with a variety of embedded operating systems. Hence, special knowledge and skills are required from forensic experts to acquire and analyze the devices.

Challenges in mobile forensics

One of the biggest forensic challenges when it comes to the mobile platform is the fact that data can be accessed, stored, and synchronized across multiple devices. As data is volatile and can be quickly transformed or deleted remotely, more effort is required for the preservation of this data. Mobile forensics is different from computer forensics and presents unique challenges to forensic examiners.

Law enforcement and forensic examiners often struggle to obtain digital evidence from mobile devices. The following are some of the reasons for this:

- **Hardware differences**: The market is flooded with different models of mobile phones from different manufacturers. Forensic examiners may come across different types of mobile models that differ in size, hardware, features, and operating system. Also, with a short product development cycle, new models emerge very frequently. As the mobile landscape changes with each passing day, it is critical for you to adapt to all challenges and remain updated on mobile device forensic techniques across various devices.
- **Mobile operating systems**: Unlike personal computers, where Windows has dominated the market for years, mobile devices widely use more operating systems, including Apple's iOS, Google's Android, RIM's BlackBerry OS, Microsoft's Windows Phone OS, HP's webOS, and many others. Even within these operating systems, there are several versions, which makes your task even more difficult.

- **Mobile platform security features**: Modern mobile platforms contain built-in security features to protect user data and privacy. These features act as a hurdle during forensic acquisition and examination. For example, modern mobile devices come with default encryption mechanisms from the hardware layer to the software layer. You might need to break through these encryption mechanisms to extract data from the devices. The FBI versus Apple encryption dispute was a watershed moment in this regard, where the security implementation of Apple prevented the FBI from breaking into an iPhone seized from an attacker in the San Bernardino case.

- **Preventing data modification**: One of the fundamental rules in forensics is to make sure that data on the device is not modified. In other words, any attempt to extract data from the device should not alter the data present on that device. But this is not practically possible with mobiles, because just switching on a device can change the data on that device. Even if a device appears to be in an off state, background processes may still run. For example, in most mobiles, the alarm clock still works even when the phone is switched off. A sudden transition from one state to another may result in the loss or modification of data.

- **Anti-forensic techniques**: Anti-forensic techniques, such as data hiding, data obfuscation, data forgery, and secure wiping, make investigations on digital media more difficult.

- **Passcode recovery**: If the device is protected with a passcode, the forensic examiner needs to gain access to the device without damaging the data on the device. While there are techniques to bypass the screen lock, they may not always work on all versions of the OS.

- **Lack of resources**: As mentioned earlier, with the growing number of mobile phones, the amount of tools required by a forensic examiner also increases. Forensic acquisition accessories, such as USB cables, batteries, and chargers for different mobile phones, have to be maintained in order to acquire those devices.

- **Dynamic nature of evidence**: Digital evidence may be easily altered either intentionally or unintentionally. For example, browsing an application on a phone might alter the data stored by that application on the device.

- **Accidental reset**: Mobile phones provide features to reset everything. Resetting a device accidentally while examining it may result in the loss of data.

- **Device alteration**: The possible ways to alter devices may range from moving application data or renaming files to modifying the manufacturer's operating system. In this case, the expertise of the suspect should be taken into account.

- **Communication shielding**: Mobile devices communicate over cellular networks, Wi-Fi networks, Bluetooth, and infrared. As device communication might alter the device data, the possibility of further communication should be eliminated after seizing the device.

- **Lack of availability of tools**: There is a wide range of mobile devices. A combination of tools needs to be used, because a single tool may not support all the devices or perform all the necessary functions. So, choosing the right tool for a particular phone might be difficult.
- **Malicious programs**: The device might contain malware or malicious software, such as a virus or a Trojan. These programs may try to spread over other devices over either a wired interface or a wireless one.
- **Legal issues**: Mobile devices might be involved in crimes that cross geographical boundaries. In order to tackle these multi-jurisdictional issues, the forensic examiner should be familiar with the nature of the crime and the regional laws.

Let's have a look at the process of evidence extraction in the next section.

The mobile phone evidence extraction process

Evidence extraction and the forensic examination of different mobile devices may differ based on various factors. However, following a consistent examination process will help the forensic examiner to ensure that the evidence gathered from each phone is well documented and that the results are reliable. There is no well-established standard process for mobile forensics.

However, the following diagram provides an overview of process considerations for the extraction of evidence from mobile devices. All methods used when extracting data from mobile devices should be tested, validated, and well documented:

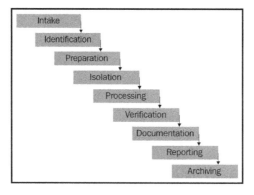

Mobile phone evidence extraction process

A great resource for handling and processing mobile devices can be found at `http://digital-forensics.sans.org/media/mobile-device-forensic-process-v3.pdf`.

As shown in the preceding diagram, forensics on a mobile device includes several phases, from the evidence intake phase to the archiving phase. The following sections provide an overview of various considerations across all the phases.

The evidence intake phase

The evidence intake phase is the starting phase and involves paperwork that captures ownership information and the type of incident the mobile device was involved in, and outlines the kind of data the requester is seeking. Developing specific objectives for each examination is the critical part of this phase. It serves to clarify your goals. Before the physical seizure process begins, you should be familiar with federal, state, and local laws pertaining to an individual's rights. If the right procedures are not followed, the investigation may be considered illegal in a court of law. The procedure and the legality may vary based on whether you are a government agent or a private party. For example, in the US, **fourth amendment** rights prevent any searching or seizure by a government agent without having a proper search warrant. The search warrant should clearly authorize the seizure of the mobile device as well as the kind of data that needs to be collected. After a successful seizure, care should be taken to ensure that a chain of custody is established not only for the device but also for the data collected.

 According to NIST (`https://csrc.nist.gov/`), chain of custody refers to a process that tracks the movement of evidence through its collection, safeguarding, and analysis life cycle by documenting each person who handled the evidence, the date/time it was collected or transferred, and the purpose of the transfer.

Also, while seizing the device, care should be taken not to modify any data present on the device. At the same time, any opportunity to help the investigation should not be missed. For example, at the time of seizing the device, if the device is unlocked, then try to disable the passcode.

The identification phase

The forensic examiner should identify the following details for every examination of a mobile device:

- The legal authority
- The data that needs to be extracted
- The make, model, and identifying information for the device
- Data storage media
- Other sources of potential evidence

We will discuss each of these in the following sections.

The legal authority

It is important for the forensic examiner to determine and document what legal authority exists for the acquisition and examination of the device, as well as any limitations placed on the media prior to the examination of the device. For example, if the investigation on the device is being conducted based on a warrant, the search should be limited only to those areas that are defined in the warrant. In short, prior to the device seizure, you need to answer the following questions:

- If a search warrant does not exist, has the device owner consented to the search?
- If a search warrant exists, is the device included within the original warrant?
- If the device is included in the warrant, does it also define what data can be collected?
- If it's a corporate investigation, is the device owned by an individual or his or her employer?
- Does the corporate policy allow collection and subsequent analysis?

Data that needs to be extracted

You will identify how in-depth the examination needs to be based upon the data requested. The goal of the examination makes a significant difference in selecting the tools and techniques to examine the phone and increases the efficiency of the examination process.

The make, model, and identifying information for the device

As part of the examination, identifying the make and model of the phone assists in determining what tools would work with the phone. When available, it is recommended to capture the following details of the seized device:

- The device manufacturer
- The device model number
- The mobile device serial number
- The color of the device
- The wallpaper visible on the device screen or lock screen wallpaper
- The presence of any hardware components (such as front camera, headphone jack, and so on)
- A description of any specific details unique to the device (scratches, broken screen, and so on)

Next, let's look at data storage media.

Data storage media

Many mobile phones provide an option to extend memory with removable storage devices. In cases when such removable media is found in a mobile phone that is submitted for examination, the storage card should be removed and processed using traditional digital forensic techniques. It is wise to also acquire the card while in the mobile device to ensure that data stored on both the handset memory and card are linked for easier analysis. This will be discussed in detail in the upcoming chapters.

Other sources of potential evidence

Mobile phones act as good sources of fingerprint and other biological evidence. Such evidence should be collected prior to the examination of the mobile phone to avoid contamination issues, unless the collection method will damage the device. Examiners should wear gloves when handling the evidence.

The preparation phase

Once the mobile phone model is identified, the preparation phase involves research regarding the particular mobile phone to be examined and the appropriate methods and tools to be used for acquisition and examination. This is generally done based on the device model, underlying operating system, its version, and so on. Also, the tools that need to be used during an examination will have to be determined based on the device in question as well as on the scope and goals of the examination.

The isolation phase

Mobile phones are, by design, intended to communicate via cellular phone networks, Bluetooth, infrared, and wireless (Wi-Fi) network capabilities. When a phone is connected to a network, new data is added to the phone through incoming calls, messages, and application data, which modifies the evidence on the phone.

Complete destruction of data is also possible through remote access or remote wipe commands. For this reason, isolation of the device from communication sources is important prior to the acquisition and examination of the device. Network isolation can be done by placing the phone in radio frequency shielding cloth and then putting the phone in airplane or flight mode. Airplane mode disables a device's communication channels, such as cellular radio, Wi-Fi, and Bluetooth. However, if the device is screen-locked, then this is not possible. Also, since Wi-Fi is now available in airplanes, some devices now have Wi-Fi access enabled in airplane mode.

An alternate solution is isolation of the phone through the use of Faraday bags, which block radio signals to or from the phone. Faraday bags contain materials that block external static electrical fields (including radio waves). Thus, Faraday bags shield seized mobile devices from external interference to prevent wiping and tracking. To work more conveniently with seized devices, Faraday tents and rooms also exist.

The processing phase

Once a phone has been isolated from communication networks, the actual processing of the mobile phone begins. One of the challenges that you will face in this phase is identifying which tools to use, as this is affected by a variety of factors such as price, ease of use, applicability, and so on. Mobile forensic software is highly expensive, and unlike with computer forensics, you may sometimes have to use multiple tools to access data. While selecting a tool, ensure that it has built-in features to maintain forensic integrity. Maintaining forensic integrity requires a tool that packages collected data in a format that probably cannot be easily modified or altered.

The phone should be acquired using a tested method that is repeatable and is as forensically sound as possible. Physical acquisition is the preferred method as it extracts the raw memory data and the device is commonly powered off during the acquisition process. On most devices, the smallest number of changes occur to the device during physical acquisition. If physical acquisition is not possible or fails, an attempt should be made to acquire the filesystem of the mobile device. A logical acquisition should always be performed as it may contain only the parsed data and provide pointers to examine the raw memory image. These acquisition methods are discussed in detail in later chapters.

The verification phase

After processing the phone, you need to verify the accuracy of the data extracted from the phone to ensure that data has not been modified. The verification of the extracted data can be accomplished in several ways:

- **Comparing the extracted data to the handset data**: Check whether the data extracted from the device matches the data displayed by the device if applicable. The data extracted can be compared to that on the device itself or a logical report, whichever is preferred. Remember, handling the original device may make changes to the only evidence—the device itself.
- **Using multiple tools and comparing the results**: To ensure accuracy, use multiple tools to extract the data and compare results.

- **Using hash values:** All image files should be hashed after acquisition to ensure that data remains unchanged. If filesystem extraction is supported, you can extract the filesystem and then compute hashes for the extracted files. Later, any individually extracted file hash is calculated and checked against the original value to verify the integrity of it. Any discrepancy in hash values must be explicable (for example, the device was powered on and then acquired again, so the hash values are different).

The documenting and reporting phase

The forensic examiner is required to document, throughout the examination process, everything related to what was done during acquisition and examination. Once you complete the investigation, the results must go through some form of peer review to ensure that the data is checked and the investigation is complete. Your notes and documentation may include information such as the following:

- The examination start date and time
- The physical condition of the phone
- Photos of the phone and individual components
- Phone status when received—turned on or turned off
- Phone make and model
- Tools used for the acquisition
- Tools used for the examination
- Data found during the examination
- Notes from peer review

Throughout the investigation, it is important to make sure that the information extracted and documented from a mobile device can be clearly presented to any other examiner or to a court. Documentation is one of your most important skills. Creating a forensic report of data extracted from a mobile device during acquisition and analysis is important. This may include data in both paper and electronic format.

Your findings must be documented and presented in a manner that means that the evidence speaks for itself when in court. The findings should be clear, concise, and repeatable. Timeline and link analysis, features offered by many commercial mobile forensic tools, will aid in reporting and explaining findings across multiple mobile devices. These tools allow you to tie together the methods behind the communication of multiple devices.

The archiving phase

Preserving the data extracted from a mobile phone is an important part of the overall process. It is also important that the data is retained in a usable format for the ongoing court process, for future reference, should the current evidence file become corrupt, and for record-keeping requirements. Court cases may continue for many years before a final judgment is arrived at, and most jurisdictions require that data be retained for long periods of time for the purposes of appeals. As the field and methods advance, new methods for pulling data out of a raw, physical image may surface, and then you can revisit the data by pulling a copy from the archives.

Now that we have understood how the evidence extraction process works, we will be looking into the different approaches in practical mobile forensics.

Practical mobile forensic approaches

Similar to any forensic investigation, there are several approaches that can be used for the acquisition and examination/analysis of data from mobile phones. The type of mobile device, the operating system, and the security setting generally dictate the procedure to be followed in a forensic process. Every investigation is distinct with its own circumstances, so it is not possible to design a single definitive procedural approach for all cases. The following details outline the general approaches followed in extracting data from mobile devices.

Understanding mobile operating systems

One of the major factors in the data acquisition and examination/analysis of a mobile phone is the operating system. From low-end mobile phones to smartphones, mobile operating systems have come a long way with a lot of features. Mobile operating systems directly affect how you can access the mobile device. For example, Android gives terminal-level access whereas iOS does not give such an option.

A comprehensive understanding of the mobile platform helps the forensic examiner make sound forensic decisions and conduct a conclusive investigation. While there is a large range of smart mobile devices, with the demise of Blackberry, currently two main operating systems dominate the market, namely Google Android and Apple iOS (followed by Windows Phone at a distant third). More information can be found at `https://www.idc.com/promo/smartphone-market-share/os`. This book covers the forensic analysis of these three mobile platforms. We will provide a brief overview of the leading mobile operating systems.

Android

Android is a Linux-based operating system, and it's a Google open source platform for mobile phones. Android is the world's most widely used smartphone operating system. Sources show that Apple's iOS stands second (`https://www.idc.com/promo/smartphone-market-share/os`). Android was developed by Google as an open and free option for hardware manufacturers and phone carriers. This makes Android the software of choice for companies who require a low-cost, customizable, lightweight operating system for their smart devices without developing a new operating system from scratch.

Android's open nature has further encouraged developers to build a large number of applications and upload them onto Google Play. Later, end users can download the applications from Android Market, which makes Android a powerful operating system. It is estimated that the Google Play Store has 3.3 million apps at the time of writing this book. More details on Android are covered in `Chapter 7`, *Understanding Android*.

iOS

iOS, formerly known as the iPhone operating system, is a mobile operating system developed and distributed solely by Apple Inc. iOS is evolving into a universal operating system for all Apple mobile devices, such as iPad, iPod Touch, and iPhone. iOS is derived from macOS and hence is based on a Unix-like operating system. iOS manages the device hardware. The technologies required to implement native applications are also provided by iOS. It also ships with various system applications, such as Mail and Safari, which provide standard system services to the user. iOS-native applications are distributed through the App Store, which is closely monitored by Apple. More details about iOS are covered in `Chapter 2`, *Understanding the Internals of iOS Devices*.

Windows Phone

Windows Phone is a proprietary mobile operating system developed by Microsoft for smartphones and pocket PCs. It is the successor to Windows Mobile and is primarily aimed at the consumer market rather than the enterprise market. The Windows Phone operating system is similar to the Windows desktop operating system, but it is optimized for devices with a small amount of storage. Windows Phone basics and forensic techniques are discussed in Chapter 12, *Windows Phone Forensics*.

Mobile forensic tool leveling system

Mobile phone forensic acquisition and analysis involves manual effort and the use of automated tools. There are a variety of tools that are available for performing mobile forensics. All the tools have their pros and cons, and it is fundamental that you understand that no single tool is sufficient for all purposes. So, understanding the various types of mobile forensic tools is important for forensic examiners.

When identifying the appropriate tools for the forensic acquisition and analysis of mobile phones, a mobile device forensic tool classification system developed by Sam Brothers (shown in the following diagram) comes in handy for examiners:

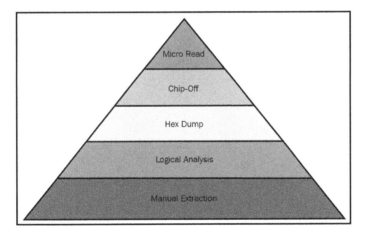

Cellular phone tool leveling pyramid (Sam Brothers, 2009)

The objective of the mobile device forensic tool classification system is to enable an examiner to categorize forensic tools based on the examination methodology of the tool. As you move from the bottom of the pyramid to the top, the methods and tools used for analysis generally become more technical and sophisticated and require longer analysis times. There are advantages and disadvantages of different techniques used at each layer. The forensic examiner should be aware of these issues before he or she applies a particular technique. Evidence can be destroyed completely if the given method or tool is not properly utilized. This risk increases as you move up in the pyramid. Thus, proper training is required to obtain the highest success rate in data extraction from mobile devices.

Each existing mobile forensic tool can be classified under one or more of the five levels. The following sections contain a detailed description of each level.

Manual extraction

The manual extraction method involves simply scrolling through the data on the device and viewing the data on the phone directly through the use of the device's keypad or touchscreen. The information discovered is then photographically documented. The extraction process is fast and easy to use, and it will work on almost every phone. This method is prone to human error, such as missing certain data due to unfamiliarity with the interface. At this level, it is not possible to recover deleted information and grab all the data.

There are some tools, such as Project-A-Phone, that have been developed to help an examiner to easily document a manual extraction. However, this might also result in the modification of data. For example, viewing an unread SMS will mark it as read.

Logical analysis

Logical analysis involves connecting the mobile device to forensic hardware or to a forensic workstation via a USB cable, an RJ-45 cable, infrared, or Bluetooth. Once connected, the computer initiates a command and sends it to the device, which is then interpreted by the device's processor. Next, the requested data is received from the device's memory and sent back to the forensic workstation. Later, you can review the data.

Most of the forensic tools currently available work at this level of the classification system. The extraction process is fast and easy to use and requires little training for you. On the flip side, the process may write data to the mobile and might change the integrity of the evidence. In addition, deleted data is not generally accessible with this procedure.

Hex dump

A hex dump, also referred to as a physical extraction, is achieved by connecting a device to a forensic workstation and pushing unsigned code or a bootloader into the phone and instructing the phone to dump memory from the phone to the computer. Since the resulting raw image is in binary format, technical expertise is required to analyze it. The process is inexpensive, provides more data to the examiner, and allows the recovery of deleted files from the device-unallocated space on most devices.

Chip-off

Chip-off refers to the acquisition of data directly from the memory chip present in the device. At this level, the chip is physically removed from the device and a chip reader or a second phone is used to extract data stored on it. This method is more technically challenging, as a wide variety of chip types are used in mobiles. The process is expensive and requires hardware-level knowledge as it involves the desoldering and heating of the memory chip. Training is required to successfully perform a chip-off extraction. Improper procedures may damage the memory chip and render all data unsalvageable. When possible, it is recommended that the other levels of extraction are attempted prior to chip-off, since this method is destructive in nature. Also, the information that comes out of memory is in a raw format and has to be parsed, decoded, and interpreted. The chip-off method is preferred in situations where it is important to preserve the state of memory exactly as it exists on the device. It is also the only option when a device is damaged but the memory chip is intact.

The chip on a device is often read using the **Joint Test Action Group (JTAG)** method. The JTAG method involves connecting to **Test Access Ports (TAPs)** on a device and forcing the processor to transfer the raw data stored on the memory chip. The JTAG method is generally used with devices that are operational but inaccessible using standard tools. Both of these techniques also work even when the device is screen-locked.

Micro read

The micro read process involves manually viewing and interpreting data seen on the memory chip. The examiner uses an electron microscope and analyzes the physical gates on the chip and then translates the gate status to 0s and 1s to determine the resulting ASCII characters. The whole process is time-consuming and costly, and it requires extensive knowledge and training on memory and the filesystem. Due to the extreme technicalities involved in micro read, it is only attempted for high-profile cases equivalent to a national security crisis after all other levels of extraction techniques have been exhausted. The process is rarely performed and is not well documented at this time. Also, there are currently no commercial tools available to perform a micro read.

Data acquisition methods

Data acquisition is the process of imaging or otherwise extracting information from a digital device and other attached media. Acquiring data from a mobile phone is not as simple as a standard hard drive forensic acquisition. The following points break down the three types of forensic acquisition methods for mobile phones: physical, logical, and manual. These methods may have some overlap with a couple of levels discussed in the mobile forensics tool leveling system. The amount and type of data that can be collected will vary depending on the type of acquisition method being used. While we cover these methods in detail in the upcoming chapters, the following is a brief description of them.

Physical acquisition

Physical acquisition of a mobile device is nothing but a bit-by-bit copy of the physical storage. With direct access to flash memory, information can be acquired from the device through physical extraction. Flash memory is non-volatile memory and is primarily used in memory cards and USB flash drives as solid-state storage. The process creates a bit-for-bit copy of an entire filesystem, similar to the approach taken in computer forensic investigations. Physical acquisition is able to acquire all of the data present on a device, including the deleted data, and access to unallocated space on most devices.

Logical acquisition

Logical acquisition is about extracting logical storage objects, such as files and directories, that reside on a filesystem. The logical acquisition of mobile phones is performed using the device manufacturer's application programming interface to synchronize the phone's contents with a computer. Many forensic tools can perform a logical acquisition. It is much easier for a forensic tool to organize and present data extracted through logical acquisition. However, the forensic analyst must understand how the acquisition occurs and whether the mobile was modified in any way during the process. Depending on the phone and forensic tools used, all or some of the data is acquired. A logical acquisition is easy to perform and only recovers the files on a mobile phone and does not recover data contained in unallocated space.

Manual acquisition

With mobile phones, physical acquisition is usually the best option, and logical acquisition is the second-best option. Manual extraction should be the last option when performing the forensic acquisition of a mobile phone. Both logical and manual acquisition can be used to validate findings in the physical data. During manual acquisition, the examiner utilizes the user interface to investigate the contents of the phone's memory. The device is used normally through keypad or touchscreen and menu navigation, and the examiner takes pictures of each screen's contents. Manual extraction introduces a greater degree of risk in the form of human error, and there is a chance of deleting evidence. Manual acquisition is easy to perform and only acquires the data that appears on a mobile phone.

Next, let's look at the amount of information that can be extracted from mobile phones.

Potential evidence stored on mobile phones

The range of information that can be obtained from mobile phones is detailed in this section. Data on a mobile phone can be found in a number of locations—SIM card, external storage card, and phone memory, for example. In addition, the service provider also stores communication-related information. This book primarily focuses on data acquired from a phone's memory. Mobile device data extraction tools recover data from a phone's memory. Even though data recovered during forensic acquisition depends on the mobile model, in general, the following data is common across all models and useful as evidence. Note that most of the following artifacts contain timestamps:

- **Address book**: This contains contact names, phone numbers, email addresses, and so on.
- **Call history**: This contains dialed, received and missed calls and call duration.
- **SMS**: This contains sent and received text messages.
- **MMS**: This contains media files such as sent and received photos and videos.
- **E-mail**: This contains sent, drafted, and received email messages.
- **Web browser history**: This contains the history of websites that have been visited.
- **Photos**: This contains pictures that were captured using the mobile phone camera, those downloaded from the internet, and those transferred from other devices.
- **Videos**: This contains videos that are captured using the mobile camera, those downloaded from the internet, and those transferred from other devices.
- **Music**: This contains music files downloaded from the internet and those transferred from other devices.
- **Documents**: This contains documents created using the device's applications, those downloaded from the internet, and those transferred from other devices.
- **Calendar**: This contains calendar entries and appointments.
- **Network communication**: This contains GPS locations.
- **Maps**: This contains places the user visited, looked-up directions, and searched and downloaded maps.
- **Social networking data**: This contains data stored by applications, such as Facebook, Twitter, LinkedIn, Google+, and WhatsApp.
- **Deleted data**: This contains information deleted from the phone.

Next, we will have a quick look at the final step of investigation: examination and analysis.

Examination and analysis

This is the ultimate step of the investigation, and it aims to uncover data that is present on the device. Examination is done by applying well-tested and scientific methods to conclusively establish results. The analysis phase is focused on separating relevant data from the rest and probing for data that is of value to the underlying case. The examination process starts with a copy of the evidence acquired using some of the techniques described previously, which will be covered in detail in coming chapters. Examination and analysis using third-party tools is generally performed by importing the device's memory dump into a mobile forensics tool that will automatically retrieve the results. Understanding the case is also crucial to performing a targeted analysis of the data. For example, a case about child pornography may require focusing on all of the images present on the device rather than looking at other artifacts.

It is important that you have a fair knowledge of how the forensic tools that are used for examination work. Proficient use of the features and options available in a tool will drastically speed up the examination process. Sometimes, due to programming flaws in the software, a tool may not be able to recognize or convert bits into a format comprehensible by you. Hence, it is crucial that you have the necessary skills to identify such situations and use alternate tools or software to construct the results. In some cases, an individual may purposefully tamper with the device information or may delete/hide some crucial data. Forensic analysts should understand the limitations of their tools and sometimes compensate for them to achieve the best possible results.

Rules of evidence

Courtrooms rely more and more on the information inside a mobile phone as vital evidence. Prevailing evidence in court requires a good understanding of the rules of evidence. Mobile forensics is a relatively new discipline, and laws dictating the validity of evidence are not widely known, and they also differ from country to country. However, there are five general rules of evidence that apply to digital forensics and need to be followed in order for evidence to be useful. Ignoring these rules makes evidence inadmissible, and your case could be thrown out. These five rules are **admissible**, **authentic**, **complete**, **reliable**, and **believable**:

- **Admissible**: This is the most basic rule and a measure of evidence validity and importance. The evidence must be preserved and gathered in such a way that it can be used in court or elsewhere. Many errors can be made that could cause a judge to rule a piece of evidence as inadmissible. For example, evidence that is gathered using illegal methods is commonly ruled inadmissible.

- **Authentic**: The evidence must be tied to the incident in a relevant way to prove something. The forensic examiner must be accountable for the origin of the evidence.
- **Complete**: When evidence is presented, it must be clear and complete and should reflect the whole story. It is not enough to collect evidence that just shows one perspective of an incident. Presenting incomplete evidence is more dangerous than not providing any evidence at all, as it could lead to a different judgment.
- **Reliable**: Evidence collected from the device must be reliable. This depends on the tools and methodology used. The techniques used and evidence collected must not cast doubt on the authenticity of the evidence. If you used some techniques that cannot be reproduced, the evidence is not considered unless those considering the evidence, such as the judge and jury, are directed to do so. This would include possible destructive methods such as chip-off extraction.
- **Believable**: A forensic examiner must be able to explain, with clarity and conciseness, what processes they used and how the integrity of the evidence was preserved. The evidence presented by you must be clear, easy to understand, and believable by the jury.

Now let's look at best practices.

Good forensic practices

Good forensic practices apply to the collection and preservation of evidence. A lack of sound forensic practices may even render the evidence collected useless before a court of law. The modification of evidence, either intentional or accidental, can affect a case. So, understanding best practices is critical for forensic examiners.

Securing the evidence

With advanced smartphone features such as *Find My iPhone* and remote wipes, securing a mobile phone in a way such that it cannot be remotely wiped is of great importance. Also, when the phone is powered on and has service, it constantly receives new data. To secure the evidence, use the right equipment and techniques to isolate the phone from all networks. With isolation, the phone is prevented from receiving any new data that would cause active data to be deleted. Depending on the case, other forensic techniques such as fingerprint matching may need to be employed to establish a connection between the device and its owner. If the device is not handled in a secure manner, physical evidence may be unintentionally tampered with and may be rendered useless.

It is also important to collect any peripherals, associated media, cables, power adapters, and other accessories that are present at the scene. At the scene of investigation, if the device is found to be connected to a personal computer, pulling it directly would stop the data transfer. Instead, it is recommended to capture the memory of the personal computer before pulling the device, as this contains significant details in many cases.

Preserving the evidence

As evidence is collected, it must be preserved in a state that is acceptable in court. Working directly on the original copies of evidence might alter it. So, as soon as you recover a raw disk image or files, create a read-only master copy and duplicate it. In order for evidence to be admissible, there must be a scientific method to validate that the evidence submitted is exactly the same as the original collected. This can be accomplished by creating a forensic hash value of the image.

 A forensic hash is used to ensure the integrity of an acquisition by calculating a cryptographically strong and non-reversible value of the image/data.

After duplicating the raw disk image or files, compute and verify the hash values for the original and the copy to ensure that the integrity of the evidence is maintained. Any changes in hash values should be documented and explicable. All further processing or examination should be performed on copies of the evidence. Any use of the device might alter the information stored on the handset. So, only perform the tasks that are absolutely necessary.

Documenting the evidence and changes

Whenever possible, a record of all visible data should be created. It is recommended to photograph the mobile device along with any of the other media found, such as cables, peripherals, and so on. This will be helpful if questions arise later on about the environment. Do not touch or lay hands on the mobile device when photographing it. Ensure that you document all the methods and tools that are used to collect and extract the evidence. Detail your notes so that another examiner can reproduce them. Your work must be reproducible; if it is not, a judge may rule it inadmissible. It's important to document the entire recovery process, including all the changes made during the acquisition and examination. For example, if the forensic tool used for the data extraction sliced up the disk image to store it, this must be documented. All changes to the mobile device, including power cycling and syncing, should be documented in your case notes.

Reporting

Reporting is the process of preparing a detailed summary of all the steps taken and conclusions reached as part of an examination. Reporting should include details about all the important actions performed by you, the results of the acquisition, and any inferences drawn from the results. Most of the forensic tools come with built-in reporting features that will autogenerate the reports while providing scope for customization at the same time. In general, a report may contain the following details:

- Details of the reporting agency
- Case identifier
- Forensic investigator
- Identity of the submitter
- Date of evidence receipt
- Details of the device seized for examination including serial number, make, and model
- Details of the equipment and tools used in the examination
- Description of steps taken during examination
- Chain of custody documentation
- Details of findings or issues identified
- Evidence recovered during the examination, ranging from chat messages, browser history, and call logs to deleted messages, and so on
- Any images captured during the examination
- Examination and analysis information
- Report conclusion

Summary

Modern mobile devices store a wide range of information, such as SMS, call logs, browser history, chat messages, location details, and so on. Hence they are often a key factor in several criminal cases, reconstruction of events, corporate and legal cases, and more. Mobile device forensics also comes with its own challenges and concepts that fall outside the boundaries of traditional digital forensics. Extreme care should be taken while handling the device, right from the evidence intake phase to the archiving phase. Examiners responsible for mobile devices must understand the different acquisition methods and the complexities of handling data during analysis. Extracting data from a mobile device is half the battle. The operating system, security features, and type of smartphone will determine the amount of access you have to the data. It is important to follow sound forensic practices and make sure that the evidence is unaltered during the investigation.

The next chapter will provide an insight into iOS forensics. You will learn about the filesystem layout, security features, and the way files are stored on an iOS device.

Section 1: iOS Forensics

This section will provide you with an overview of iOS devices such as iPhones and iPads, as well as an overview of the operating systems and filesystems they run. You will learn about the different types of forensic acquisition methods, including logical acquisition and filesystem acquisition, the process of jailbreaking, performing forensic analysis on the most common artifact sources, and how to work with popular mobile forensic software.

This section will consist of the following chapters:

- Chapter 2, Understanding the Internals of iOS Devices
- Chapter 3, Data Acquisition from iOS Devices
- Chapter 4, Data Acquisition from iOS Backups
- Chapter 5, iOS Data Analysis and Recovery
- Chapter 6, iOS Forensic Tools

Understanding the Internals of iOS Devices

2

According to Apple, there were 1.4 billion active Apple devices in 2019, 900 million of which were running on iOS. While iOS is the leading **operating system (OS)** for tablets worldwide, Android continues to be the leading OS for smartphones. Regardless of the statistics, if you are a forensic examiner, the chances are that you will need to conduct an examination of an iOS device.

In order to perform a forensic examination of an iOS device, you as the examiner must understand the internal components and inner workings of that device. Developing an understanding of the underlying components of a mobile device will help you understand the criticalities involved in the forensic process, including what data can be acquired, where the data is stored, and what methods can be used to access the data from that device. So, before we delve into the examination of iOS devices, it is necessary to gain an understanding of the different models that exist and their internal components. Throughout this book, we will perform forensic acquisition and analysis on iOS devices, including the iPhone, iPad, and Apple Watch.

The goal of this chapter is to introduce you to iOS device technology. We will cover details that may often get overlooked but will help you during your forensic investigation. You must understand the different iOS devices and how data is stored on these devices before you can successfully extract it.

In this chapter, we will cover the following topics in detail:

- iPhone models and hardware
- iPad models and hardware
- The **Hierarchical File System (HFS)** Plus and **Apple File System (APFS)** filesystems
- The iPhone OS

iPhone models and hardware

The iPhone is among the most popular smartphones on the market. Apple released the first-generation iPhone in June 2007. Since the first release, the iPhone became extremely popular due to its many groundbreaking features and usability. The introduction of the iPhone has since redefined the entire world of mobile computing. Consumers have started looking for faster and more efficient phones. Various iPhone models now exist, with different features and storage capabilities to serve consumer requirements.

The iPhones released since the third edition of *Practical Mobile Forensics*—the iPhone XR, XS, XS Max, 11, and 11 Pro—can be challenging when it comes to dealing with filesystem forensic acquisition methods. Just like the devices released since the iPhone 5, there is no method or tool available to physically recover data from these devices, unless they are jailbroken. However, logical acquisition can be obtained if the iPhone is unlocked. Acquisition methods for data extraction are available and will be discussed in `Chapter 3`, *Data Acquisition from iOS Devices*, and `Chapter 4`, *Data Acquisition from iOS Backups*. Now, let's learn how to identify the correct hardware model.

Identifying the correct hardware model

Before examining an iPhone, it is necessary to identify the correct hardware model and the firmware version installed on the device. Knowing the iPhone's details helps you to understand the criticalities and possibilities of obtaining evidence from an iPhone. For example, in many cases, the device passcode is required in order to obtain a logical image. Depending on the iOS version, device model, and passcode complexity, it may be possible to obtain the device passcode using a brute-force attack.

There are various ways to identify the hardware of a device. The easiest way to identify the hardware of some devices is to observe the model number displayed on the back of the device. To make this task even simpler, you can use Apple's Knowledge Base articles. More information on iPhone models can be found at `https://support.apple.com/en-in/ HT201296`.

The firmware version of an iPhone can be found by accessing the **Settings** option and then navigating to **General | About | Software Version**, as shown in the following screenshot. The purpose of the firmware is to enable certain features and assist with the general functioning of the device:

The iPhone About screen, displaying the software version 13.2

Alternatively, the `ideviceinfo` command-line tool that is available in the `libimobiledevice` software library (`http://www.libimobiledevice.org/`) can be used to identify the iPhone model and its iOS version.

To obtain the iPhone model and its iOS version information on a Windows 10 workstation, follow these steps:

1. Download the latest binaries from the following link: `https://dev.azure.com/ libimobiledevice-win32/imobiledevice-net/_build/results?buildId= 419` (click on **Artifacts** | **Binaries** to start downloading).
2. Unzip the archive with x86 or x64 binaries, depending on your workstation's version.
3. Open Command Prompt and change the directory to the one with binaries (use the `cd` command for this).
4. Connect the iPhone to your workstation using a **Universal Serial Bus** (**USB**) cable (for the latest iOS versions, the passcode is also required), and run the `ideviceinfo` command with the `-s` option, as shown in the following code:

```
$ ideviceinfo -s
```

The output of the `ideviceinfo` command displays the iPhone identifier, its internal name, and the iOS version, as shown in the following screenshot:

```
C:\Users\0136\Desktop\binaries\libimobiledevice.1.2.1-r419-win-x64>ideviceinfo.exe -s
BasebandCertId: 524245983
BasebandKeyHashInformation:
 AKeyStatus: 64
 SKeyStatus: 2
BasebandSerialNumber: sHODAZgntV0AAAAA
BasebandVersion: 1.02.14
BoardId: 4
BuildVersion: 17B84
CPUArchitecture: arm64e
ChipID: 32816
DeviceClass: iPhone
DeviceColor: 1
DeviceName: OlegтАЩs iPhone
DieID: 8563692629688366
HardwareModel: N104AP
HasSiDP: true
PartitionType: GUID_partition_scheme
ProductName: iPhone OS
ProductType: iPhone12,1
ProductVersion: 13.2
ProductionSOC: true
ProtocolVersion: 2
SupportedDeviceFamilies[1]:
 0: 1
TelephonyCapability: true
UniqueChipID: 8563692629688366
UniqueDeviceID: 00008030-001E6CA21128802E
WiFiAddress: f8:87:f1:f2:b0:78
```

The output from ideviceinfo displaying firmware version 13.2

Some other tools, such as iExplorer, will provide access to similar iOS device information, as shown in the following screenshot. The methods for recovering iPhone device information will work on iPad devices as well. Here, iExplorer is being used to obtain device information from an iPhone:

```
Device info

ActivationState - Activated
BasebandStatus - BBInfoAvailable
BasebandVersion - 1.02.14
BluetoothAddress - f8:87:f1:f2:21:45
BuildVersion - 17B84
CPUArchitecture - arm64e
DeviceClass - iPhone
DeviceColor - 1
DeviceName - Oleg's iPhone
FirmwareVersion - iBoot-5540.40.51
HardwareModel - N104AP
HardwarePlatform - t8030
IntegratedCircuitCardIdentity - 89701010063711442239
InternationalMobileEquipmentIdentity - 353989105391061
MLBSerialNumber - C7H94061QTDL73X67
MobileSubscriberCountryCode - 250
MobileSubscriberNetworkCode - 01
ModelNumber - MWLT2
PartitionType - GUID_partition_scheme
PhoneNumber -
ProductType - iPhone12,1
ProductVersion - 13.2
ProtocolVersion - 2
RegionInfo - RU/A
SerialNumber - C7CZJ36QN735
SIMStatus - kCTSIMSupportSIMStatusReady
TimeZone - Europe/Moscow
UniqueDeviceID - 00008030-001E6CA21128802E
WiFiAddress - f8:87:f1:f2:b0:78
```

iExplorer displaying device info

Every release of the iPhone comes with improved or newly added features. As previously stated in this chapter, knowing the iPhone's details helps you to understand the criticalities and possibilities of obtaining evidence from it. You must know the model of the device to ensure that the tools and methodologies being deployed support that particular iPhone. Additionally, the internal storage size of the iPhone must be determined to ensure that the evidence container is large enough for the entire forensic image. Most tools will not alert you if there is not enough disk space on the evidence drive until space has run out. This will waste time and force you to acquire the device a second time. Finally, the network capabilities of the device must also be noted so that you can properly isolate the device to prevent remote accessing or wiping during the examination. This will be discussed further in `Chapter 3`, *Data Acquisition from iOS Devices*.

Again, some familiarity with iPhone device hardware will aid you in determining how to handle the device during a forensic investigation. Certain models enforce full-disk encryption, while older models do not. Encrypted devices require additional steps during an acquisition—if access is even possible. You must be prepared for all hurdles you may be required to clear during the acquisition and analytical stages of the investigation. In addition to this, knowing the capabilities that the iPhone has—and the initial and current iOS version—makes a difference in the data you will be able to recover from the device. Apple is not consistent with data storage locations across iOS versions. Therefore, you must know the original version installed when the phone was first in use to ensure that the forensic tools do not overlook data that could aid in the investigation.

More information about identifying iPhone models can be found at `https://support.apple.com/en-us/HT201296`.

Understanding the iPhone hardware

The iPhone is a collection of modules, chips, and electronic components from different manufacturers. Due to the complexities of the iPhone, the list of hardware components is extensive, and each device should be researched for internal components.

For example, the iPhone 11 has an A13 Bionic processor; 64 GB, 128 GB, or 256 GB storage; 4 GB of RAM; a 6.1-inch Liquid Retina **liquid-crystal display (LCD)**; and a dual-lens 12 MP rear camera array.

Internal images for all iPhones can be found in the teardown section of `https://www.ifixit.com/Device/iPhone`.

iPad models and hardware

The Apple iPhone changed the way cell phones are produced and used. Similarly, the iPad, a version of the tablet computer introduced in January 2010, quashed the sales of notebooks. With the iPad, individuals can shoot videos, take photos, play music, read books, browse the internet, and do much more. Various iPad models now exist—for example, iPad Air 3 and iPad Pro—with different features and storage capabilities. More information on identifying iPad models can be found at `https://support.apple.com/en-in/HT201471`.

As with the iPhone, not all versions of the iPad are supported for filesystem acquisition. Additionally, Apple changes data storage locations in iOS versions, which affects iPad devices as well. You must be aware of the different models, the released and currently installed iOS version, the storage capability, the network access vectors, and more.

Understanding the iPad hardware

One of the key factors of the success of Apple iOS devices is the proper selection of their hardware components. Just like the iPhone, the iPad is also a collection of modules, chips, and electronic components from different manufacturers. Internal images for all iPads can be found in the teardown section of `https://www.ifixit.com/Device/iPad`.

The HFS Plus and APFS filesystems

To better understand the forensic process of an iOS device, it is useful to know about the filesystem that is used. Originally, the filesystem used in the iPhone and other Apple iOS devices was HFSX. This is a variation of HFS Plus, with one major difference. HFSX is case-sensitive, whereas HFS Plus is case-insensitive. Other differences will be discussed later in this chapter. APFS was introduced in June 2016 as a replacement for HFS Plus and became the default filesystem for iOS devices with the release of iOS 10.3, and for macOS devices with the release of macOS 10.13.

The HFS Plus filesystem

In 1996, Apple developed a new filesystem, HFS, to accommodate the storage of large datasets. In an HFS filesystem, the storage medium is represented as volumes. HFS volumes are divided into logical blocks of 512 bytes. The logical blocks are numbered from first to last on a given volume and will remain static with the same size as physical blocks—that is, 512 bytes. These logical blocks are grouped together into allocation blocks, which are used by the HFS filesystem to track data in a more efficient way. HFS uses a 16-bit value to address allocation blocks, which limits the number of allocation blocks to 65,535. To overcome the inefficient allocation of disk space and some of the limitations of HFS, Apple introduced the HFS Plus filesystem (`http://dubeiko.com/development/FileSystems/HFSPLUS/tn1150.html`).

The HFS Plus filesystem was designed to support larger file sizes. Sectors on HFS volumes are usually 512 bytes in size. These sectors form allocation blocks. The number of such blocks depends on the size of the volume. HFS Plus uses block addresses of 32 bits to address allocation blocks. HFS Plus uses *journaling* by default. Journaling is the process of logging every transaction to the disk, which helps prevent filesystem corruption. The key characteristics of the HFS Plus filesystem include the following: efficient use of disk space, Unicode support for filenames, support for name forks, file compression, journaling, dynamic resizing, dynamic defragmentation, and an ability to boot on OSes other than macOS.

The HFS Plus volume

The HFS Plus volume contains a number of internal structures to manage the organization of data. These structures include a header, an alternate header, and five special files: an allocation file, an extents overflow file, a catalog file, an attributes file, and a startup file. Among the five files, three files (the extents overflow file, the catalog file, and the attributes file) use a B-Tree structure. This is a data structure that allows data to be efficiently searched, viewed, modified, or removed. The HFS Plus volume structure is shown in the following diagram:

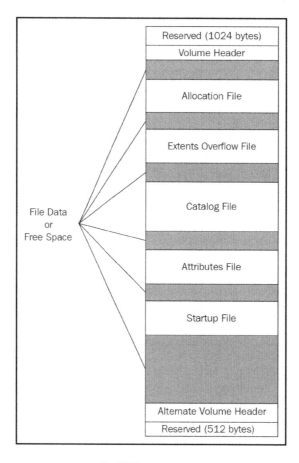

The HFS Plus volume structure

The volume structure is described as follows:

- **Reserved (1024 bytes)**: This is reserved for bootloader information.
- **Volume Header**: This stores volume information, such as the size of allocation blocks, a timestamp of when the volume was created, and metadata about each of the five special files.
- **Allocation File**: This file is used to track which allocation blocks are in use by the system. The file format consists of 1 bit for every allocation block. If the bit is set, the block is in use. If it is not set, the block is free.
- **Extents Overflow File**: This file records the allocation blocks that are allocated when the file size exceeds eight blocks, which helps in locating the actual data when referred. Bad blocks are also recorded in the file.
- **Catalog File**: This file contains information about the hierarchy of files and folders, which is used to locate any file and folder within the volume.
- **Attributes File**: This file contains inline data attribute records, fork data attribute records, and extension attribute records.
- **Startup File**: This file contains the information needed to assist in booting a system that does not have HFS Plus support.
- **Alternate Volume Header**: This is a backup of the volume header, and it's mainly used for disk repairing.
- **Reserved (512 bytes)**: This is reserved for use by Apple, and it is used during the manufacturing process.

Next, let's look at the APFS filesystem.

The APFS filesystem

APFS is a new filesystem for iOS, macOS, tvOS, and watchOS. It is a 64-bit filesystem and supports over 9 quintillion files on a single volume. The following is a list of its main features:

- **Clones**: These are instantaneous copies of files or directories. Modifications are written elsewhere and continue to share the unmodified blocks; the changes are saved as deltas of the cloned file.
- **Snapshots**: **Point-in-Time** (**PIT**) read-only instances of the filesystem.
- **Space sharing**: This allows multiple filesystems to share the same underlying free space on a physical volume.

- **Encryption**: There are three modes, as follows:
  - No encryption
  - Single-key encryption
  - Multi-key encryption with per-file keys for file data and a separate key for sensitive metadata

Depending on the hardware, the **Advanced Encryption Standard-XEX-based tweaked codebook mode with ciphertext stealing (AES-XTS)** or the **Advanced Encryption Standard-Cipher Blocker Chaining (AES-CBC)** encryption mode is used.

- **Crash protection**: This is a novel copy-on-write metadata scheme; it's used to ensure that filesystem updates are crash-protected.
- **Sparse files**: These allow the logical size of files to be greater than the physical space they occupy on the disk.
- **Fast directory sizing**: This quickly computes the total space used by a directory hierarchy, allowing it to be updated as the hierarchy evolves.

The APFS structure

So, APFS is structured in a single container that may contain one or more volumes. The APFS structure is presented in the following diagram:

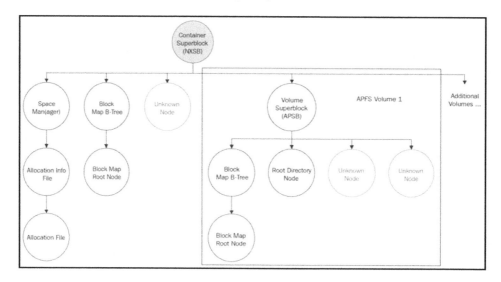

Overview of the APFS structure

Each filesystem structure in APFS starts with a block header. The block header starts with a checksum (Fletcher's checksum algorithm is used) for the whole block and also contains the copy-on-write version of the block, the block ID, and the block type.

The APFS structure can be explained as follows:

- The **Container Superblock** contains information on the block size, the number of blocks and pointers to the space manager for this task, the block IDs of all volumes, and a pointer to a block map B-Tree (which contains entries for each volume, along with its ID and offset).
- **Nodes** are used for storing different kinds of entries. They can be part of a B-Tree or exist on their own and can contain either flexible or fixed-sized entries.
- The **Space Man(ager)** manages the allocated blocks in the APFS container, and stores the number of free blocks and a pointer to the **Allocation Info File**.
- The **Allocation Info File** stores the allocation file's length, version, and the offset.
- The **B-Trees** manage multiple nodes and contain the offset of the root node.
- A **Volume Superblock** contains the name of the volume, its ID, and a timestamp.

As for allocation files, they are simple bitmaps and do not have a block header and type ID.

Disk layout

By default, the filesystem is configured as two logical disk partitions: the system (root or firmware) partition and the user data partition.

The system partition contains the OS and all of the preloaded applications used with the iPhone. The system partition is mounted as read-only unless an OS upgrade is in progress or the device is jailbroken. The partition is updated only when a firmware upgrade is performed on the device. During this process, the entire partition is formatted by iTunes without affecting any of the user data. The system partition takes only a small portion of storage space, normally between 0.8 GB and 4 GB, depending on the size of the NAND drive. As the system partition was designed to remain in a factory state for the entire lifetime of the iPhone, there is typically little useful evidentiary information that can be obtained from it. If the iOS device is jailbroken, the files containing information regarding the jailbreak and user data may be resident on the system partition. Jailbreaking an iOS device allows the user root access to the device, but voids the manufacturer warranty. Jailbreaking will be discussed later in this chapter.

The user data partition contains all the user-created data, ranging from music and contacts to third-party application data. The user data partition occupies most of the NAND memory and is mounted to the `/private/var` directory on the device. Most of the evidentiary information can be found in this partition. During a filesystem acquisition, the user data partition contents should be captured and saved as a `.tar` file. Acquired data can be easily extracted and parsed by most commercial mobile forensic tools.

The iPhone OS

iOS is Apple's most advanced and feature-rich proprietary mobile OS. It was released with the first generation of the iPhone. When introduced, it was named iPhone OS, and it was later renamed iOS to reflect the unified nature of the OS that powers all Apple iOS devices, such as the iPhone, iPod touch, iPad, and Apple TV. iOS is derived from core OS X technologies and is streamlined to be compact and efficient for mobile devices.

It utilizes a multi-touch interface, where simple gestures are used to operate and control the device, such as swiping your finger across the screen to move to the successive page or pinching your fingers to zoom. In simple terms, iOS assists with the general functioning of the device.

The iOS architecture

iOS is an intermediary between the device hardware components and the applications on the screen. The applications don't interact with the underlying hardware directly. Instead, they do it through a well-defined system interface that protects them from hardware changes. This abstraction makes it easy to build applications that work on devices with different hardware capabilities.

The iOS architecture consists of four layers: the **Cocoa Touch** layer, the **Media** layer, the **Core Services** layer, and the **Core OS** layer. Each layer consists of several frameworks that help to build an application, as illustrated in the following diagram:

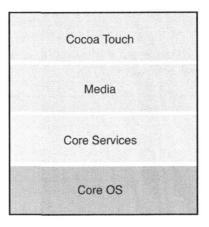

The iOS layers

These layers can be described as follows:

- **Cocoa Touch**: This layer contains the key frameworks required to develop the visual interface for iOS applications. Frameworks in this layer provide the basic application infrastructure and support key technologies, such as touch-based input, multitasking, and many high-level system services.

- **Media**: This layer provides the graphics, audio, and video frameworks to create the best multimedia experience available on a mobile device. The technologies in this layer help developers to build applications that look and sound great.

- **Core Services**: This layer provides the fundamental system services that are required for the applications. Not all of these services are used by developers, though many parts of the system are built on top of them. This layer contains technologies that enable support for location services, iCloud, and social media.

- **Core OS**: This layer is the base layer and sits directly on top of the device hardware. This layer deals with low-level functionalities and provides services such as networking (**Berkeley Software Distribution** (BSD) sockets), memory management, threading (**Portable Operating System Interface** (POSIX) threads), filesystem handling, external accessories access, and **Inter Process Communication** (IPC).

Now that we have learned about the iOS architecture, let's have a look at iOS security.

iOS security

Newer versions of iOS have been designed with security at their core. At the highest level, the iOS security architecture is as follows:

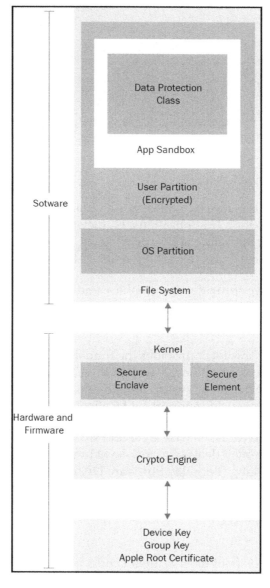

The iOS security architecture

Apple iOS devices such as iPhone, iPad, and iPod Touch are designed with layers of security. Low-level hardware features safeguard from malware attacks, and the high-level OS features prevent unauthorized use. A brief overview of the iOS security features is provided in the following sections.

Passcodes, Touch ID, and Face ID

Passcodes restrict unauthorized access to the device. Once a passcode is set, each time you turn on or wake up the device, it will ask for the passcode to access the device. iOS devices support simple as well as complex passcodes. iOS 9 released the option to use a six-digit simple passcode instead of the legacy four-digit option. The iPhone 5S and later also supports Touch ID fingerprints as a passcode, which are backed up with a simple or complex passcode. The iPhone X and later support a new biometric way of locking the device—Face ID—so that users can use their faces as the passcodes. And it's even more secure, as the chance that a stranger will unlock your iPhone with Touch ID is 1 in 50,000, but with Face ID it is 1 in 1,000,000.

Code signing

Code signing prevents users from downloading and installing unauthorized applications on the device. Apple says the following about it:

> *"Code Signing is the process by which your compiled iOS application is sealed and identified as yours. Also, iOS devices won't run an application or load a library unless it is signed by a trusted party. To ensure that all apps come from a known and approved source and have not been tampered with, iOS requires that all executable code be signed using an Apple-issued certificate."*

Sandboxing

Sandboxing mitigates post-code-execution exploitation by placing the application into a tightly restricted area. Applications installed on the iOS device are sandboxed, and one application cannot access the data stored by another. Essentially, a sandbox is a mechanism that enforces fine-grained controls that limit an application's access to files, network resources, hardware, and more.

Encryption

On iOS devices (starting with the iPhone 4), the entire filesystem is encrypted with a filesystem key, which is computed from the device's unique hardware key. This key is stored in effaceable storage, which exists between the OS and hardware levels of the device. This is the reason that **Joint Test Action Group (JTAG)** and chip-off methods are not useful acquisition methods, as the entire data dump will be encrypted.

Data protection

Data protection is designed to protect data at rest and to make offline attacks difficult. It allows applications to leverage the user's device passcode, in concert with the device hardware encryption, to generate a strong encryption key. Later, the strong encryption key is used to encrypt the data stored on the disk. This key protects data from unauthorized access when the device is locked, so critical information is secured even if the device is compromised.

Address Space Layout Randomization (ASLR)

ASLR is an exploit mitigation technique introduced with iOS 4.3. ASLR randomizes the application object's location in the memory, making it difficult to exploit the memory corruption vulnerabilities.

Privilege separation

iOS runs with the **principle of least privilege (PoLP)**. It contains two user roles: *root* and *mobile*. The most important processes in the system run with root user privileges. All other applications to which the user has direct access, such as the browser and third-party applications, run with mobile user privileges.

Stack-smashing protection

Stack-smashing protection is an exploit mitigation mechanism. It protects the device against buffer overflow attacks by placing a random and known value (called a stack canary) between a buffer and the control data on the stack.

Data Execution Prevention (DEP)

DEP is an exploit mitigation technique mechanism through which a processor can distinguish the portions of memory that are executable code from data. For example, in a code injection attack, an attacker tries to inject a vector and execute it. But DEP prevents this because it recognizes the injected part as data and not code.

Data wiping

iOS provides the **Erase All Content and Settings** option to wipe the data on an iPhone. This type of data wipe erases user settings and information by removing the encryption keys that protect the data. As the encryption keys are erased from the device, it is not possible to recover the deleted data, not even during forensic investigations. Other wiping methods are available that overwrite the data in the device memory. More information on wiping can be found at `https://support.apple.com/en-in/HT201274`.

Activation Lock

Activation Lock, introduced with iOS 7, is a theft deterrent that works by leveraging **Find My iPhone**. When Find My iPhone is enabled, it enables **Activation Lock**, and a user's Apple ID and password will be required to turn off Find My iPhone, to erase the device, and to reactivate it.

The App Store

The App Store is an application distribution platform for iOS, developed and maintained by Apple. It is a centralized online store where users can browse and download both free and paid apps. These apps expand the functionality of a mobile device. As of the first quarter of 2019, there were 2.2 million applications in the App Store.

Apps available in the App Store are generally written by third-party developers. Developers use Xcode and the iOS **software development kit (SDK)** to develop applications. Later, they submit the app to Apple for approval. Apple follows an extensive review process to check the app against the company's guidelines. If Apple approves the app, it is published to the App Store, where users can download or buy it. The strict review process makes the App Store less prone to malware, but not 100% secure.

XcodeGhost, the Apple malware that infected 50 applications within the Apple App Store, was detected in September 2015. This malware was built into Xcode, which made it harder to detect, and was reported to affect more than 500 million users worldwide. Once detected, Apple immediately removed the infected applications.

Jailbreaking

Jailbreaking is the process of removing limitations imposed by Apple's mobile OS through the use of software and hardware exploits. Jailbreaking permits unsigned code to run and gain root access on the OS. The most common reason for jailbreaking is to expand the limited feature set imposed by Apple's App Store and to install unapproved apps. Jailbreaking can aid in forensic acquisition but will void the user's warranty, potentially *brick* the device, and may not support being restored to the factory settings.

 If you jailbreak a device, it's best to assume that it will forever be jailbroken and the warranty is no longer valid.

Many publicly available jailbreaking tools add an unofficial application installer to the device, such as Cydia, which allows users to install many third-party applications, tools, tweaks, and apps from an online file repository. The software downloaded from Cydia opens up endless possibilities on a device that a non-jailbroken device would never be able to do. The most popular jailbreaking tools are Pangu, TaiG, Electra, and UncOver. Not all iOS versions are jailbreakable. The following table will help you to choose the appropriate jailbreak tool according to the device you have and its iOS version:

Version	Release date	Tool
iPhone OS 1.0	June 29, 2007	(no name)
iPhone OS 2.0	July 11, 2008	PwnageTool
iPhone OS 3.0	June 17, 2009	PwnageTool
iOS 4.0	June 21, 2010	PwnageTool
iOS 5.0	October 12, 2011	redsn0w
iOS 6.0	September 19, 2012	redsn0w
iOS 7.0 - 7.0.6	September 18, 2013	evasi0n7
iOS 7.1 - 7.1.2	May 29, 2014	Pangu
iOS 8.0 - 8.1	September 17, 2014	Pangu8
iOS 8.1.1 - 8.4	November 17, 2014	TaiG, PP Jailbreak
iOS 8.4.1	August 13, 2015	EtasonJB

iOS 9.0	September 16, 2015	Pangu9
iOS 9.1	October 21, 2015	Pangu9
iOS 9.3.5	August 25, 2016	Phoenix
iOS 10.0 - 10.1.1	September 13, 2016	Yalu
iOS 11.0 - 11.1.2	September 19, 2017	LiberiOS
iOS 11.0 - 11.1.2	September 19, 2017	Electra1112
iOS 11.0 - 11.4.1	July 7, 2018	Electra1131
iOS 11.0 - 11.4.1	October 14, 2018	Unc0ver
iOS 12.0 - 12.2, 12.4 - 12.4.2	September 17, 2019	Chimera, Unc0ver
iOS 12.3 - 13.2.3	November 10, 2019	checkra1n

We have now learned about the jailbreaking process and have had a look at the different jailbreaking tools currently available.

Summary

The first step in the forensic examination of an iOS device should be identifying the device model. The model of an iOS device can be used to help you as the examiner develop an understanding of the underlying components and capabilities of the device, which can be used to drive the methods for acquisition and examination. Legacy iOS devices should not be disregarded, because they may surface as part of an investigation. You must be aware of all iOS devices, as old devices are sometimes still in use and may be tied to a criminal investigation.

The next chapter will provide tools that will aid in obtaining data from iOS devices to later forensically examine. Not all tools are created equal, so it's important to know the best tools to get the job done properly.

Data Acquisition from iOS Devices

3

An iOS device that's been recovered from a crime scene can be a rich source of evidence. Think about how personal a smartphone is to a user; nothing else that's digital comes close. We rarely leave our homes or even walk around outside them without our smartphones within arm's reach. It's literally a glimpse into the most personal aspects of a human, almost like a diary of our everyday activity. According to several news references, Oscar Pistorius' iPads were examined by a mobile expert and presented during his trial to show his internet activity hours before the death of his girlfriend. When an iOS device can provide access to a so-called *smoking gun*, you, as the examiner, must ensure that you know how to properly handle, acquire, and analyze the device.

There are different ways to acquire forensic data from an iOS device. Though each method will have its pluses and minuses, the fundamental principle of any acquisition method is to obtain as much data as possible.

In this chapter, we will cover the following topics:

- iOS device operating modes
- Password protection and potential bypasses
- Logical acquisition
- Filesystem acquisition

Operating modes of iOS devices

Before we dive into forensic techniques and acquisition methods, it's important to know the different operating modes of an iOS device. Many forensic tools and methods require you to place the device in one of the operating modes. Understanding the iOS device's operating modes is required in order to perform a particular action on the device.

While most commercial tools will demonstrate the proper steps to get the device in a particular mode, you must understand what that mode represents. iOS devices are capable of running in different operating modes: normal mode, recovery mode, and **Device Firmware Update** (DFU) mode. Some forensic tools require you to know which mode the device is currently utilizing. We will define each mode in this section.

 Note that when the term *iPhone* is mentioned, it should be understood that the statement remains true for all iOS devices.

Normal mode

When an iPhone is switched on, its operating system is booted; this mode is known as normal mode. Most regular activities (calling, texting, and so on) that are performed on an iPhone will be run in normal mode.

When an iPhone is turned on, internally, it goes through a *secure boot chain*, as shown in the following diagram. This does not occur for jailbroken devices. Each step in the boot-up process contains software components that are cryptographically signed by Apple to ensure integrity:

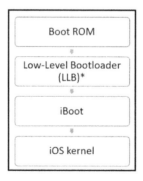

A secure boot chain of an iPhone in normal mode

*The boot ROM, in turn, verifies whether the Low-Level Bootloader (LLB) is signed by Apple and loads it. The LLB is loaded and verified by the boot ROM, but this only occurs on devices with an A9 or earlier A-series processor

The *boot ROM*, known as the *secure ROM*, is **read-only memory** (**ROM**) and is the first significant piece of code that runs on an iPhone (`https://www.apple.com/business/docs/ iOS_Security_Guide.pdf`). An explanation of the boot process for iOS devices is defined in the following steps:

1. The boot ROM code contains the Apple root **certificate authority** (**CA**) public key, which is used to verify the signature of the next stage before allowing it to load.
2. When the iPhone is started, the application processor executes the code from the boot ROM.
3. The boot ROM, in turn, verifies whether the **Low-Level Bootloader** (**LLB**) is signed by Apple and loads it. The LLB is loaded and verified by the boot ROM, but this only occurs on devices with an A9 or earlier A-series processor.
4. When the LLB finishes its tasks, it verifies and loads the second-stage boot loader (iBoot). iBoot verifies and loads the iOS kernel.
5. The iOS kernel, in turn, verifies and runs all the user applications.

When an iOS device is in this state, it's possible to gain a part that is accessible to the user through forensic acquisition. Most often, this includes a logical acquisition, which will be discussed later in this chapter.

Recovery mode

During the boot-up process, if one step is unable to load or verify the next step, then the boot-up is stopped and the iPhone displays the screen shown in the following screenshot:

iOS device recovery mode

This mode is known as recovery mode and is required to perform upgrades or restore the iPhone. To enter recovery mode, perform the following steps:

1. Turn off the device.
2. Hold down the iPhone Home button and connect the device to a computer via a USB cable. The device should turn on.
3. Continue holding the Home button until the Connect to iTunes screen appears. Then, you can release the Home button (on a jailbroken iOS device, this screen may appear with different icons). Most forensic tools and extraction methods will alert you regarding the current state of the iOS device.
4. To exit recovery mode, reboot the iPhone. On iPhone 6s and earlier, this can be completed by holding down the Home and Sleep/Power buttons until the Apple logo appears. On iPhone 7 and iPhone 7 Plus, this can be done by holding the Side button and Volume Down button together. On iPhone 8 and later, you do this by clicking the Volume Up button, then clicking the Volume Down button, and then holding down the Side button.

You can read more about recovery mode on iOS devices at `https://support.apple.com/en-in/HT201263`.

Normally, the process of rebooting returns the iPhone from recovery mode to normal mode. This same methodology applies to the Apple Watch. You may experience a situation where the iPhone constantly reboots into recovery mode. This is known as a recovery loop. A recovery loop may occur when the user or examiner attempts to jailbreak the iOS device and an error occurs. To get the device out of a recovery loop, the device must be connected to iTunes so that a backup can be restored to the device.

This makes changes to the evidence, so ensure that you have validated your acquisition methods on a test device prior to attempting to use your methods on real evidence.

DFU mode

During the boot-up process, if the Boot ROM is unable to load or verify the LLB or iBoot (on newer devices), the iPhone enters **Device Firmware Upgrade** (**DFU**) mode. DFU mode is a low-level diagnostic mode and is designed to perform firmware upgrades for iPhones.

To enter DFU mode, perform the following steps for iPhone 8 and later:

1. Connect the device to your workstation via a USB cable.
2. Press the Volume Up button and quickly release it.
3. Press the Volume Down button and quickly release it.
4. Hold the Side button and press the Volume Down button again.
5. After 5 seconds, release the Side button, but continue holding the Volume Down button until you see the Recovery screen.

Follow these steps for iPhone 7:

1. Connect the device to your workstation via a USB cable.
2. At the same time, press and hold the Side and Volume Down buttons.
3. Release the Side button, but continue to hold the Volume Down button until you see the Recovery screen.

Follow these steps for iPhone 6s and earlier:

1. Connect the device to your workstation via a USB cable.
2. At the same time, press and hold the Home and the Top (or Side) buttons.
3. Release the Top (or Side) button and continue holding the Home button.

 On iPhone 6s and earlier, nothing will be displayed on the screen when the device is in DFU mode.

To verify whether the iPhone is in DFU mode on macOS, launch a **System Report** and go to the **USB** option. You should see something similar to the following screenshot:

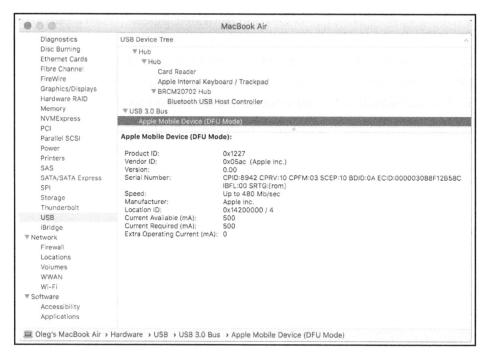

The MacBook system information displaying a device in DFU mode

Next, we will have a quick look at the tools that are required to set up the forensic environment.

Setting up the forensic environment

Nowadays, we have a few tools that can be used by mobile forensic examiners to acquire and analyze iOS devices using both macOS and Windows systems as the hosts. For example, *Elcomsoft iOS Forensic Toolkit* has both macOS and Windows versions; as for free and open source tools, the `libimobiledevice` library can be used – not only on macOS and Windows forensic workstations, but even on Linux!

We are going to introduce you to these tools with hands-on exercises, of course, including practical logical and filesystem acquisitions, and even jailbreaking, later in this chapter. But let's start with password protection and potential bypasses, since, without the passcode, we can't extract anything from a modern iOS device.

Password protection and potential bypasses

We want to start with the bad news: if you are examining an iPhone that runs iOS 8 or newer, and especially if it's a newer device, for example, the iPhone 6s, your chances of unlocking it are not good at all.

Of course, there are some hardware-based solutions, such as IP-BOX 3, but all of them work only occasionally, and using one of them can even result in bricking the device. With iOS 11, this problem becomes even more severe – even if the device under examination is not passcode protected, you will need the passcode anyway as it must be entered to confirm the trust between the device and your workstation.

So, what should a mobile forensic examiner do? Use the lockdown files! The lockdown files, which are stored as a `plist` file on *trusted computers*, allow you to trick the device into believing it's unlocked or *trusted* on the forensic workstation.

The lockdown files are located in the following locations:

- `/var/db/lockdown` on macOS
- `C:\ProgramData\Apple\Lockdown` on Windows 7 and later releases

You must be aware that unlocking with a lockdown file only works if the device was unlocked with a passcode at least once after the last reboot.

There are also some advanced techniques that exist. These include fingerprint molds to trick Touch ID, masks to trick Face ID, and NAND mirroring to bypass passcode entry limits.

The first technique was first demonstrated by Jason Chaikin. He demonstrated how to bypass Touch ID by lifting another person's fingerprint with common molding materials, such as dental mold and Play-Doh.

The second technique was demonstrated as a proof of concept by the Vietnamese cybersecurity firm Bkav. They created a mask that can be used to trick the Face ID feature using a combination of three-dimensional printing, makeup, and two-dimensional images.

The last technique was demonstrated by Sergei Skorobogatov, a senior research associate at the Cambridge Computer Laboratory's Security Group. This technique allows you to bypass passcode entry limits by soldering off the iPhone's flash memory chip and cloning it. This technique should work on any iOS device up to iPhone 6s Plus.

Logical acquisition

A logical acquisition captures a part of what is accessible to the user; in other words, what is included in an iTunes backup. It means that we won't get any deleted files, but, thanks to SQLite databases' free lists and unallocated space, we can recover deleted records, including SMS and other chats, browsing history, and so on. We will discuss recovering SQLite data and deleted artifacts in Chapter 5, *iOS Data Analysis and Recovery*.

Logical acquisition is the simplest way to ascertain whether the device is unlocked as it simply uses the built-in backup mechanism. Most tools and methods that support the logical acquisition of iOS devices will fail if the device is locked. Some think that if a physical image is captured, there is little to no need for a logical acquisition. However, not all data is parsed in a physical image, which is why having access to a logical image, which results in readable data, will assist you in digging deep into the physical image for artifacts to support your forensic investigation.

Logical acquisition is the fastest, easiest, and cheapest way to gain access to data stored on an iOS device. There are a variety of tools, ranging from commercial to free, that are capable of capturing logical images. Most of these tools require that the device be unlocked, or access to the plist file from the host machine be readily available.

Practical logical acquisition with libimobiledevice

Having the theory under your belt is good, but putting this into practice is much better. Let's create a logical image of an iPhone running iOS 13.2 with libimobiledevice, which should already be installed on your workstation, as we used it for device information gathering in the previous chapter.

OK, let's start:

1. First of all, let's make our backups encrypted. Connect the iOS device to your workstation and start the Command Prompt. Change the directory to the one containing libimobiledevice and type in the following command:

```
idevicebackup2.exe backup encryption on <your_password>
```

2. If you see **Backup encryption has been enabled successfully**, then you've done everything right and the backups will be encrypted. This will help you, the forensics examiner, to gain more information regarding users' passwords, Safari browsing history, and much more.

3. It's time to create the backup—our iOS device logical image. To do this, type in the following command:

```
idevicebackup2 backup --full
<the_folder_you_want_the_image_to_be_saved>
```

That's it. You can see the logical imaging process in the following screenshot:

```
Backup directory is "D:\Backup"
Started "com.apple.mobilebackup2" service on port 49994.
Negotiated Protocol Version 2.1
Starting backup...
Enforcing full backup from device.
Backup will be encrypted.
Requesting backup from device...
Full backup mode.
[=                                               ]   2% Finished
Receiving files
[================================================] 100% (110.7 MB/110.7 MB)
[===                                             ]   5% Finished
Receiving files
[================================================] 100% (131.1 MB/131.1 MB)
[================================================] 100% (131.1 MB/131.1 MB)
[=====                                           ]  10% Finished
Receiving files
[================================================] 100% (7.1 MB/7.1 MB)
[=====                                           ]  10% Finished
Receiving files
[================================================] 100% (7.0 MB/7.0 MB)
[======                                          ]  10% Finished
Receiving files
[========                                        ]  18% FinishedB/233.6 MB)
```

iPhone logical imaging with libimobiledevice

Next, let's look at logical acquisition with the Belkasoft Acquisition Tool.

Practical logical acquisition with the Belkasoft Acquisition Tool

Since logical acquisition is the most common option for modern iOS devices, we'll demonstrate how to use a few more free tools. The first one is the Belkasoft Acquisition Tool. This tool can be used not only for iOS device acquisition, but also for hard drives, and even cloud data.

Let's acquire an iPhone running iOS 13.2.3 using the Belkasoft Acquisition Tool:

1. Launch the Belkasoft Acquisition Tool and choose the **Mobile device** option:

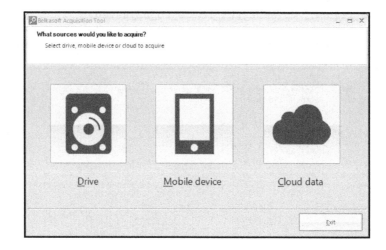

Choosing the source

2. In the next window, choose the **Apple** option:

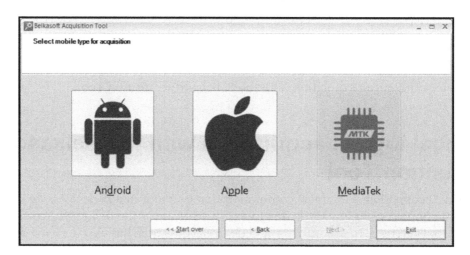

Choosing the mobile type

3. Now, choose the acquisition method and the image path:

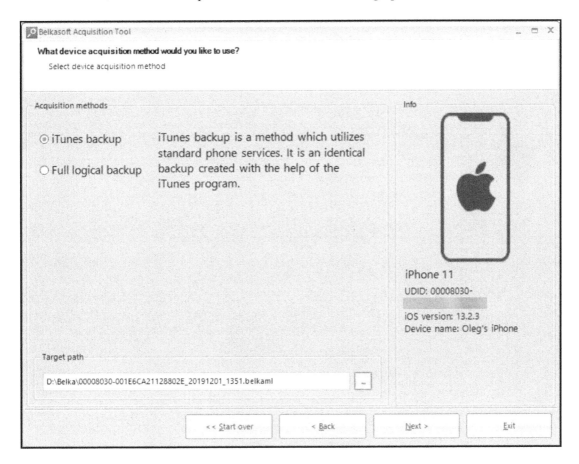

What device acquisition method would you like to use?

Select device acquisition method

Acquisition methods

Info

⊙ iTunes backup

○ Full logical backup

iTunes backup is a method which utilizes standard phone services. It is an identical backup created with the help of the iTunes program.

iPhone 11

UDID: 00008030-

iOS version: 13.2.3

Device name: Oleg's iPhone

Target path

D:\Belka\00008030-001E6CA21128802E_20191201_1351.belkaml

| << Start over | < Back | Next > | Exit |

Choosing the acquisition method

The tool is able to create an iTunes backup if the device isn't jailbroken and perform filesystem extraction if it is.

4. Wait for the task to finish successfully. You will find your device's logical image in the folder you chose in the previous step:

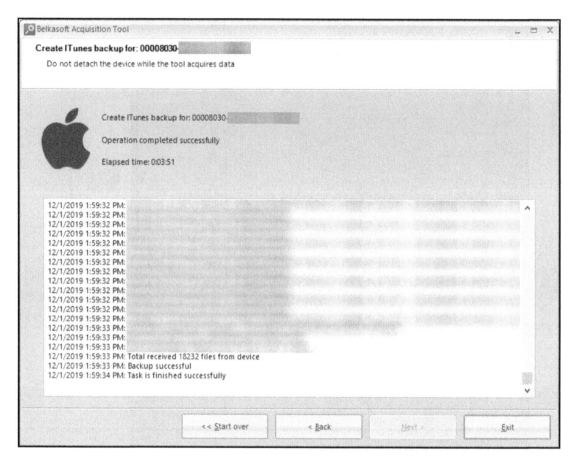

Creating the backup

The backup can be analyzed both by Belkasoft Evidence Center and by many other mobile forensic tools.

Practical logical acquisition with Magnet ACQUIRE

Another free tool capable of logical acquisition is **ACQUIRE** from Magnet Forensics. Let's perform a logical acquisition again, this time using a device running iOS 12.2:

1. Launch **Magnet ACQUIRE** and choose the device you want to image from the list:

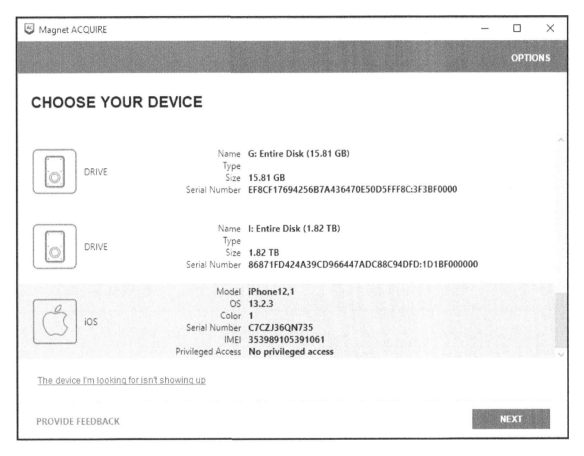

Choosing the device

2. Choose the type of image you want to acquire. We want to acquire a logical image and our device is not jailbroken, so we are going to choose the **Quick** option:

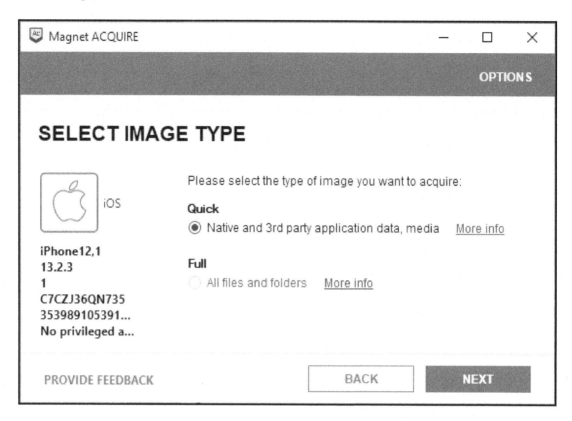

Choosing the image type

3. You can add a description of the evidence source if needed, and choose the folder where you want the image to be saved:

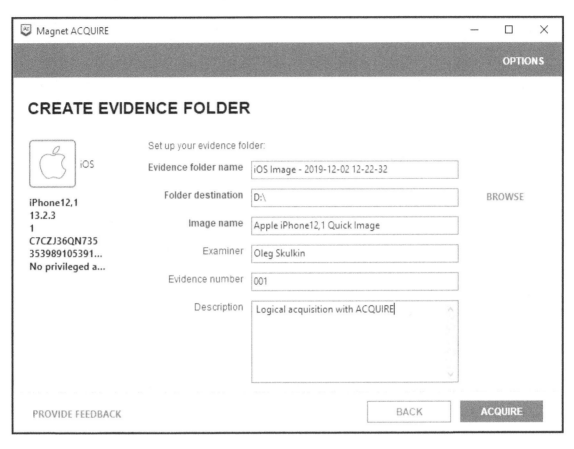

Choosing the destination folder, image name, and image information

4. Wait for the tasks to finish successfully; you'll see a summary of the acquisition process:

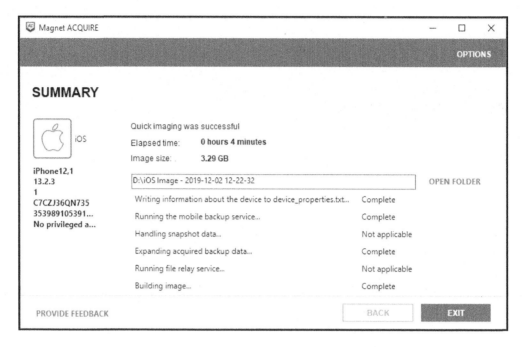

Creating the image

All extracted data will be saved to the destination folder in a ZIP archive. Also, the destination folder will contain a TXT file with the acquisition's process log and image information.

The next section will walk you through jailbreaking and filesystem acquisition.

Filesystem acquisition

Secure Enclave has brought new challenges to iOS forensic examiners. We can't extract the encryption keys that are required to decrypt the device image, so performing physical acquisition is useless. But there is filesystem acquisition. Unfortunately, in most cases, it requires the iOS device to be jailbroken. The next section will show you how to jailbreak an iPhone running iOS 11.4.1 with Electra and an iPhone running iOS 13.2 with Checkra1n.

Practical jailbreaking

To perform filesystem acquisition, we need our iOS device to be jailbroken. The steps to jailbreak an iOS device running 11.4.1 are as follows:

1. Download `Electra` from: `https://github.com/coolstar/electra-ipas/raw/master/Electra1141-1.3.2.ipa`.

2. Download `Cydia Impactor` (`http://www.cydiaimpactor.com/`), run it, and connect the device to your workstation:

Running Cydia Impactor

3. Drag and drop the `Electra IPA` file to the `Cydia Impactor` window.

4. Type any Apple ID in the new window (you can register a new one for every device you examine).

5. Log on with this Apple ID to `https://appleid.apple.com/` and generate an app-specific password under the **Security** section. Paste this password into the next window. Wait for the process to finish.

6. On the phone, go to **Settings** | **General** | **Device Management** | **Apple ID** and tap **Trust**:

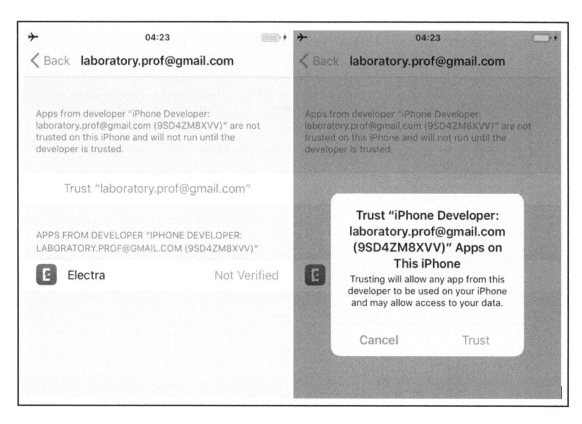

Verifying the developer

7. Put the phone into Airplane mode, turn Siri off, and reboot the device.

8. Tap the **Electra** icon on the Springboard and then choose **Jailbreak**. If the process finishes successfully, you will find the **Cydia** icon on the Springboard:

Jailbreaking the device

Now, the phone is jailbroken and ready for filesystem acquisition.

`Checkra1n` is based on a bootrom vulnerability and exploit and supports a wide range of iOS devices, even those running the latest (at the time of writing) iOS 13.2. Here are the steps to jailbreak an iOS device running 13.2:

1. Download `Checkra1n` from: `https://checkra.in/`.
2. Run the application. At the time of writing, `Checkra1n` is only available for macOS.
3. Connect the device and put it into DFU mode:

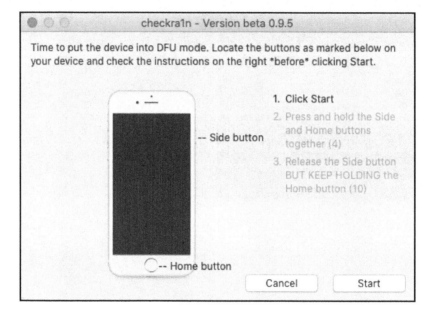

Putting the device into DFU mode

4. Wait for the exploitation process to finish:

Exploitation process

Once the device has been rebooted, you will find the checkra1n icon on the Springboard – the device is now jailbroken and ready for filesystem acquisition.

 For more jailbreaking techniques, please refer to the *Jailbreaking* section of Chapter 2, *Understanding the Internals of iOS Devices*.

Practical filesystem acquisition with free tools

It's time to perform filesystem acquisition. All we'll need is iproxy from libimobiledevice:

1. Open a Command Prompt window and run iproxy with the following parameters:

```
D:\libimobiledevice-Compiled-Windows-ios11>iproxy.exe 4444 22
waiting for connection
accepted connection, fd = 4
waiting for connection
Number of available devices == 1
Requesting connecion to device handle == 18 (serial: d53f03254b03c3a4704d0d4dcd86999fb9eece19), port 22
```

2. Open another Command Prompt window, change the directory to the one you want your image to be stored in, and run the following command:

```
ssh root@127.0.0.1 -p 4444 "tar -cf - /private/var/" > userdata.tar
```

 To connect via SSH, you will be prompted for the necessary password. The default password for SSH is *alpine*.

Once the process has finished, you'll find the created filesystem image in the directory you changed to before running the preceding command. It's a TAR archive and can be opened with many archivers, such as 7-Zip:

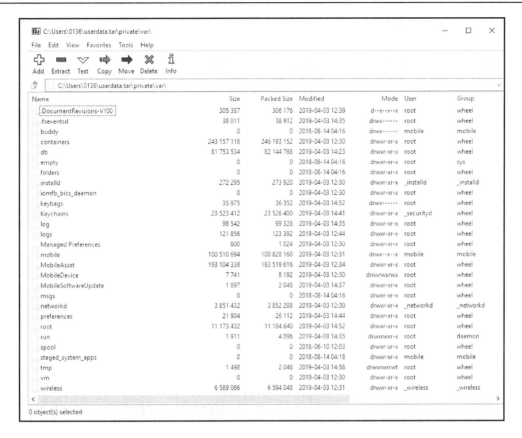

Filesystem image contents

Next, let's look at the *Elcomsoft iOS Forensic Toolkit*.

Practical filesystem acquisition with Elcomsoft iOS Forensic Toolkit

Of course, commercial tools are more stable and reliable. One of the tools that's capable of filesystem acquisition is the Elcomsoft iOS Forensic Toolkit. Here, we are going to acquire a jailbroken iOS device running iOS 12.4.3.

The steps to do this are as follows:

1. Connect the device to your workstation and start `Toolkit.cmd`.

2. Choose the port to use for SSH connection (the default is `22`, but since we used checkra1n for jailbreaking, the port is `44` instead) and type in the password (the default is `alpine`):

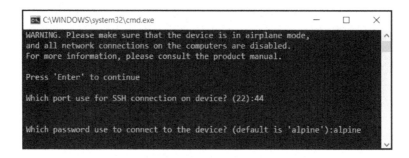

3. To acquire the device filesystem, type *F*:

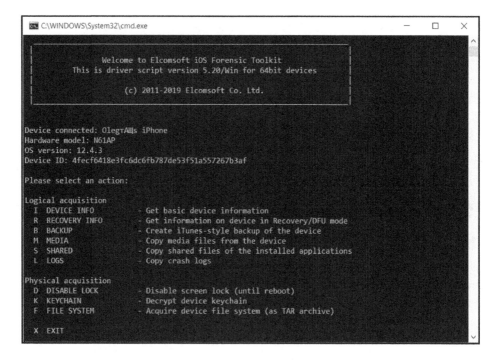

4. Choose the image name and start the process.

Once the process has finished, we'll have a filesystem image ready to be analyzed with a mobile forensic tool of our choice.

Summary

The first step in iOS device forensic examination is to acquire the data from the device. There are several different ways to acquire data from an iOS device. This chapter covered logical and filesystem acquisition techniques, as well as jailbreaking and methods to bypass passcodes.

While filesystem acquisition is the best method for forensically obtaining a majority of the data from iOS devices, backup files may exist or be the only method to extract data from the device.

The next chapter will discuss iOS device backup files in detail, including user, forensic, encrypted, and iCloud backup files, and the methods that you can perform to conduct your forensic examination.

Data Acquisition from iOS Backups

In the previous chapter, we covered techniques to acquire data from an iOS device, which included logical and filesystem acquisition. This chapter covers techniques to acquire a backup of files from the device onto a computer or iCloud, using Apple's synchronization protocol.

The physical acquisition of an iOS device provides the most data in an investigation, but you can also find a wealth of information in iOS backups. iOS device users have several options to back up the data present on their devices. Users can choose to back up the data to their computer, using the Apple iTunes software, or to the Apple cloud storage service known as iCloud. Every time an iPhone is synced with a computer or to iCloud, it creates a backup by copying the selected files from the device. The user can determine what is contained in the backup, so some backups may be more inclusive than others. Also, the user can back up to both a computer and iCloud and the data derived from each location may differ. This often occurs due to the limitations of iCloud's free storage. The user may simply back up photos and contacts to iCloud but may take a complete backup of all the data on their computer. As previously mentioned, physical acquisition provides the best access to all data on the iOS device; however, backups may be the only available source of digital evidence, especially if we are dealing with the most recent iOS devices.

In this chapter, we will cover the following topics:

- Working with iTunes backups
- Creating and analyzing backups with iTunes
- Extracting unencrypted backups
- Handling encrypted backup files
- Working with iCloud backups

Working with iTunes backups

A wealth of information is stored on any computer that has been previously synced with an iOS device. These computers, commonly referred to as host computers, can have historical data and passcode bypass certificates. In a criminal investigation, a search warrant can be obtained to seize a computer that belongs to a suspect, in order to access the backup and lockdown certificates. For all other cases, consent or permissible access is required. iOS backup file forensics mainly involves analyzing an offline backup produced by an iPhone or an iPad. Apple Watch data will be contained within the iPhone backup to which it is synced.

The iTunes backup method is also useful in cases where other acquisition types are not feasible. In this situation, you essentially create an iTunes backup of the device and analyze it using forensic software. Thus, it is important for you to completely understand the backup process and the tools involved, to ensure tools are capable of creating a forensic backup without contaminating the devices with other existing data in iTunes.

iPhone backup files can be created using the iTunes software, which is available for the macOS and Windows platforms. iTunes is a free utility provided by Apple for data synchronization and management between iOS devices and the computer. iTunes uses Apple's proprietary synchronization protocol to copy data from the iOS device to a computer. For example, an iPhone can be synced with a computer using a cable or Wi-Fi. iTunes provides an option for an encrypted backup, but, by default, it creates an unencrypted backup whenever an iPhone is synced. Encrypted backups, when cracked, provide additional access to data stored on the iOS device. This will be discussed later in this chapter.

Users often create backup files to protect their data in the event that their device is damaged or lost. Either a forensic backup is created to act as the best evidence or data is simply extracted from existing iOS backup files to search for legacy information. For example, if you are under investigation and you delete files or wipe your iPhone, your backup files on your iCloud and your Mac still exist. Depending on whether iTunes or iCloud was used, multiple backups for the same device may exist. You will have to analyze each backup forensically to uncover artifacts relating to the investigation.

iTunes is configured to automatically initiate the synchronization process once the iOS device is connected to the computer. To avoid unintended data exchange between the iOS device and the computer, disable the automatic synchronization process before connecting your evidence to the forensic workstation. The screenshot in *Step 2* of the following process illustrates the option that disables automatic syncing in iTunes version 12.9.4.102.

To disable auto-syncing in iTunes, perform the following steps:

1. Navigate to **Edit | Preferences | Devices**.
2. Check **Prevent iPods, iPhones, and iPads from syncing automatically** and click on the **OK** button, as illustrated in the following screenshot:

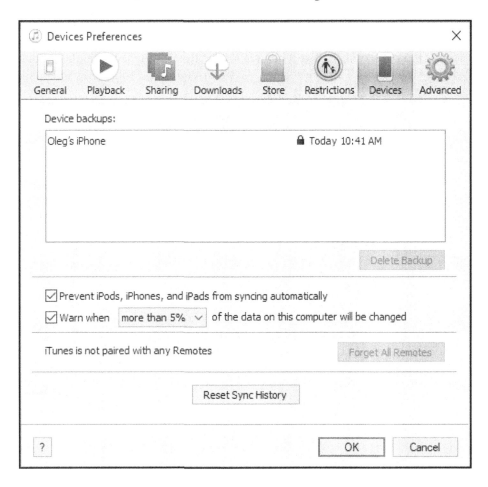

Disabling automatic syncing in iTunes

3. As seen in the preceding screenshot, iOS backup files exist on the system. If this were a forensic workstation, these backup files wouldn't exist or would be permanently removed to prevent cross-contamination.

4. Once you verify the synchronization settings, connect the iOS device to the computer using a **Universal Serial Bus (USB)** cable. If the connected device is not protected with a passcode or it was already connected to the computer recently, iTunes immediately recognizes the device; otherwise, you'll have to enter the passcode. This can be verified by the iPhone icon displayed on the left-hand side of the iTunes interface, as illustrated in the following screenshot:

An iPhone recognized by iTunes

5. Before iTunes can access the iPhone, you must enable **Trust** between the computer and the phone. You will be prompted to press **Continue** on the computer (as highlighted in the following screenshot) and select **Trust** on the iPhone. With iOS 11, you must also enter the device's passcode:

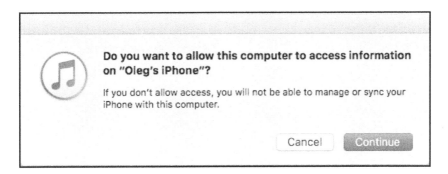

Do you want to allow this computer to access information on "Oleg's iPhone"?

If you don't allow access, you will not be able to manage or sync your iPhone with this computer.

Cancel   Continue

iTunes prompts for access permissions

6. Once iTunes recognizes the device, a single click on the iPhone icon displays the iPhone summary, including the iPhone's name, capacity, firmware version, serial number, free space, and phone number. The iPhone **Summary** page also displays the options to create backups. The process of creating a backup will be discussed in the following section.

Now, we are ready to start backing up the device. The next section will walk you through this process.

Creating and analyzing backups with iTunes

In this section, we are going to walk you through backing up an iOS device with Apple iTunes. We are using iTunes version 12.10.2.3 and an iPhone running iOS version 13.2. Perform the following steps:

1. Connect the device and click on the iPhone icon displayed on the left-hand side of the iTunes interface.

2. Go to the **Backups** section, where you can choose the backup destination (local computer or **iCloud**), and whether it's encrypted, as illustrated in the following screenshot:

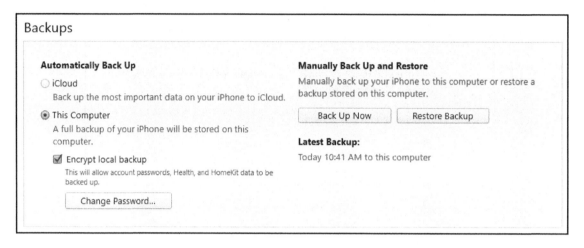

 Encrypted iTunes backups contain data that unencrypted ones don't, including passwords, Wi-Fi settings, and web browsing history, so make sure you are creating encrypted backups for forensic purposes.

3. Click on the **Back Up Now** button and wait for the process to complete. Once it's complete, the latest backup date and time will be changed.

If you want to use iTunes and save the backup to an external drive, observe the following instructions (we are using iTunes version 12.10.2.3 and Windows 10):

1. Rename the original backup folder.
2. Connect the external drive and create a backup folder on it.
3. Open Command Prompt and type the following command:

```
mklink /J "C:\Users\<username>\AppData\Roaming\Apple
Computer\MobileSync\Backup" "f:\Backup"
```

4. Now, you can create a regular local backup, and it will be saved to your external drive.

Now, we have the backup ready for further analysis. Let's look inside in order to understand its structure.

Understanding the backup structure

When the iPhone is backed up to a computer, the backup files are stored in a backup directory, which exists as a 40-character hexadecimal string and corresponds to the **Unique Device Identifier** (UDID) of the device. The newest devices have changed the UDID format—now it's a 24-character string, so their backups are named accordingly. The backup process may take a considerable amount of time, depending on the size of the data stored on the iPhone during the first backup. The location of the backup directory in which your backup data is stored depends on the computer's operating system. The following table displays a list of the common operating systems and the default locations of the iTunes backup directory:

Operating system	Backup directory location
Windows XP	`C:\Documents and Settings\<username>\Application Data\Apple Computer\MobileSync\Backup\`
Windows Vista/7/8/10	`C:\Users\<username>\AppData\Roaming\Apple Computer\MobileSync\Backup\`
macOS	`~/Library/Application Support/MobileSync/Backup/` (~ represents the home folder)

During the first sync, iTunes creates a backup directory and takes a complete backup of the device. Currently, on subsequent syncs, iTunes only backs up the files that are modified on the device and updates the existing backup directory. This has not always been true since, in the past, a new backup was created every time the iOS device was backed up. Also, when a device is updated or restored, iTunes automatically initiates a backup and takes a *differential backup*. A differential backup has the same name as the backup directory but is appended with a dash (–), the **International Organization for Standardization (ISO)** date of the backup, a dash (–), and the time in a 24-hour format with seconds (`[UDID]+ '-' + [Date]+'-'+[Time stamp]`).

The iTunes backup may make a copy of everything on the device, including contacts, **Short Message Service (SMS)** messages, photos, calendars, music, call logs, configuration files, documents, the keychain, network settings, offline web application cache, bookmarks, cookies, application data (if selected), and more. For example, emails and passwords will not be extracted if the backup is not encrypted. The backup also contains device details, such as the serial number, UDID, **Subscriber Identification Module (SIM)** details, and phone number. This information can also be used to prove a relationship between the backup and the mobile device.

The backup directory contains four standard files, along with the individual files (up to iOS 9) or folders (iOS 10 and newer). Up to iOS 9, these four files were `info.plist`, `manifest.plist`, `status.plist`, and `manifest.mbdb`, but starting from iOS 10, we have the following standard files:

- `info.plist`
- `manifest.plist`
- `status.plist`
- `manifest.db`

These files store details about the backup and the device from which it was derived.

info.plist

The `info.plist` file stores details about the backed-up device, and typically contains the following information:

- `Applications`: This is the list of applications installed on the device.
- `Build version`: This is the iOS build version number.
- `Device name and display name`: This is the name of the device, which typically includes the owner's name.
- `GUID`: This is the **Globally Unique Identifier (GUID)** of the device.
- `ICCID`: This is the **Integrated Circuit Card Identifier (ICCID)**, which is the serial number of the SIM.
- `IMEI`: This is the **International Mobile Equipment Identity (IMEI)**, which is used to uniquely identify the mobile phone.
- `Installed Applications`: This is the list of installed applications.
- `Last backup date`: This is the timestamp of the last successful backup.
- `MEID`: This is the **Mobile Equipment Identifier (MEID)** of the device.
- `Phone Number`: This is the phone number of the device at the time of backup.
- `Product Name`: This is the name of the device (for example, iPhone X).
- `Product type and product version`: This is the device's model and firmware version.
- `Serial Number`: This is the serial number of the device.

- `Target Identifier` and `Unique Identifier`: This is the UDID of the device.
- `iTunes Files`: This contains information about photos, folders, voice memos, and iTunes preferences.
- `iTunes Settings`: This contains information about deleted applications and applications library.
- `iTunes version`: This is the version of iTunes used to create the backup.

Let's now take a look at the `manifest.plist` file.

manifest.plist

The `manifest.plist` file describes the contents of the backup, and typically contains the following information:

- `Backup keybag`: `Backup keybag` contains a set of data protection class keys that are different from the keys in `System keybag`, and backed-up data is re-encrypted with the new class keys. Keys in `Backup keybag` facilitate the storage of backups in a secure manner.
- `Version`: This is the backup version.
- `Date`: This is the timestamp of when a backup was created or last updated.
- `ManifestKey`: This is the key used to encrypt `manifest.db` (wrapped with protection class 4).
- `WasPasscodeSet`: This identifies whether a passcode was set on the device when it was last synced.
- `Lockdown`: This contains device details, the last backup computer's name, and other remote syncing profiles.
- `Applications`: This is a list of third-party applications installed on the backed-up device, their version numbers, and bundle identifiers.
- `IsEncrypted`: This identifies whether the backup is encrypted. For encrypted backups, the value is `True`; otherwise, it is `False`.

Next, we will look at the `status.plist` file.

status.plist

The status.plist file stores details about the backup status, and typically contains the following information:

- IsFullBackup: This identifies whether the backup was a full backup of the device.
- UUID: This is the UUID of the device.
- Date: This is the timestamp of the last time the backup was modified.
- BackupState: This identifies whether the backup is a new backup or one that has been updated.
- SnapshotState: This identifies whether the backup process has finished successfully.

Now, we will look at the manifest.db file.

manifest.db

manifest.db is an SQLite database that contains a list of all the files and folders extracted from the iPhone via the backup mechanism. The Files table of the database includes the following columns:

- fileID: This is a **Secure Hash Algorithm 1 (SHA1)** hash of the domain, plus the – symbol and file or folder relative path. For example, ae94e0607ca39a88c18aca095cb5b4f8471291a0 is the SHA1 hash for CameraRollDomain-Media/PhotoData/Thumbnails/V2/DCIM/102APPLE.
- domain: This is the domain to which the file or folder belongs (all files in iOS are divided into multiple domains—for example, CameraRollDomain and HomeDomain).
- relativePath: This is the relative path to the file (including the filename) or folder.
- flags: These are the file flags.

- `file`: This is an embedded `.plist` file. These `.plist` files include the following important pieces of information, among others:
    - `LastModified`: This is the file's last modification timestamp in Unix format.
    - `Birth`: This is the file creation timestamp in Unix format. The fields are shown in the following screenshot:

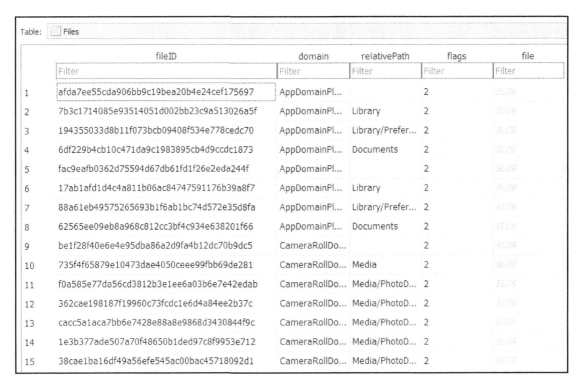

	fileID	domain	relativePath	flags	file
	Filter	Filter	Filter	Filter	Filter
1	afda7ee55cda906bb9c19bea20b4e24cef175697	AppDomainPl...		2	*BLOB*
2	7b3c1714085e93514051d002bb23c9a513026a5f	AppDomainPl...	Library	2	*BLOB*
3	194355033d8b11f073bcb09408f534e778cedc70	AppDomainPl...	Library/Prefer...	2	*BLOB*
4	6df229b4cb10c471da9c1983895cb4d9ccdc1873	AppDomainPl...	Documents	2	*BLOB*
5	fac9eafb0362d75594d67db61fd1f26e2eda244f	AppDomainPl...		2	*BLOB*
6	17ab1afd1d4c4a811b06ac84747591176b39a8f7	AppDomainPl...	Library	2	*BLOB*
7	88a61eb49575265693b1f6ab1bc74d572e35d8fa	AppDomainPl...	Library/Prefer...	2	*BLOB*
8	62565ee09eb8a968c812cc3bf4c934e638201f66	AppDomainPl...	Documents	2	*BLOB*
9	be1f28f40e6e4e95dba86a2d9fa4b12dc70b9dc5	CameraRollDo...		2	*BLOB*
10	735f4f65879e10473dae4050ceee99fbb69de281	CameraRollDo...	Media	2	*BLOB*
11	f0a585e77da56cd3812b3e1ee6a03b6e7e42edab	CameraRollDo...	Media/PhotoD...	2	*BLOB*
12	362cae198187f19960c73fcdc1e6d4a84ee2b37c	CameraRollDo...	Media/PhotoD...	2	*BLOB*
13	cacc5a1aca7bb6e7428e88a8e9868d3430844f9c	CameraRollDo...	Media/PhotoD...	2	*BLOB*
14	1e3b377ade507a70f48650b1ded97c8f9953e712	CameraRollDo...	Media/PhotoD...	2	*BLOB*
15	38cae1ba16df49a56efe545ac00bac45718092d1	CameraRollDo...	Media/PhotoD...	2	*BLOB*

The manifest.db contents

You can easily export this .plist embedded binary using, for example, **DB Browser for SQLite (DB4S)**. To do this, observe the following steps:

1. Open manifest.db using the **Open Database** button.
2. Go to the **Browse Data** tab.
3. Click on a cell from in the **file** column.
4. On the **Edit Database Cell** pane, use the **Export** button to save the data as a .plist file, as illustrated in the following screenshot:

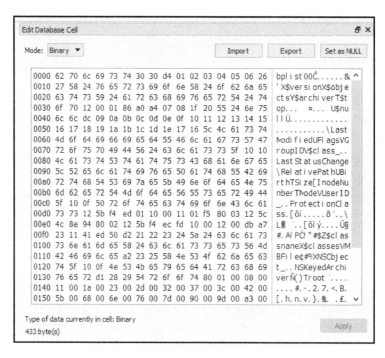

Exporting an embedded .plist file with DB4S

Since iOS 10, files are no longer named with 40-character hexadecimal strings. Instead, you will see a list of folders named with 2-character hexadecimal strings, which contain the files you used to see in previous versions, as illustrated in the following screenshot:

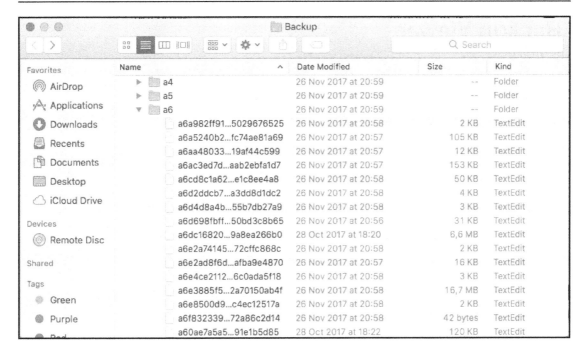

iPhone backup files

Now that you understand the backup structure, let's learn how to extract valuable data from it.

Extracting unencrypted backups

There are many free and commercial tools available to analyze data from unencrypted backups. These tools analyze the `manifest.db` database, restore the filenames, and create the file structure that users see on the iOS device. Some popular tools include iBackup Viewer, iExplorer, and commercial forensic tools such as Belkasoft Evidence Center, Magnet AXIOM, and UFED Physical Analyzer.

iBackup Viewer

iBackup Viewer is a free tool for both Windows and macOS that can be downloaded from `http://www.imactools.com/iphonebackupviewer/`.

The tool expects the backup to be located in the default location, but you can change it to the location of your choice—for example, an external drive.

To extract the backup, observe the following steps:

1. If the backup you want to analyze is not saved in the default location, click on the **Preferences** hyperlink on the main screen and choose the correct location, as illustrated in the following screenshot:

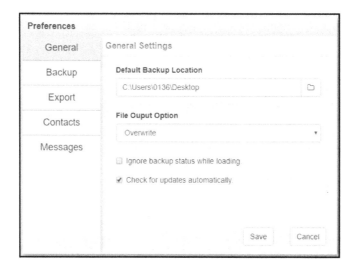

Choosing the backup location

2. You will see the backups available in the location you chose. Click on the one you want to examine.

You will see potential evidence sources that are available, including contacts, call history, messages, the calendar, notes, voicemails, and browsing history, as shown in the following screenshot:

Potential evidence sources

3. It's important to note that you can browse the backup as a filesystem, using the Raw Data mode (the last icon in the previous screenshot), as shown in the following screenshot:

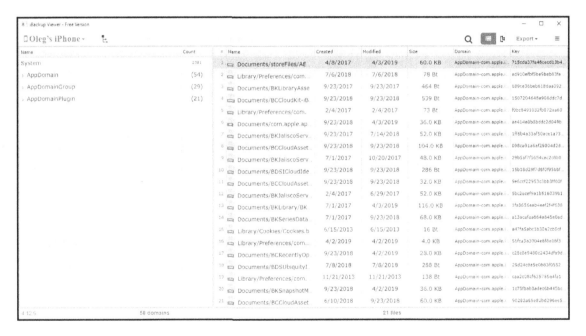

The Raw Data mode

With the help of this tool, you can easily view and export files of interest. Of course, it's not the only tool capable of solving such tasks. Let's look at another one—iExplorer.

iExplorer

A free version of iExplorer is available at `https://macroplant.com/iexplorer`. This tool supports both Windows and macOS and is capable of browsing iTunes backups, too. Here is how to use it:

1. Launch iExplorer and click on **Browse iTunes Backups**.
2. To add a backup from a custom location, click on **Add/Modify Backup Location**.
3. Now, click on the **Add Backup Location** button and choose the path, as illustrated in the following screenshot:

Adding a custom path

4. The backups from your custom location should now be available.

Also, there is an interesting option—iExplorer can gather SQLite databases for you. To do this, click on the **Raw Databases** button to take you to the following screen (you will learn more about SQLite forensics in the following chapter):

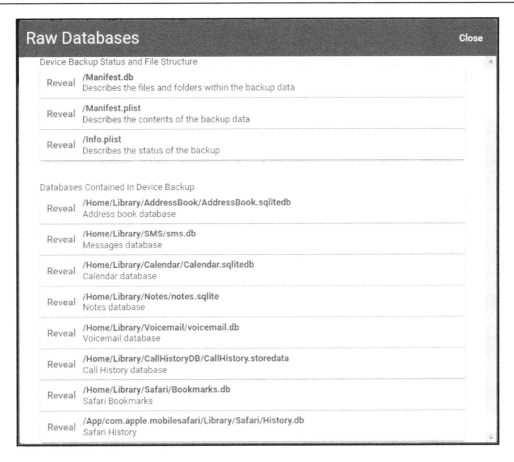

iExplorer Raw Databases option

You can also browse the backup as a list of files and folders with the help of iExplorer; use the left pane for this. Also, you can use the **Backup Explorer** button and then the main pane to browse the backup.

As you can see, there are enough tools capable of extracting valuable pieces of data from an iTunes backup, even if it's encrypted. Of course, it's usually possible if you know the password. But what if you don't? You will learn how to bypass it in the next section.

Handling encrypted backup files

For encrypted backups, the backup files are encrypted using the **Advanced Encryption Standard-256 (AES-256)** algorithm in the **Cipher Block Chaining (CBC)** mode, with a unique key and a null **initialization vector (IV)**. The unique file keys are protected with a set of class keys from `Backup keybag`. The class keys in `Backup keybag` are protected with a key derived from the password set in iTunes through 10,000 iterations of the **Password-Based Key Derivation Function 2 (PBKDF2)**. In iOS 10.2 this mechanism was upgraded, so now, there are 10,000,000 iterations.

Many free and commercial tools provide support for encrypted backup file parsing if the password is known. Unfortunately, it's not always true, so sometimes forensic examiners have to crack such passwords. The next section will walk you through this process, with Elcomsoft Phone Breaker.

Elcomsoft Phone Breaker

Elcomsoft Phone Breaker is a **graphics processing unit (GPU)**-accelerated commercial tool from Elcomsoft, developed for the Windows platform. The tool can decrypt an encrypted backup file when the backup password is not available. The tool provides an option to launch a password brute-force attack on the encrypted backup if the backup password is not available. Elcomsoft Phone Breaker tries to recover the plain-text password that protects the encrypted backup, using a dictionary and brute-force attacks. Passwords that are relatively short and simple can be recovered in a reasonable amount of time. However, if the backup is protected with a strong and complex password, breaking it can take forever.

The tool is available here (including free trial version): `https://www.elcomsoft.com/eppb.html`.

To brute-force the backup password, perform the following steps:

1. Launch the Elcomsoft Phone Breaker tool and the tool's main screen will appear, as shown in the following screenshot:

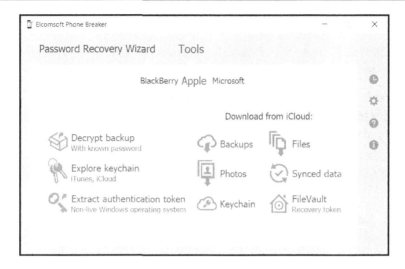

Elcomsoft Phone Breaker's main screen

2. Navigate to **Password Recovery Wizard** | **Choose source** | **iOS device backup**. Navigate to the backup file you want to crack, and select the `Manifest.plist` file.

3. Configure the brute-force pattern in the **Attacks** section and click on the **Start** button to start the brute-force attack, as illustrated in the following screenshot:

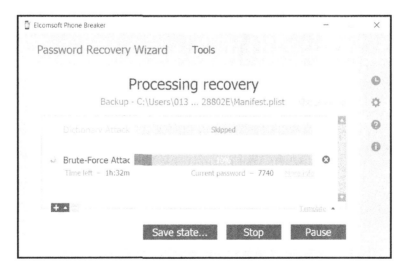

Password recovery process

If the brute-force attack is successful, the tool displays the password on the main screen.

If you have an iPhone running iOS 11 or later, and its passcode, you can reset the actual password and make a backup with a new known password. Here is how to do it:

1. On the iPhone, go to **Settings** | **General** | **Reset**.
2. Choose **Reset All Settings** and enter the device's passcode. It's important to note that no data will be deleted.
3. Once the settings are reset, you can create a new backup with a password of your choice.

 If the **Screen Time** password is set, you will need it as well to reset the backup password.

Working with iCloud backups

iCloud is a cloud storage and cloud computing service by Apple, launched in October 2011. The service allows users to keep data such as calendars, contacts, reminders, photos, documents, bookmarks, applications, notes, and more in sync across multiple compatible devices (iOS devices running with iOS 5 or later; computers with macOS X 10.7.2 or later; and Microsoft Windows), using a centralized iCloud account. The service also allows users to wirelessly and automatically back up their iOS devices to iCloud. iCloud also provides other services, such as *Find My iPhone* (to track a lost phone and wipe it remotely) and *Find My Friends* (to share locations with friends and notify the user when a device arrives at a certain location).

Signing up with iCloud is free, and is simple to perform with an Apple ID. When you sign up for iCloud, Apple grants you access to 5 GB of free remote storage. If you need more storage, you can purchase the upgrade plan. To keep your data secure, Apple forces users to choose a strong password when creating an Apple ID to use with iCloud. The password must have a minimum of eight characters, including a number, an uppercase letter, and a lowercase letter.

iOS devices running on iOS 5 and later allow users to back up the device settings and data to iCloud. Data backed up includes photos, videos, documents, application data, device settings, messages, contacts, calendars, emails, and keychain, as shown in the following screenshot. You can turn on iCloud backup on your device by navigating to **Settings** | **Passwords & Accounts** | **iCloud** | **iCloud**:

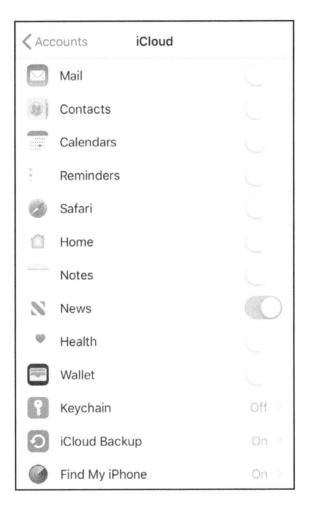

iCloud backup options on the iPhone

iCloud can automatically back up your data when your phone is plugged in, locked, and connected to Wi-Fi. That is to say, iCloud backups represent a fresh and near-real-time copy of information stored on the device, as long as space is available to create a current backup.

You can also initiate an iCloud backup from a computer by connecting the device to iTunes and choosing the **iCloud** option. iCloud backups are incremental; that is, once the initial iCloud backup is completed, all the subsequent backups only copy the files that are changed on the device. iCloud secures your data by encrypting it when it is transmitted over the internet, storing it in an encrypted format on the server, and using secure tokens for authentication.

Apple's built-in apps (for example, **Mail** and **Contacts**) use a secure token to access iCloud services. Using secure tokens for authentication eliminates the need to store the iCloud password on devices and computers.

Extracting iCloud backups

Online backups stored on the iCloud are commonly retrieved when the original iOS device is damaged, upgraded, or lost. To extract a backup from iCloud, you must know the user's Apple ID and password. With the known Apple ID and password, you can log on to `https://www.icloud.com/` and get access to contacts, notes, emails, calendars, photos, reminders, and more. You can also use forensic tools to extract data from iCloud. For example, you can use **Belkasoft Acquisition Tool**, a free tool from Belkasoft that can be downloaded from: `https://belkasoft.com/get`.

To extract the iCloud data, perform the following steps:

1. Launch Belkasoft Acquisition Tool.
2. Choose the **Cloud** option.
3. Choose **iCloud**.
4. Type the Apple ID login and password, and click **Next**.
5. Choose the artifacts you want to download and the target folder in which you want to place them, as illustrated in the following screenshot:

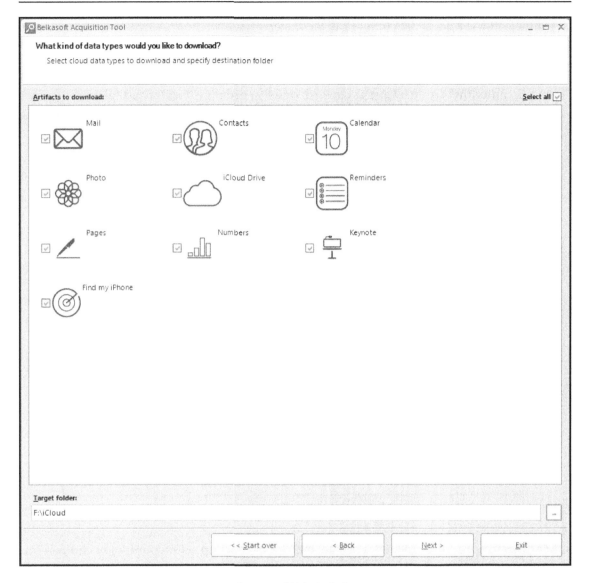

Data types available for downloading

6. Enter the verification code.
7. Wait for the process to complete. You'll find the files in the folder you've chosen.

If you prefer full backups, the best choice is Elcomsoft Phone Breaker.

To download the iCloud backup, follow these steps:

1. Launch Elcomsoft Phone Breaker.
2. Choose the **Backups** option.
3. Enter the Apple ID and password, or use a previously extracted token.
4. If Apple ID is protected with **two-factor authentication** (**2FA**), enter the code in the corresponding field.
5. Choose the backup you want to download, as illustrated in the following screenshot:

Choosing the backup for downloading

Once downloading is completed, you can analyze the backup with your tool of choice—for example, one of the tools discussed throughout this chapter.

Summary

iOS device backups contain essential information that may be your only source of evidence. Information stored in iOS backups includes photos, videos, contacts, emails, call logs, user accounts and passwords, applications, and device settings. This chapter explained how to create backup files and retrieve data from iTunes and iCloud backups, including encrypted backup files, wherever possible.

The following chapter, Chapter 5, *iOS Data Analysis and Recovery*, goes further into the forensic investigation by showing you how to analyze the data recovered from the backup files.

5
iOS Data Analysis and Recovery

A key aspect of iOS-device forensics is to examine and analyze the data acquired to interpret the evidence. In the previous chapters, you learned various techniques to acquire data from iOS devices. Any type of acquired image contains hundreds of data files that are often parsed by the tools described in earlier chapters. Even when the data is parsed by the forensic tool, a manual analysis may be required to uncover additional artifacts or to simply validate your findings.

This chapter will help you understand how data is stored on iOS devices, and it will walk you through the key artifacts that should be examined in each investigation to recover the most data possible.

In this chapter, we will be covering the following topics:

- Interpreting iOS timestamps
- Working with SQLite databases
- Key artifacts – important iOS database files
- Property lists
- Other important files
- Recovering deleted SQLite records

Interpreting iOS timestamps

Before examining the data, it is important to understand different timestamp formats that are used on iOS devices. Timestamps found on iOS devices are presented either in the *Unix timestamp* or *Mac absolute time* format. You, as the examiner, must ensure that the tools properly convert the timestamps. Access to the raw SQLite files will allow you to verify these timestamps manually. You'll learn how to decode each timestamp format in the next few sections.

Unix timestamps

A Unix timestamp is the number of seconds that have elapsed since Unix epoch time, which started at midnight on January 1, 1970. A Unix timestamp can be converted easily, using the `date` command on a Mac workstation or using an online Unix epoch converter, such as `https://www.epochconverter.com/`.

The `date` command is shown in the following code snippet:

```
$ date -r 1557479897
Fri May 10 12:18:17 MSK 2019
```

You may come across Unix timestamps in a millisecond or nanosecond format as well. This is not a big problem; there are a number of online converters, such as `http://currentmillis.com/`, as highlighted in the following screenshot:

A Unix timestamp in milliseconds converted with http://currentmillis.com/

The Unix epoch is the most common format for iOS devices, but there are others as well, including Mac absolute time and WebKit/Chrome time.

Mac absolute time

iOS devices adopted the use of Mac absolute time with iOS 5. Mac absolute time is the number of seconds that have elapsed since Mac epoch time, which started at midnight on January 1, 2001. The difference between the Unix epoch time and the Mac time is exactly 978,307,200 seconds. It means you can easily convert the Mac time to the Unix epoch and use the same methods to finally convert it to a human-readable timestamp. Of course, there are a few online converters, such as `https://www.epochconverter.com/coredata`, as shown in the following screenshot:

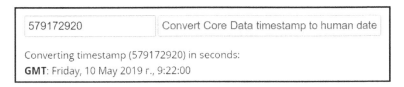

579172920	Convert Core Data timestamp to human date

Converting timestamp (579172920) in seconds:
GMT: Friday, 10 May 2019 г., 9:22:00

A Mac timestamp converted with https://www.epochconverter.com/coredata

Of course, there are offline tools for timestamp conversion as well. We'll introduce you to one of them in the next section.

WebKit/Chrome time

When analyzing iOS application data, especially for web browsers such as Google Chrome, Safari, and Opera, you may face another timestamp format—*WebKit/Chrome time*. This is the number of microseconds since midnight on January 1, 1601. There is also an online converter for this: `https://www.epochconverter.com/webkit`.

If you don't like or don't want to use online converters for some reason, you can also use a free tool: Digital Detective's DCode. This tool can be used to convert timestamps in a number of different formats, including Unix time (both seconds and milliseconds), Mac absolute time, and WebKit/Chrome time, as shown in the following screenshot:

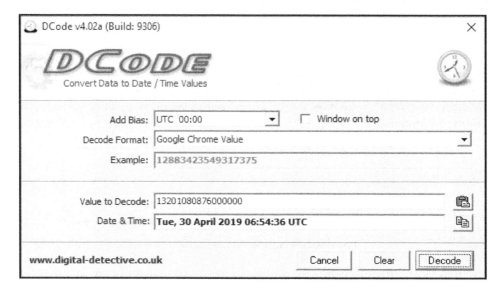

A WebKit/Chrome timestamp converted with DCode

Many commercial mobile forensic suites will easily convert extracted timestamps for you automatically, but in some cases, it's extremely important to validate it, so it's a must for you to clearly understand the timestamp formats.

Working with SQLite databases

SQLite is an open source, in-process library that implements a self-contained, zero-configuration, and transactional SQL database engine. This is a complete database with multiple tables, triggers, and views that are contained in a single cross-platform file. As SQLite is portable, reliable, and small, it is a popular database format that appears on many mobile platforms.

Apple iOS devices, as with other smartphones and tablets, make heavy use of SQLite databases for data storage. Many of the built-in applications—such as Phone, Messages, Mail, Calendar, and Notes—store data in SQLite databases. Apart from this, third-party applications installed on the device also leverage SQLite databases for data storage.

SQLite databases are created with or without a file extension. They typically have the `.sqlitedb` or `.db` file extensions, but some databases are given other extensions as well.

Data in SQLite files is broken up into tables that contain the actual data. To access the data stored in the files, you need a tool that is able to read it. Most commercial mobile forensic tools—such as Belkasoft Evidence Center, Magnet AXIOM, and Cellebrite **Universal Forensic Extraction Device (UFED)** Physical Analyzer—provide support for the examination of SQLite databases. If you don't own one of these tools, some good free tools are as follows:

- **DB Browser for SQLite (DB4S)**: This can be downloaded from `http://sqlitebrowser.org/`.
- **SQLite command-line client**: This can be downloaded from `http://www.sqlite.org/`.
- **SQLiteStudio** (`https://sqlitestudio.pl`): This is a free cross-platform SQLite manager with support for Windows 9x/2k/XP/2003/Vista/7/8/10, macOS, and Linux.
- **SQLiteSpy**: This is a free **graphical user interface (GUI)** tool for Windows. You can download it from
  `http://www.yunqa.de/delphi/doku.php/products/sqlitespy/index`.

macOS includes the SQLite command-line utility (`sqlite3`) by default. This command-line utility can be used to access individual files and run SQL queries against a database. In the following sections, we will use both the `sqlite3` command-line utility and other SQLite tools and browsers to retrieve data from various SQLite databases. Before retrieving the data, the basic commands that you will need to learn are explained in the following sections.

Connecting to a database

Manual examination of iOS SQLite database files is possible with the use of free tools. The following is an example of how to examine a database using native Mac commands in the Terminal:

1. Make sure that your device image is mounted as read-only to prevent changes being made to the original evidence.

2. To connect to an SQLite database from the command line, run the `sqlite3` command in the Terminal by entering your database file. This will give you an SQL prompt where you can issue SQL queries, as shown in the following code block:

```
$ sqlite3 sms.db
SQLite version 3.28.0 2019-04-15 14:49:49
Enter ".help" for usage hints.
```

3. To disconnect, use the `.exit` command. This exits the SQLite client and returns to the Terminal.

The next section will walk you through the analysis of databases, using `sqlite3` built-in commands.

Exploring SQLite special commands

Once you connect to a database, you can use a number of built-in SQLite commands that are known as *dot commands* and that can be used to obtain information from the database files.

You can obtain the list of special commands by issuing the `.help` command in the SQLite prompt. These are SQLite-specific commands, and they do not require a semicolon at the end. The most commonly used dot commands include the following:

- `.tables`: This lists all of the tables within a database. The following screenshot displays the list of tables found inside the `sms.db` database:

```
sqlite> .tables
_SqliteDatabaseProperties   kvtable
attachment                  message
chat                        message_attachment_join
chat_handle_join            message_processing_task
chat_message_join           sync_deleted_attachments
deleted_messages            sync_deleted_chats
handle                      sync_deleted_messages
```

- `.schema table-name`: This displays the `SQL CREATE` statement that was used to construct the table. The following screenshot displays the schema for the `handle` table from the `sms.db` database:

```
sqlite> .schema handle
CREATE TABLE handle ( ROWID INTEGER PRIMARY KEY AUTOINCREMENT UNIQUE, id TEXT NOT NULL,
country TEXT, service TEXT NOT NULL, uncanonicalized_id TEXT, UNIQUE (id, service) );
```

- `.dump table-name`: This dumps the entire content of a table into SQL statements. The example in the following screenshot displays the dump of the `handle` table, which is found inside the `sms.db` database:

```
sqlite> .dump deleted_messages
PRAGMA foreign_keys=OFF;
BEGIN TRANSACTION;
CREATE TABLE deleted_messages (ROWID INTEGER PRIMARY KEY AUTOINCREMENT UNIQUE,
  guid TEXT NOT NULL);
COMMIT;
```

- `.output file-name`: This redirects the output to a file on the disk instead of showing it on the screen.
- `.headers on`: This displays the column title whenever you issue a `SELECT` statement.
- `.help`: This displays the list of available SQLite dot commands.
- `.exit`: This disconnects from the database and exits the SQLite command shell.
- `.mode`: This sets the output mode; it could be `.csv`, HTML, tabs, and so on.

Make sure that there is no space between the SQLite prompt and the dot command; otherwise, the entire command will be ignored.

Exploring standard SQL queries

In addition to the SQLite dot commands, standard SQL queries such as `SELECT`, `INSERT`, `ALTER`, and `DELETE` can be issued to SQLite databases on the command line. Unlike the SQLite dot commands, standard SQL queries expect a semicolon at the end of the command.

Most of the databases that you will examine will contain only a reasonable number of records, so you can issue a `SELECT *` statement, which prints all of the data contained in the table. This will be covered in detail throughout this chapter.

Accessing a database using commercial tools

While a manual examination of iOS SQLite database files is possible with the use of free tools, most examiners prefer commercial support prior to digging manually into the files for examination. The following is an example of how to examine a database using SQLite, which is included in Belkasoft Evidence Center.

To open and analyze a database, you just need to follow a few simple steps, listed here:

1. Launch Belkasoft Evidence Center and navigate to **View | SQLite Viewer**, and choose the database file you want to examine.
2. Once the database is chosen, it's immediately opened with SQLite Viewer and is ready to be examined, as illustrated in the following screenshot:

sms.db database opened with Belkasoft Evidence Center's SQLite Viewer

Why does an examiner need to use such commercial viewers instead of free and open-source ones? For example, this particular viewer supports even damaged or partially overwritten SQLite databases. What's more, the tool supports the extraction of data from freelists, **Write-Ahead Log (WAL)**, and unallocated space, as illustrated in the following screenshot:

Carved data from unallocated space		Unallocated	
Offset	Length		Data
8196	4092		080ba6000fcc0fb00f2d...

	00	01	02	03	04	05	06	07	08	09	0a	0b	0c	0d	0e	0f	
d40	68	74	74	70	73	3a	2f	2f	61	77	61	79	2e	76	6b	2e	https://away.vk.
d50	63	6f	6d	2f	61	77	61	79	2e	70	68	70	3f	61	64	61	com/away.php?ada
d60	61	74	6f	3d	41	51	73	7a	53	57	30	57	4c	77	5a	63	ato=AQszSW0WLwZc
d70	45	30	6c	73	41	44	51	58	4f	44	39	30	64	53	67	2a	E01sADQXOD90dSg*
d80	57	47	6f	69	61	56	67	39	53	47	68	30	44	30	67	70	WGoiaVg9SGh0D0gp
d90	46	78	63	68	62	45	63	47	42	6c	45	59	4b	6a	6f	47	FxchbEcGBlEYKjoG
da0	43	53	55	6e	43	6a	6b	65	58	56	6b	47	45	68	34	2a	CSUnCjkeXVkGEh4*
db0	4b	68	46	42	47	58	67	48	52	54	34	6b	41	56	49	50	KhFBGXgHRT4kAVIP
dc0	50	68	35	34	46	77	49	68	4e	44	38	32	65	52	74	51	Ph54FwIhND82eRtQ
dd0	44	78	49	38	48	6a	4d	31	4a	31	78	7a	4c	41	77	69	DxI8HjM1J1xzLAwi
de0	61	77	34	7a	61	6b	55	47	52	46	38	43	4f	68	73	50	aw4zakUGRF8COhsP
df0	47	51	5a	78	58	68	38	72	54	33	77	62	45	41	73	36	GQZxXh8rT3wbEAs6
e00	49	57	35	6a	46	57	4e	79	46	32	77	78	41	6b	5a	75	IW5jFWNyF2wxAkZu
e10	4a	6b	52	44	44	53	41	4b	4f	52	77	4d	66	51	4d	50	JkRDDSAKORwMfQMp
e20	5a	78	63	61	5a	41	38	69	46	6d	31	63	48	57	38	57	ZxcaZA8iFm1cHW8W
e30	52	43	45	6a	44	33	78	30	48	6d	68	70	43	51	51	6c	RCEjD3x0HmhpCQQl
e40	45	43	45	57	62	6c	6b	42	65	32	73	42	54	51	4a	35	ECEWblkBe2sBTQJ5
e50	45	32	31	76	48	51	77	57	42	54	41	47	4c	6e	4d	42	E21vHQwWBTAGLnMB
e60	52	45	6c	68	49	53	34	6a	4c	78	59	51	57	54	74	62	RElhIS4jLxYQWTtb

Unallocated space of the database as seen in Belkasoft Evidence Center's SQLite Viewer

Of course, there are some free and open source tools available for SQLite data recovery. You'll learn more about such tools in the following sections.

Key artifacts – important iOS database files

Filesystems and backups that you extracted as per the instructions in Chapter 3, *Data Acquisition from iOS Devices*, and Chapter 4, *Data Acquisition from iOS Backups*, should contain the following SQLite databases that may be important to your investigation. If these files are not recovered, make sure that you acquired the iOS device correctly. The files that are shown in the following sections are extracted via logical acquisition from a device running iOS. As Apple adds new features to the built-in applications with every iOS release, the format of the files may vary for different iOS versions.

Address book contacts

The address book contains a wealth of information about the owner's personal contacts. With the exception of third-party applications, the address book contains contact entries for all of the contacts that are stored on the device. The address book database can be found at /HomeDomain/Library/AddressBook.sqlitedb. The AddressBook.sqlitedb file contains several tables, of which the following three are of particular interest:

- ABPerson: This contains the name, organization, notes, and more for each contact.
- ABMultiValue: This contains phone numbers, email addresses, website **Uniform Resource Locators (URLs)**, and more for the entries in the ABPerson table. The ABMultiValue table uses a record_id file to associate the contact information with a ROWID from the ABPerson table.
- ABMultiValueLabel: This table contains labels to identify the kind of information stored in the ABMultiValue table.

Some of the data stored within the AddressBook.sqlitedb file could be from third-party applications. You should manually examine the application file folders to ensure that all the contacts are accounted for and examined.

While all the following commands can be run natively on a Mac, we are going to use DB4S to examine the most common databases found on iOS devices. This is a free tool that simplifies the process and provides a clear view of the data to you. Once the database is loaded, you can draft queries to examine the data most relevant to you and export the address book into a .csv file named AddressBook.csv, as shown in the following screenshot:

The AddressBook.sqlitedb file in DB4S

In the preceding screenshot, you can see the suggested query to parse data from both the `ABPerson` and `ABMultiValue` tables.

Address book images

In addition to the address book's data, each contact may contain an image associated with it. This image is displayed on the screen whenever the user receives an incoming call from a particular contact. These images can be created by third-party applications that have access to the contacts on the device. Often, the contact is linked to a third-party application profile photo. The address book images database can be found at
`/HomeDomain/Library/AddressBook/AddressBookImages.sqlitedb`.

The address book images can be parsed manually, but using commercial software makes this process much more practical. Most free and commercial tools will provide access to the address book images. However, some tools will not make the link between the graphic and the contact, which may require some manual rebuilding. Sometimes, the free solutions work best when parsing simple data from iOS devices. Next, we will examine the address book images in iExplorer, which was introduced in `Chapter 4`, *Data Acquisition from iOS Backups*.

In the example in the following screenshot, iExplorer matched contact data with the image automatically:

Examining address book images in iExplorer

The same thumbnails can be found in the ABThumbnailImage table, in the data column. You can match the photo to the contact manually, using the record_id column from the ABThumbnailImage table of AddressBookImages.sqlitedb and the ROWID column from the ABPerson table of AddressBook.sqlitedb.

Call history

Phone or FaceTime calls placed, missed, and received by the user are logged in the call history along with other metadata, such as call duration, and date and time. The call history database can be found at /HomeDomain/Library/CallHistoryDB/CallHistory.storedata. The CallHistory.storedata file was introduced with iOS 8 and is currently in use at the time of writing (iOS 13.2).

The ZCALLRECORD table in the CallHistory.storedata database contains the call history. It's important to note that only a limited number of calls may be stored in the active database. Just because the database removes the oldest record when space is needed does not mean this data is deleted. It's simply in the free pages of the SQLite database file, and it can be recovered using forensic tools or manually. The most important columns in the ZCALLRECORD table are the following:

- ZDATE: This column contains the timestamps of calls in Mac absolute time format.
- ZDURATION: This column contains the duration of calls.
- ZLOCATION: This column contains the locations of phone numbers.
- ZADDRESS: This column contains the phone numbers.
- ZSERVICE_PROVIDER: This column contains the service providers—for example, Phone, WhatsApp, Telegram, and so on.

You can run the following queries in DB4S to parse the call history. Afterward, you can export it into a .csv file, as shown in the following screenshot:

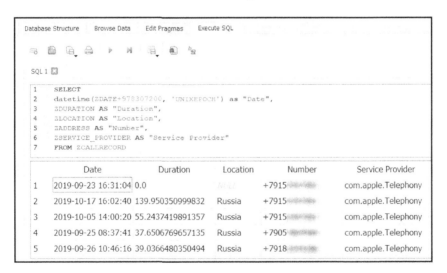

Examining CallHistory.storedata in DB4S

This time, the query is quite simple as all columns of interest are in the same table. Notice we used datetime to convert Mac absolute timestamps to human-readable dates.

Short Message Service (SMS) messages

The SMS database contains text and multimedia messages that were sent from and received by the device, along with the phone number of the remote party, date and time, and other carrier information. Starting with iOS 5, iMessage data is also stored in the SMS database. iMessage allows users to send SMS and **Multimedia Messaging Service (MMS)** messages over a cellular or Wi-Fi network to other iOS or macOS users, thus providing an alternative to SMS. The SMS database can be found at `/HomeDomain/Library/SMS/sms.db`.

You can run the following queries in DB4S to parse the SMS messages. Afterward, you can export it into a `.csv` file, as shown in the following screenshot:

Examining sms.db in DB4S

There's another interesting subdirectory that can be found at `/HomeDomain/Library/SMS/`—`Drafts`. Inside, there are more subfolders, each of which contains a `message.plist` file. Each file is a property list with draft messages the user started to type but didn't send. You'll learn more about property lists in the next sections.

Calendar events

Calendar events that have been manually created by the user or synced using a mail application or other third-party applications are stored in the `Calendar` database. The `Calendar` database can be found at

`/HomeDomain/Library/Calendar/Calendar.sqlitedb`.

The `CalendarItem` table in the `Calendar.sqlitedb` file contains the calendar events summary, description, start date, end date, and more. You can run the following queries in DB4S to parse the calendar, as illustrated in the following screenshot:

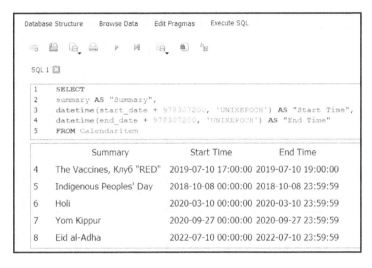

Examining calendar.sqlitedb in DB4S

As you can see, the `CalendarItem` table stores dates in Mac absolute time format, so we added `978307200` to reveal actual timestamps, with the help of the `datetime` function.

Notes

The `Notes` database contains the notes that are created by the user using the device's built-in `Notes` application. `Notes` is the simplest application, often containing the most sensitive and confidential information. The `Notes` database can be found at

`/HomeDomain/Library/Notes/notes.sqlite`.

The `ZNOTE` and `ZNOTEBODY` tables in the `notes.sqlite` file contain each note's title, content, creation date, modification date, and more. You can run the following queries to parse the `Notes` database:

Examining notes in DB4S

This query merges data from two tables, so we use `ZOWNER` from `ZNOTEBODY`, `Z_PK` from `ZNOTE`, and a `WHERE` clause to do it.

Safari bookmarks and history

The Safari browser used on an iOS device allows users to bookmark their favorite websites. The `Bookmarks` database can be found at `/HomeDomain/Library/Safari/Bookmarks.db`. Bookmark data can be extracted with a very simple query, as illustrated in the following screenshot:

Examining bookmarks in DB4S

Browsing history can be found in `History.db`, at `/HomeDomain/Library/Safari/`. The most important pieces of information about visited websites can be extracted from `history_items` and `history_visits` tables, as shown in the following screenshot:

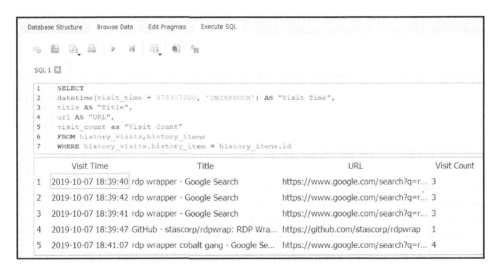

Examining history in DB4S

In addition to Safari, other browsers can be used to store data on an iOS device. For this reason, we recommend using a tool built to parse internet history, to ensure that data is not overlooked. Good forensic tools for solving this task are AXIOM by Magnet Forensics, Physical Analyzer by Cellebrite, and some others.

Voicemail

The `Voicemail` database contains metadata about each voicemail that is stored on the device, which includes the sender's phone number, callback number, timestamp and message duration, and more. The voicemail recordings are stored as **Adaptive Multi-Rate (AMR)** audio files that can be played by any media player that supports the AMR codec (for example, QuickTime Player). The `Voicemail` database can be found under `/HomeDomain/Library/Voicemail/voicemail.db`.

Recordings

The `Recordings` database contains metadata about each recording stored on the device, which includes the timestamp, its duration, its location on the device, and more. The database can be found at `/MediaDomain/Media/Recordings`. The metadata can be extracted with the query shown in the following screenshot:

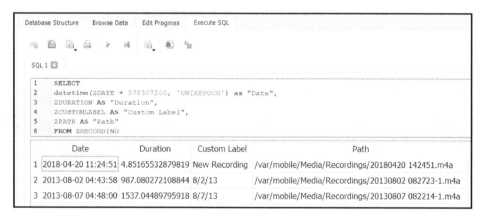

Examining recordings in DB4S

As you can see in the preceding screenshot, actual files with recordings are stored in the same directory.

Device interaction

There is an SQLite database that records how the user interacts with different applications. This database is called `interactionC.db` and is located at `/HomeDomain/Library/CoreDuet/People`. The `ZINTERACTIONS` table contains information about whether the user reads a message, sends a message, performs a call, and so on. You can extract this information from the table with the query shown in the following screenshot:

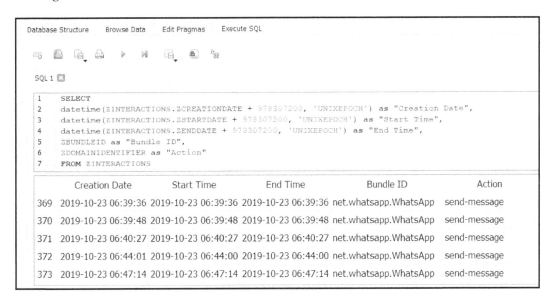

Examining interactions in DB4S

Also, make sure you examined the `ZCONTACTS` table—it contains information about contacts who were involved in the user's interactions with the device, if applicable.

Phone numbers

You can obtain information about all phone numbers utilized by the user, even if they changed phones and restored from a backup, by analyzing the `CellularUsage.db` file located at `/WirelessDomain/Library/Databases`. The query to extract this data is shown in the following screenshot:

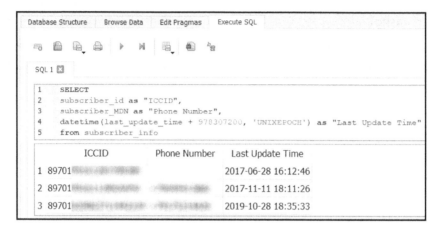

Extracting phone numbers

As you can see, there is not only phone numbers available, but also the **Subscriber Identity Module (SIM)** card's **Integrated Circuit Card Identifier (ICCID)**.

Property lists

A property list, commonly referred to as a `plist`, is a structured data format used to store, organize, and access various types of data on an iOS device as well as a macOS device. `plist` files are binary-formatted, and they can be viewed using a property List Editor, which is capable of reading or converting the binary format to an **American Standard Code for Information Interchange (ASCII)** format.

`Plist` files may or may not have a `.plist` file extension. To access the data stored in these files, you need a tool that can read them. Some of the good free tools include the following:

- plist Editor Pro, which can be downloaded from `http://www.icopybot.com/plist-editor.htm`.
- The `plutil` command-line utility on macOS.

You can view `plist` files using Xcode. macOS includes the `plutil` command-line utility by default. This command-line utility can easily convert the binary-formatted files into human-readable files. In addition to this, most commercial forensic tools include great support for parsing `plist` files.

The following screenshot displays the `com.apple.mobile.ldbackup.plist` file:

Key	Type	Value
⊟ Root	dict	
Version	string	2.0
LastiTunesBackupTZ	string	GMT+3
RequiresEncryption	integer	0
WillEncrypt	boolean	true
LastiTunesBackupDate	integer	581862772
CloudBackupEnabled	boolean	true
LastCloudBackupTZ	string	GMT+3
LastCloudBackupDate	integer	594465315

The com.apple.mobile.ldbackup.plist in plist Editor Pro

As you can see, this `plist` uncovers the last local and cloud backup dates (in Mac absolute time, of course), the time zone it was created in, as well as the fact that the backup is encrypted.

Important plist files

Raw disk images or the backup that you extracted in `Chapter 3`, *Data Acquisition from iOS Devices*, and `Chapter 4`, *Data Acquisition from iOS Backups*, should contain the following `plist` files that are important for an investigation. The files displayed are extracted from an iOS 13.2 device backup. The file locations may vary for your iOS version.

The following are the `plist` files that contain data that may be relevant to your investigation:

plist file	Description
/HomeDomain/Library/Preferences/com.apple.commcenter.shared.plist	Contains the phone number in use
/HomeDomain/Library/Preferences/com.apple.identityservices.idstatuscache.plist	Contains information about the email address used for the Apple ID and the phone numbers of the individuals the user interacted with via FaceTime or iMessage using this ID
/HomeDomain/Library/Preferences/com.apple.mobile.ldbackup.plist	Contains the timestamps of the last iTunes and iCloud backups, the last iTunes backup time zone, and if it was encrypted or not
/HomeDomain/Library/Preferences/com.apple.MobileBackup.DemotedApps.plist	Contains the list of unused applications that were automatically offloaded by the operating system
/HomeDomain/Library/Preferences/com.apple.mobilephone.speeddial.plist	Contains the list of the user's favorite contacts, including their names and phone numbers
/HomeDomain/Library/Preferences/com.apple.preferences.datetime.plist	Contains information about the time zone set by the user
/RootDomain/Library/Caches/locationd/clients.plist	Contains the list of applications that use location Services
/RootDomain/Library/Preferences/com.apple.MobileBackup.plist	Contains information about the last restoration from the backup, including the restore start date, file transfer duration, number of files transferred, source device **Unique Device Identifier (UDID)**, and so on
/SystemPreferencesDomain/SystemConfiguration/com.apple.mobilegestalt.plist	Contains the device name assigned by the user
/SystemPreferencesDomain/SystemConfiguration/com.apple.wifi.plist	Contains information about wireless access points used by the device owner
/WirelessDomain/Library/Preferences/com.apple.commcenter.plist	Contains information about the device phone number, network carrier, ICCIDs, and **international mobile subscriber identities (IMSIs)**

Of course, `plist` files don't contain as much information as SQLite databases, but they can still be useful during your forensic examinations. Next, we'll look at some other files that may be also useful.

Other important files

Apart from SQLite and `plist` files, several other locations may contain information that could be valuable to an investigation.

The other sources include the following:

- Local dictionary
- Photos
- Thumbnails
- Wallpaper
- Downloaded third-party applications

Let's look at each of them.

Local dictionary

The list of words added by the device user to the dictionary are stored in a `LocalDictionary` plaintext file, located at `/KeyboardDomain/Library/Keyboard/`. As the file is plaintext, you can use your favorite text editor.

Photos

Photos are stored in a directory located at `/CameraRollDomain/Media/DCIM`, which contains the photos taken with the device's built-in camera, screenshots, selfies, photo stream, recently deleted photos, and accompanying thumbnails. Some third-party applications will also store photos taken in this directory. Every photo stored in the `DCIM` folder contains **Exchangeable Image File Format (EXIF)** data. `EXIF` data stored in the photo can be extracted using `ExifTool`, which can be downloaded from `https://sno.phy. queensu.ca/~phil/exiftool/`. `EXIF` data may contain geographical information when a photo is tagged with the user's geolocation if the user has enabled location permissions on the iOS device.

Thumbnails

Another source of important artifacts related to photos is the `ithmb` files. You can find these files at `/CameraRollDomain/Media/PhotoData/Thumbnails`. These files contain thumbnails not only for actual photos on the device but also for deleted ones. And, of course, there is a tool for parsing such files, `iThmb Converter`, which can be downloaded from `http://www.ithmbconverter.com/en/download/` and is shown in the following screenshot:

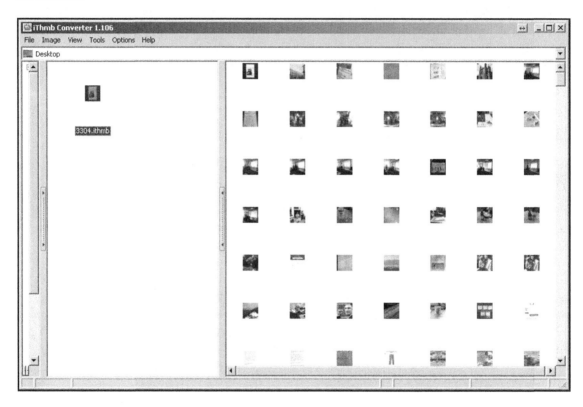

Examining 3304.ithmb with iThmb Converter

As these files may contain thumbnails of deleted photos, they mustn't be overlooked by forensic examiners. What's more, some of them contain quite big thumbnails, so it will be clear what was pictured.

Wallpaper

The current background wallpapers set for the iOS device can be recovered from the `LockBackgroundThumbnail.jpg` and `LockBackgroundThumbnaildark.jpg` files that are found in `/HomeDomain/Library/SpringBoard`.

The wallpaper picture may contain identifying information about the user that could help in a missing person's case or that could be found on an iOS device recovered from a theft investigation.

Downloaded third-party applications

Third-party applications that are downloaded and installed from the App Store—including applications such as Facebook, WhatsApp, Viber, Threema, Tango, Skype, and Gmail—contain a wealth of information that is useful for an investigation. Some third-party applications use Base64 encoding, which needs to be converted for viewing purposes as well as encryption. Applications that encrypt the database file may prevent you from accessing the data residing in the tables. Encryption varies among these applications, based on the application and iOS versions.

A subdirectory with a **universally unique identifier (UUID)** is created for each application that is installed on the device in the `/private/var/mobile/Containers/Data/Application` directory. Most of the files stored in the application's directory are in the SQLite and `plist` format. Each file must be examined for relevance. We recommend using Belkasoft Evidence Center, Cellebrite UFED Physical Analyzer, Elcomsoft Phone Viewer, and Magnet AXIOM when possible to extract these artifacts quickly, before going back and manually running queries and parsing the data.

Also, information about installed applications can be gathered from the `applicationState.db` database, located at `/HomeDomain/Library/FrontBoard`. This is another SQLite database and can be analyzed with an appropriate viewer of the examiner's choice.

Recovering deleted SQLite records

SQLite databases store the deleted records within the database itself, so it is possible to recover deleted data, such as contacts, SMS messages, calendars, notes, email, voicemail, and more by parsing the corresponding SQLite database. If an SQLite database is vacuumed or defragmented, the likelihood of recovering the deleted data is minimal. The amount of cleanup that these databases require relies heavily on the iOS version, the device, and the user's settings on the device.

A SQLite database file comprises one or more fixed-size pages, which are used just once. SQLite uses a B-tree layout of pages to store indices and table content. Detailed information on the B-tree layout can be found at `https://github.com/NotionalLabs/SQLiteZer/blob/master/_resources/Sqlite_carving_extractAndroidData.pdf`.

Commercial forensic tools provide support to recover deleted data from SQLite database files, but they don't always recover all of the data, nor do they support extracting data from all databases on an iOS device. It is recommended that each database containing key artifacts be examined for deleted data. The key artifacts or databases already discussed in this book should be examined using free parsers, hex viewers, or even your forensic tool to determine whether the user deleted artifacts that are relevant to the investigation.

To carve an SQLite database, you can examine the data in raw hex or use `sqliteparse.py`, a free Python script developed by Mari DeGrazia. The Python script can be downloaded from `https://github.com/mdegrazia/SQlite-Deleted-Records-Parser`.

The following example recovers the deleted records from the `notes.sqlitedb` file and dumps the output to the `output.txt` file. This script should work on all database files recovered from iOS devices. To validate your findings from running the script, simply examine the database in a hex viewer to ensure nothing is overlooked. The code can be seen here:

```
$python sqliteparse.py -f notes.sqlitedb -r -o output.txt
```

In addition to this, performing a `strings` dump of the database file can also reveal deleted records that may have been missed, as shown in the following command:

```
$strings notes.sqlitedb
```

Should you prefer a GUI, Mari DeGrazia kindly created one and placed it on her GitHub page.

Another open-source tool you can use to recover deleted SQLite records is Undark. You can download it here: http://pldaniels.com/undark/. To use the tool, run the following command:

```
./undark -i sms.db > sms_database.csv
```

It's important to note that Undark does not differentiate between current and deleted data, so you will get the whole set of data, both actual and deleted.

Summary

This chapter covered various data analysis techniques and specified the locations for common artifacts within the iOS device's filesystem. When writing this chapter, we aimed to cover the most popular artifacts that tie into most investigations. Clearly, it is impossible to cover them all. We hope that once you learn how to extract data from SQLite and plist files, intuition and persistence will assist you in parsing the artifacts that were not covered.

Keep in mind that most open-source and commercial tools are able to pull active and deleted data from common database files, such as contacts, calls, SMS messages, and more, but they often overlook the third-party application database files. Our best advice is to know how to recover the data manually, just in case you need to validate your findings or testify as to how your tool functions.

We covered techniques to recover deleted SQLite records that prove useful in most iOS device investigations. Again, the acquisition method, encoding, and encryption schemas can affect the amount of data that you can recover during your examination.

In the next chapter, *iOS Forensic Tools*, we will introduce you to the most popular mobile forensic tools—Cellebrite UFED Physical Analyzer, Magnet AXIOM, Elcomsoft Phone Viewer, and Belkasoft Evidence Center.

6
iOS Forensic Tools

An examiner like you must not only know how to use forensic tools but must also understand the methods and acquisition techniques that are deployed by the tools you use in your investigations. Apart from saving time, forensic tools also make the process of forensic analysis a lot easier. However, each tool has its flaws. You must catch any mistakes and know how to correct them by leveraging another tool or technique. It's impossible for a tool to support all devices. You are responsible for learning and using the best tools to complete the job. As we discussed in the previous chapters, you must understand how data is stored on iOS devices to ensure that the tool is capturing all the accessible data.

Currently, there are a number of commercial tools, such as Cellebrite UFED Physical Analyzer, BlackBag BlackLight, Oxygen Forensic Detective, Belkasoft Evidence Center, MSAB XRY, Magnet AXIOM, and others, which are available for the forensic acquisition and analysis of iOS devices. For familiarity purposes, this chapter will walk you through the usage of a few of them and provide details on the steps required to perform acquisitions and the analysis of iOS devices.

In this chapter, we will cover the following topics:

- Working with Cellebrite UFED Physical Analyzer
- Working with Magnet AXIOM
- Working with Belkasoft Evidence Center
- Working with Elcomsoft Phone Viewer

Working with Cellebrite UFED Physical Analyzer

As per the vendor, Cellebrite **Universal Forensic Extraction Device (UFED)** empowers law enforcement, antiterrorism, and security organizations to capture critical forensic evidence from mobile phones, smartphones, PDAs, and portable handset varieties, including updates for newly released models. The tool enables forensically sound data extraction, decoding, and analysis techniques to obtain existing and deleted data from different mobile devices. As of February 2019, UFED supports data extraction from almost 28,000 mobile devices.

Features of Cellebrite UFED Physical Analyzer

The following are the features of Cellebrite UFED Physical Analyzer:

- Supports different types of acquisition
- Extracts the device keys that are required to decrypt physical images, as well as keychain items
- Decrypts physical images and keychain items
- Reveals device passwords (not available for all locked devices)
- Allows you to open an encrypted raw disk image file with a known password
- Supports passcode recovery attacks
- Supports advanced analysis and decoding of extracted application data
- Provides access to physical and logical data extracted in the same user interface, making analysis easier
- Generates reports in several popular formats, including Microsoft Excel, PDF, and HTML
- Dumps the raw filesystem partition so that it can be imported and examined in another forensic tool
- Creates a binary image file, in addition to the UFED shortcut file, for ease of importing into other forensic tools for verification

Let's now look at advanced logical acquisition and analysis.

Advanced logical acquisition and analysis with Cellebrite UFED Physical Analyzer

As we mentioned previously, Physical Analyzer can be used not only for parsing different types of forensic artifacts from acquired images but also for performing both logical and filesystem (and even physical, for older devices) types of extraction from iOS devices. Due to the fact that physical acquisition is actually only for older devices, the best option is an advanced logical acquisition.

We are going to acquire and analyze data from an iPhone running iOS 13.2.3. Let's get started:

1. Connect the device through the appropriate cable to your workstation. Make sure it's trusted and launch the Physical Analyzer.

2. Go to **Extract | iOS Device Extraction**. The **iOS Device Data Extraction Wizard** window will pop up:

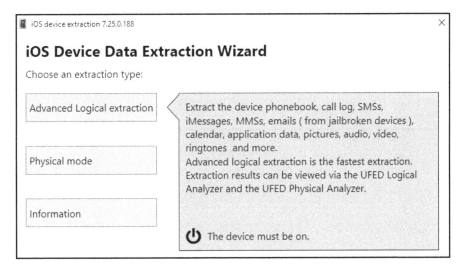

Choosing an extraction type

3. Since we are dealing with a modern iOS device, let's choose **Advanced Logical extraction**. If the device is recognized, you'll see the device's name, its UDID, and also its iOS version:

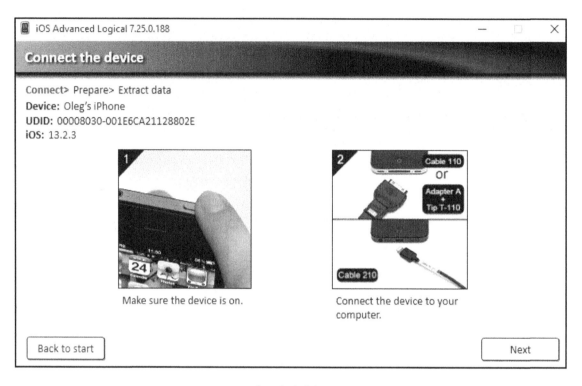

Connecting the device

In our case, the iPhone's iTunes backup is protected with a known password, so the best method is **Method 1**:

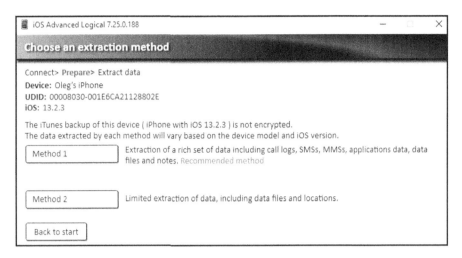

Choosing an extraction method

4. If you want the backup to be encrypted (recommended), you can choose this option on the next page:

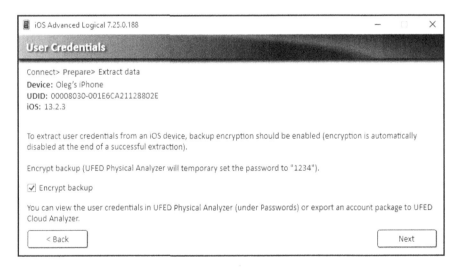

Choosing whether the backup should be encrypted or not

5. It's time to choose where the data will be saved; in our case, it's the root of the D:\ drive:

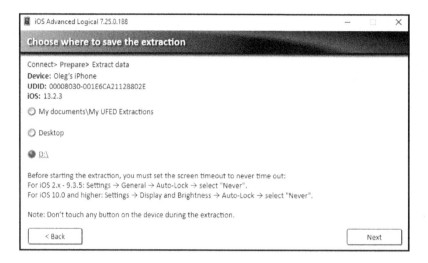

Choosing where to save the extraction

5. Now, the acquisition process will start. Make sure the device is connected until the end of the process:

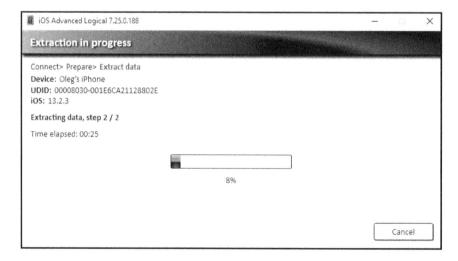

Extracting the data

Once the extraction process has finished, the extracted data will be parsed with powerful Physical Analyzer plugins. As a result, you will get a set of artifacts divided into a number of categories:

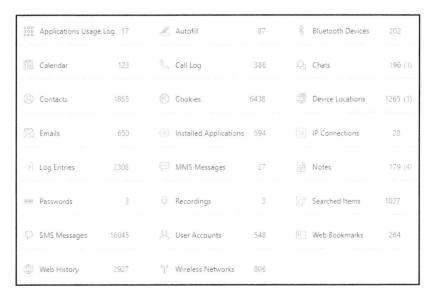

Phone data extracted and parsed by Physical Analyzer

The same can be said about the data files:

Data files extracted by Physical Analyzer

As you may have already noticed, there are red numbers in brackets – these are deleted records that have been recovered by Physical Analyzer's plugins. As you already know, it's not a miracle that deleted data can be recovered from SQLite databases, which are widely used in iOS.

Talking about SQLite databases, there is another amazing feature of Physical Analyzer that might be useful for adding custom artifacts to your mobile forensics reports and parsing unknown apps data – the SQLite wizard. You can find it under **Tools** | **SQLite wizard**:

1. Let's start by choosing a database. Of course, it's good to choose an app that isn't parsed by Physical Analyzer automatically. In our example, this is an app called **Scan**:

Selecting a database

2. Make sure you have selected the **Include deleted rows** option; this will help you recover data automatically but, of course, it will increase the number of false positive records:

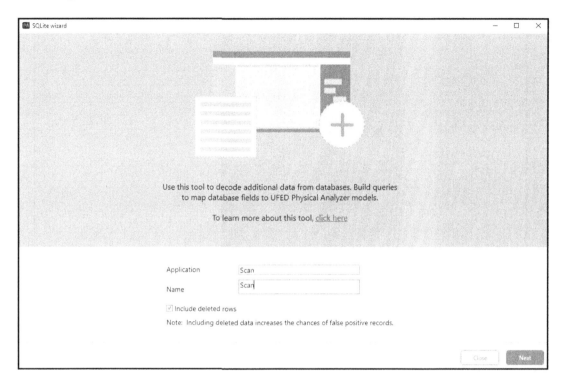

Starting the SQLite wizard

So, our app is used for scanning QR codes and contains four columns of interest – the scan date and time, latitude, longitude, and scan result. All of the rows are part of ZSCSCANEVENT:

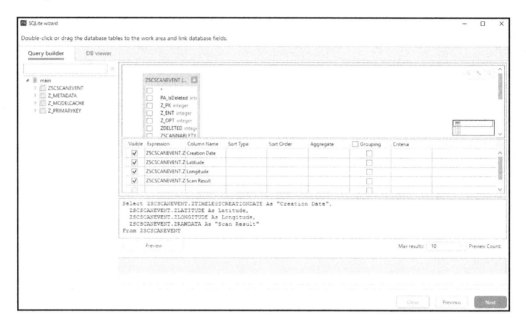

Choosing database tables and columns

3. The next step is selecting the timestamp. You've already learned quite a bit about iOS timestamps and should recognize the format in ZTIMELESSCREATIONDATE, but even if you don't, the SQLite wizard does this for you:

Selecting the timestamp format

4. The generic model will suit any database, but there are some existing Physical Analyzer models that can be used for typical content, such as *Chats* or *Contacts*. In our case, we are using the generic model:

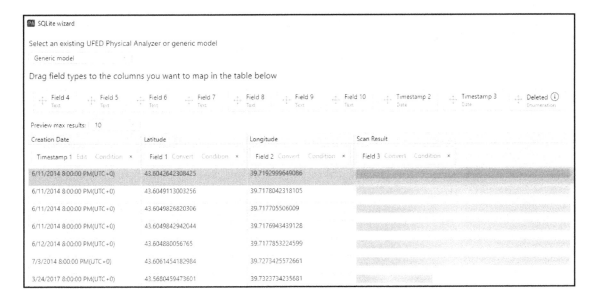

Choosing the model

Once you've chosen the model and field types for the column, you can run the query and add the new parsed artifacts to your extraction and, afterward, to your report.

Working with Magnet AXIOM

Magnet AXIOM is one of the most useful digital forensics tools on the market. It can be used for both computer and mobile forensics; the recent version of the suite introduced the newest feature – cloud forensics. As for iOS forensics, it can be used both for logical and filesystem acquisitions and supports all iOS versions – from the oldest to the latest. Of course, it can also be used for parsing iTunes backups and physical images created by third-party tools such as Elcomsoft iOS Forensic Toolkit.

One of the best features of Magnet AXIOM is its ability to start processing extraction data on the fly so that you don't have to wait for the acquisition process to be finished to start your forensic analysis.

Features of Magnet AXIOM

The following are the features of Magnet AXIOM:

- Supports logical and filesystem (for jailbroken devices) acquisitions
- Supports both encrypted and unencrypted iTunes backups
- Recovers more than 500 artifact types
- Works with other popular mobile forensics tools such as Cellebrite UFED and XRY
- Includes built-in SQLite and plist viewers
- Creates so-called **Portable Cases** so that you can share the whole set of data with your teammates and third parties
- Can generate reports in several popular formats, such as Microsoft Excel, PDF, and HTML

Logical acquisition and analysis with Magnet AXIOM

As you may recall, the most common acquisition for modern iOS devices is a logical type. Here is how you would acquire an iOS device with Magnet AXIOM:

1. Start by creating a new case:

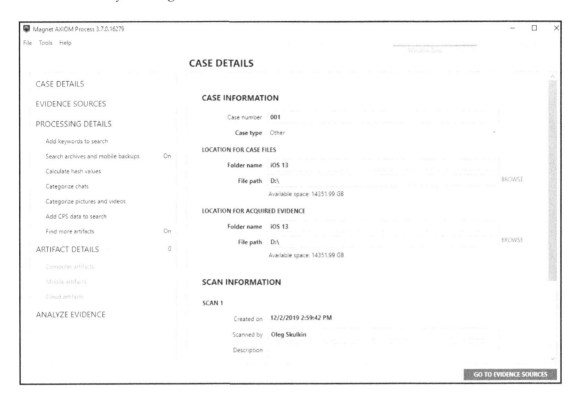

Creating a new case

2. Since we are dealing with an iOS device, we will choose the **MOBILE** option:

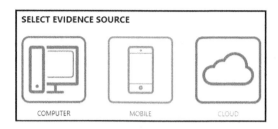

Selecting the evidence source

3. There are a number of options to choose from, but in our case, the **iOS** option is the right one:

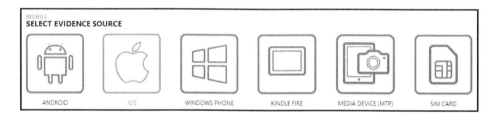

Selecting the evidence source

4. There are three options for acquiring evidence – we can choose an already acquired image (for example, a iTunes backup or a filesystem image acquired by a third-party tool), extract data from the device, or use GrayKey for acquisition. Let's choose the second option:

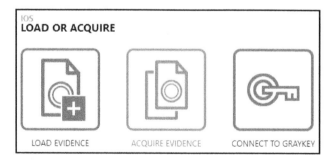

Choosing to acquire evidence

5. Our device is recognized and ready to be imaged. If you don't see your device, use the **UNKNOWN** option:

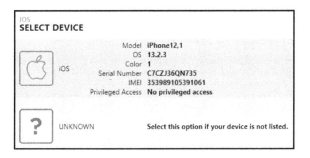

Selecting the device

6. There are two types of extraction – **Quick** and **Full**. The **Full** option will only be available if the device you want to acquire is jailbroken. In our case, it's not:

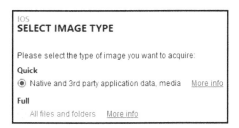

Choosing the image type

7. You will be prompted to enter the password for the backup. As you may recall, this way, you can get more data, so it's highly recommended:

Encrypting the backup

8. Before acquisition and processing are started, you can, for example, choose keywords of interest, use Magnet.AI to categorize chats, or configure Dynamic App Finder:

ADD KEYWORDS TO SEARCH

Provide the keywords and regular expressions that you want to include in your search. If a keyword gets a hit during the search, it's added to a Keywords filter in AXIOM Examine.

> ADD KEYWORDS TO SEARCH

CATEGORIZE CHATS WITH MAGNET.AI

Enable chat categories so that AXIOM Examine automatically categorizes chat conversations, based on the categories you select, and tags them in the Artifacts explorer.

> CATEGORIZE CHATS WITH MAGNET.AI

SEARCH ARCHIVES AND MOBILE BACKUPS

Container files such as archives and mobile backups can be found within other evidence sources. Configure options on this page to search any containers found during your search.

> SEARCH ARCHIVES AND MOBILE BACKUPS

CALCULATE HASH VALUES

Import hashes for non-relevant files so they don't appear in your case.

> CALCULATE HASH VALUES

CATEGORIZE PICTURES AND VIDEOS

Import hashes for known media files and JSON files from Project VIC and CAID so that AXIOM categorizes them automatically.

> CATEGORIZE PICTURES AND VIDEOS

Processing details

Dynamic App Finder is a Magnet IEF and AXIOM feature that's capable of finding potential mobile chat app databases located in images. You can read more about this feature at: `https://www.magnetforensics.com/ mobile-forensics/using-dynamic-app-finder-to-recover-more- mobile-artifacts/`.

9. You can customize **MOBILE ARTIFACTS** from here. For example, if you are only interested in chats artifacts, it's better to choose only these types of artifacts as they will shorten the processing time:

☑ CHAT (38 of 38)

☑ CLOUD STORAGE (1 of 1)

☑ CUSTOM ARTIFACTS (335 of 335)

☑ DOCUMENTS (10 of 10)

☑ EMAIL (12 of 12)

☑ ENCRYPTION (1 of 1)

☑ INTERNET OF THINGS (4 of 4)

☑ MEDIA (8 of 8)

☑ MOBILE (1 of 1)

☑ OPERATING SYSTEM (56 of 56)

☑ PEER TO PEER (1 of 1)

☑ SOCIAL NETWORKING (15 of 15)

☑ TRANSPORTATION & TRAVEL (3 of 3)

☑ WEB RELATED (35 of 35)

Selecting mobile artifacts

10. The **ANALYZE EVIDENCE** button will start the acquisition and analysis process:

IMAGING IN PROGRESS

Elapsed time: **18 seconds**

Initializing backup...	Complete
Running the mobile backup service...	**In progress**
Handling snapshot data...	Pending
Expanding acquired backup data...	Pending
Running file relay service...	Pending
Building image...	Pending
Moving image to destination...	Pending
Calculating image hashes...	Pending

Imaging the evidence source

11. There are two windows for Magnet AXIOM – **Process** and **Examine**. The first can be used to monitor the process of acquiring and processing the evidence source, while the second can be used to analyze the extracted and parsed data. As we mentioned previously, you can start the analysis before the processing phase has ended. All you need to do is click on **LOAD NEW RESULTS** in **Magnet Examine**:

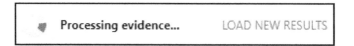

Processing evidence...   LOAD NEW RESULTS

Loading new results

12. Once the processing stage is over, you can find the parsed data in the **MOBILE** section of **Magnet Examine**:

MOBILE	2,291
Apple Contacts - iOS	397
Calendar Events	122
Installed Applications	1,338
iOS Call Logs	223
iOS Wi-Fi Profiles	209
Owner Information	2

The MOBILE section

But, of course, it won't include everything; there are other valuable sections that you can find evidence that has been extracted from the iOS device, such as **CHAT**, **MEDIA**, and **DOCUMENTS**.

Working with Belkasoft Evidence Center

Belkasoft Evidence Center is another popular digital forensics tool capable of performing the acquisition and analysis of iOS devices. Like AXIOM, it can be used for computer, mobile, and cloud forensics.

One of the best features of Belkasoft Evidence Center is its ability to deal with damaged iTunes backups. So, if you have a backup that none of your tools is able to process, try Belkasoft Evidence Center; according to our experience, it will process it successfully.

Features of Belkasoft Evidence Center

The following are the features of Belkasoft Evidence Center:

- Supports logical and filesystem (for jailbroken devices) acquisitions
- Supports both encrypted and unencrypted iTunes backups
- Supports damaged iTunes backups
- Recovers more than 700 artifact types
- Works with other popular mobile forensics tools, such as Cellebrite UFED and XRY
- Includes built-in SQLite and plist viewers
- Includes a free scripting module, BelkaScript, that allows examiners to write their own scripts to automate some common tasks
- Can generate reports in several popular formats, such as Microsoft Excel, PDF, and HTML

Logical acquisition and analysis with Belkasoft Evidence Center

Since backup processing and analysis is one of the best features of Belkasoft Evidence Center, we are going to walk you through this process here:

1. Let's start by creating a new case:

Creating a new case

2. There are multiple options here – you can process a previously acquired image, such as an iTunes backup, or choose to extract data from a device first. Let's start with logical acquisition. Choose the **Mobile** option:

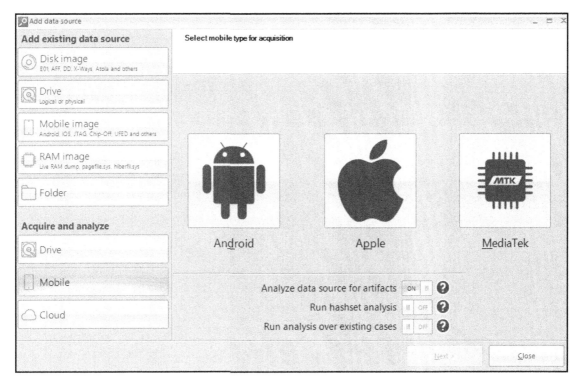

Choosing the data source

3. Since we're dealing with an iOS device, choose **Apple**. You'll see a list of devices that are available:

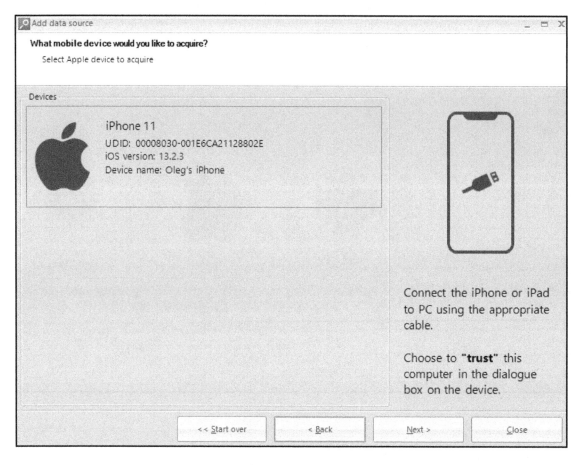

Devices available for acquisition

4. Our device isn't jailbroken, so our choice is either logical acquisition or iTunes backup:

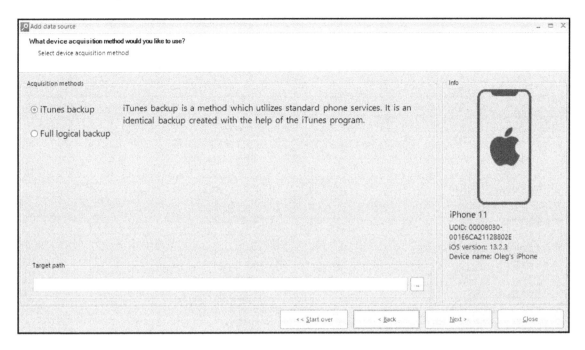

Choosing the acquisition method

5. Once acquisition has been completed, you can choose artifacts of interest. Make sure you choose only iOS-related artifacts; this will decrease the processing time:

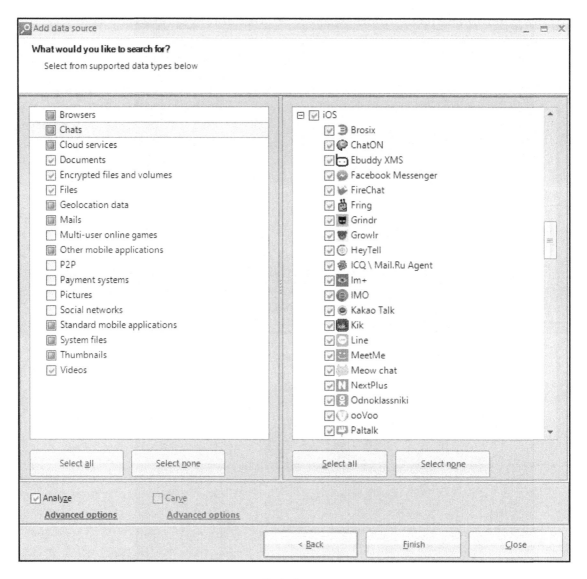

Choosing data types

6. Once processing is finished, extracted artifacts will be shown in the **Overview** tab:

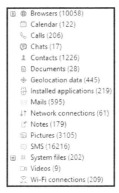

Overview tab

7. Finally, if you want to browse the filesystem of your forensic image, use the **File System** tab:

Data sources
  <BelkaImage> 00008030-001E6CA21128802E_20191203_1501.belkaml
    <ITunes10Encrypted> Oleg's iPhone
      AppDomain-com.alfabank.app
      AppDomain-com.allgoritm.Youla
      AppDomain-com.apple.AccountAuthenticationDialog
      AppDomain-com.apple.ActivityMessagesApp
      AppDomain-com.apple.Animoji.StickersApp
      AppDomain-com.apple.appleseed.FeedbackAssistant
      AppDomain-com.apple.AppSSOUIService
      AppDomain-com.apple.AppStore
      AppDomain-com.apple.AuthKitUIService
      AppDomain-com.apple.AXUIViewService
      AppDomain-com.apple.BarcodeScanner
      AppDomain-com.apple.BusinessChatViewService
      AppDomain-com.apple.calculator
      AppDomain-com.apple.carkit.DNDBuddy
      AppDomain-com.apple.CarPlaySettings
      AppDomain-com.apple.CarPlaySplashScreen
      AppDomain-com.apple.clips
      AppDomain-com.apple.CloudKit.ShareBear
      AppDomain-com.apple.compass
      AppDomain-com.apple.CompassCalibrationViewService
      AppDomain-com.apple.CoreAuthUI
      AppDomain-com.apple.CTCarrierSpaceAuth
      AppDomain-com.apple.CTNotifyUIService
      AppDomain-com.apple.datadetectors.DDActionsService
      AppDomain-com.apple.DemoApp
      AppDomain-com.apple.Diagnostics
      AppDomain-com.apple.DiagnosticsService
      AppDomain-com.apple.facetime
      AppDomain-com.apple.findmy

The File System tab

Other available tabs may be useful too – the **Dashboard** tab shows you all the available information about the case you are currently working on, the **Task Manager** tab allows you to monitor processing progress, and the **Search Results** tab shows you keyword search results.

Working with Elcomsoft Phone Viewer

Elcomsoft Phone Viewer is a tool capable of parsing and viewing data extracted from not only iOS devices but also from BlackBerry 10 and Windows Phone devices. It provides read-only, forensically sound access to logical and filesystem images, as well as to data that's been extracted from the cloud.

Features of Elcomsoft Phone Viewer

The following are the features of Elcomsoft Phone Viewer:

- Analyzes online activities, including web browsing history, bookmarks, and open tabs.
- Provides access to synced data, passwords, and user data, including messages, call logs, and contacts.
- It categorizes multimedia files so that it's easier for you to understand whether a photo was received in a message or was taken with the phone's camera.
- Aggregates location data from different sources.
- Supports logical images, filesystem images, and iTunes and iCloud backups.

Filesystem analysis with Elcomsoft Phone Viewer

Elcomsoft Phone Viewer doesn't support device acquisition but can parse and help you view data that has been extracted with Elcomsoft iOS Forensic Toolkit, Elcomsoft Cloud eXtractor, or almost any other tool capable of iOS device acquisition.

To explore a filesystem image that was previously created with Elcomsoft iOS Forensic Toolkit, follow these steps:

1. Launch Elcomsoft Phone Viewer and choose the appropriate data source. In our case, this is **iOS device image**:

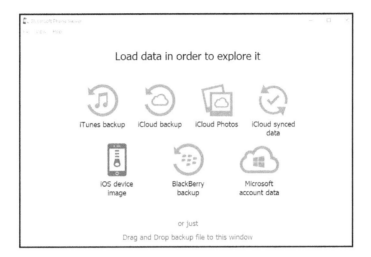

Choosing data source

2. Choose the file you want to import and the artifact you want to parse:

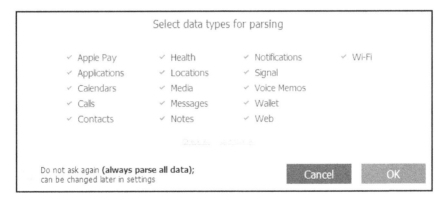

Choosing data types

3. Wait for the extraction process to finish:

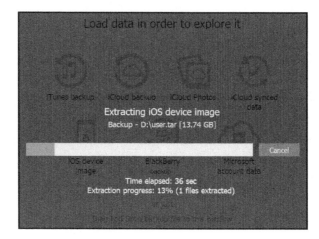

Extraction process

As a result, you'll get the device's information, as well as the parsed artifacts split into multiple categories:

Parsed artifacts

Now, you can easily view, filter, and export any data that may be of interest for your examination – all you need to do is click on the corresponding icon.

Summary

Forensic tools are helpful for an examiner as they not only save time but also make the process a lot easier. However, not everyone has a budget large enough to purchase commercial tools to obtain iOS acquisition. While free tools exist for acquisition, support may be limited and multiple extractions may be required to obtain the same amount of data as a commercial tool.

For jailbroken devices, the iOS device can be connected to a forensic workstation for live examination through SSH, which is how some of the tools acquire the necessary data. However, this is not a method that is recommended for those new to mobile forensics. For such purposes, this chapter introduced you to several available iOS forensic tools and included the steps you need to follow to perform acquisition and analysis.

You should take further steps to validate and understand each tool that might be used as part of an investigation. We recommend that you acquire test devices with known data to ensure that nothing is overlooked, the evidence hasn't been altered, and that the methods provide you with access to the data of interest, where possible.

The next chapter will introduce Android forensics and cover the fundamental concepts of the Android platform.

Section 2: Android Forensics

2

This section will cover everything you need to know about forensics on Android devices. We will start by understanding the Android platform and its filesystem and then cover the topics of setup, acquisition/extraction, and recovery. We will also look at Android malware and how to reverse engineer Android apps using open source tools.

This chapter consists of the following chapters:

- Chapter 7, Understanding Android
- Chapter 8, Android Forensic Setup and Pre-Data Extraction Techniques
- Chapter 9, Android Data Extraction Techniques
- Chapter 10, Android Data Analysis and Recovery
- Chapter 11, Android App Analysis, Malware, and Reverse Engineering

Understanding Android 7

In the previous chapters, we covered details about iOS devices, including the filesystem structure, key artifacts, backup files, and acquisition and analysis methods. Starting with this chapter, we will focus on the Android platform and how to perform forensics on Android devices. Having a good understanding of the Android ecosystem, security constraints, filesystems, and other features would prove useful during a forensic investigation. Gaining knowledge of these fundamentals would help a forensic expert to make informed decisions while conducting an investigation.

We will cover the following topics in this chapter:

- The evolution of Android
- The Android architecture
- Android security
- The Android file hierarchy
- The Android filesystem

The evolution of Android

Android is a Linux-based mobile operating system developed for touchscreen mobile devices. It is developed by a consortium of companies known as the **Open Handset Alliance (OHA)**, with the primary contributor and commercial marketer being Google. The Android operating system has evolved significantly since its inaugural release date. Android was officially launched to the public in 2008, with Android version 1.0. With the Android 1.5 Cupcake release in 2009, the tradition of naming Android versions after confectionery was born. The version names were also released in alphabetical order for the next 10 years. However, in 2019, Google announced that they were ending the confectionery-based naming, and were using numerical ordering for future versions. In the initial years, Android versions were updated more than twice a year, but in more recent years, version updates are done once per year. The most recent major Android update is Android 11, the eleventh major version of the Android operating system, announced by Google on February 19, 2020.

The following is an overview of Android version history as of the time of writing:

Version	Version name	Release year
Android 1.0	Apple Pie	2008
Android 1.1	Banana Bread	2009
Android 1.5	Cupcake	2009
Android 1.6	Donut	2009
Android 2.0	Eclair	2009
Android 2.2	Froyo	2010
Android 2.3	Gingerbread	2010
Android 3.0	Honeycomb	2011
Android 4.0	Ice Cream Sandwich	2011
Android 4.1	Jelly Bean	2012
Android 4.4	KitKat	2013
Android 5.0	Lollipop	2014
Android 6.0	Marshmallow	2015
Android 7.0	Nougat	2016
Android 8.0	Oreo	2017
Android 9.0	Pie	2018
Android 10.0	Q	2019
Android 11	R	2020

This evolution has also dramatically impacted the security considerations of Android and how forensics techniques are applied. For example, the initial versions of Android did not have a **Full Disk Encryption** (**FDE**) mechanism to store data in an encrypted format within the device. As a result, extracting data from the device was much easier for a forensic investigator than it is currently. With each Android version update, more and more security features, such as app permissions, **trusted execution environment** (**TEE**), and secure kernel, have been added to improve the security of the platform overall but at the same time complicate the process of data extraction. We shall cover these security features in detail in the other sections of this chapter.

Now that we know about the history and versions of Android, we will take a look at the Android architecture in the next section.

The Android architecture

To effectively understand forensic concepts when dealing with Android, you should have a basic understanding of the Android architecture. Just like a computer, any computing system that interacts with the user and performs complicated tasks requires an operating system to handle the tasks effectively. This operating system (whether it's a desktop operating system or a mobile phone operating system) is responsible for managing the resources of the system, to provide a way for the applications to talk to the hardware or physical components to accomplish certain tasks. Android is currently the most popular mobile operating system designed to power mobile devices. You can find out more about this at `https://developer.android.com/about/android.html`.

Android, as an open source operating system, releases its code under the Apache License, one of the many open source licenses. Practically, this means anyone (especially device manufacturers) can access it, freely modify it, and use the software according to the requirements of any device. This is one of the primary reasons for its wide acceptance. Notable players that use Android include Samsung, HTC, Sony, and LG.

As with any other platform, Android consists of a stack of layers running one above the other. To understand the Android ecosystem, it's essential to have a basic understanding of what these layers are and what they do.

The following diagram summarizes the various layers involved in the Android software stack:

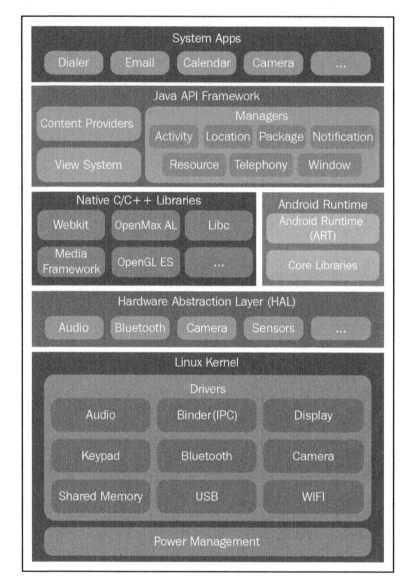

Android architecture
This image is modified based on work created and shared by the Android Open Source Project: https://developer.android.com/guide/platform
License: https://creativecommons.org/licenses/by/4.0/

Each of these layers performs several operations that support specific operating system functions. Each layer provides services to the layers lying on top of it. Let's look at them in a little more detail.

The Linux kernel layer

The Android operating system is built on top of the Linux kernel, with some architectural changes made by Google. There are several reasons for choosing the Linux kernel. Most importantly, Linux is a portable platform that can be compiled easily on different hardware. The kernel acts as an abstraction layer between the software and hardware present on the device. Consider the case of a camera. What happens when you take a photo using the camera button on your device? At some point, the hardware instruction (pressing a button) has to be converted to a software instruction (to take a picture and store it in the gallery). The kernel contains drivers to facilitate this process. When the user presses the button, the instruction goes to the corresponding camera driver in the kernel, which sends the necessary commands to the camera hardware, similar to what occurs when a key is pressed on a keyboard. In simple words, the drivers in the kernel command control the underlying hardware. As shown in the Android architecture model, the kernel contains drivers related to Wi-Fi, Bluetooth, **Universal Service Bus** (**USB**), audio, display, and so on.

The Linux kernel is responsible for managing the core functionality of Android, such as process management, memory management, security, and networking. Linux is a proven platform when it comes to security and process management. Android has taken leverage of the existing Linux open source operating system to build a solid foundation for its ecosystem. Each version of Android has a different version of the underlying Linux kernel. The Oreo Android version is known to use Linux kernel 3.18 or 4.9, whereas the Pie version is known to use Linux kernel 4.4, 4.9, or 4.14. Android Q, targets Linux kernel 4.9, 4.14, or 4.19. The actual kernel depends on the individual device.

The Hardware Abstraction Layer

The device hardware capabilities are exposed to the high-level Java framework through the **Hardware Abstraction Layer** (**HAL**). The HAL consists of several library modules that implement interfaces for a specific type of hardware component. This allows hardware vendors to implement functionality without changing the higher-level system.

Libraries

The next layer in the Android architecture consists of Android's native libraries. The libraries are written in C or C++, and help the device to handle different kinds of data. For example, the SQLite libraries are useful for storing and retrieving the data from a database. Other libraries include Media Framework, WebKit, Surface Manager, and **Secure Sockets Library (SSL)**.

The Media Framework library acts as the main interface to provide a service to the other underlying libraries. The WebKit library provides web pages in web browsers, and the Surface Manager library maintains the graphics. In the same layer, we have **Android Runtime (ART)** and core libraries. ART is responsible for running applications on Android devices. The term *runtime* refers to the time from when an application is launched until it is shut down.

Dalvik Virtual Machine (DVM)

All the applications that you install on the Android device are written in the Java programming language. When a Java program is compiled, we get bytecode. A **virtual machine (VM)** is an application that acts as an operating system—that is, it is possible to run an instance of the Windows operating system on a Mac, or vice versa, using a VM. **Java Virtual Machine (JVM)** is one such VM that can execute the previously mentioned bytecode. But Android versions before Android 5.0 used something called DVM to run their applications.

DVM runs Dalvik bytecode, which is Java bytecode converted by the **Dalvik Executable (DEX)** compiler. Thus, the .class files are converted to dex files using the dx tool. Dalvik bytecode, when compared with Java bytecode, is more suitable for low-memory and low-processing environments. Also, note that JVM's bytecode consists of one or more .class files, depending on the number of Java files that are present in an application, but Dalvik bytecode is composed of only one dex file. Each Android application runs its own instance of DVM. This is a crucial aspect of Android security and will be addressed in detail in Chapter 8, *Android Forensic Setup and Pre-Data Extraction Techniques*.

The following diagram provides an insight into how Android's DVM differs from Java's JVM:

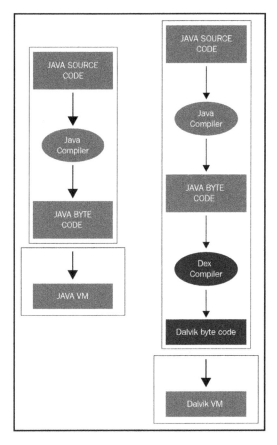

JVM versus DVM

Now that we have understood the basic differences between JVM and DVM, let's quickly have a look at ART.

ART

From the Android 5.0 Lollipop version onward, Dalvik was replaced by ART. Earlier versions of Android used **just-in-time** (**JIT**) compilation with Dalvik (frequently executed operations are identified and dynamically compiled to native machine code). This native execution of these frequently used bytecodes, called traces, provides significant performance improvements.

Unlike Dalvik, ART uses **ahead-of-time** (**AOT**) compilation, which compiles entire applications into native machine code upon their installation. This automatically increases the install time for an application, but a major advantage is that this eliminates Dalvik's interpretation and trace-based JIT compilation, and thereby increases efficiency and reduces power consumption. ART uses a utility called `dex2oat` that accepts `DEX` files as input and generates a compiled app executable for the target device. With ART, the **optimized DEX (.odex)** files have been replaced with the **Executable and Linkable Format (ELF)** executables.

The Java API framework layer

The application framework is the layer responsible for handling the basic functioning of a phone, such as resource management, handling calls, and so on. This is the block through which the applications installed on the device directly talk to it. The following are some of the important blocks in the application framework layer:

- **Telephony Manager**: This block manages all the voice calls.
- **Content Provider**: This block manages the sharing of data between different applications.
- **Resource Manager**: This block manages various resources used in applications.

The final layer is the system apps layer, which will be discussed next.

The system apps layer

This is the topmost layer where the user can interact directly with the device. There are two kinds of applications—preinstalled applications and user-installed applications. Preinstalled applications—such as dialer, web browser, and contacts—come along with the device. User-installed applications can be downloaded from different places, such as Google Play Store, Amazon Marketplace, and so on. Everything that you see on your phone (contacts, mail, camera, and so on) is an application.

So far, we have learned about the Android architecture and the important building blocks. We shall now dive into some of the inherent security features in the Android operating system.

Android security

Android was designed with a specific focus on security. Android as a platform offers and enforces certain features that safeguard the user data present on the mobile through multilayered security. There are certain safe defaults that will protect the user, and there are certain offerings that can be leveraged by the development community to build secure applications. As a forensic investigator, understanding the internals of Android security is crucial as it helps to identify the best techniques to apply in a given situation, the technical limitations of certain techniques, and so on.

The next few sections will help us understand more about Android's security features and offerings.

 A detailed explanation on Android security can be found at `https://source.android.com/security/`.

Secure kernel

The kernel is at the heart of the security of any operating system. By choosing Linux, which has evolved as a trusted platform over the years, Android has established a very solid security foundation. Most of the security features that are inherent to the Linux kernel are automatically adopted by Android. For example, the user-based permission model of Linux has, in fact, worked well for Android. As mentioned earlier, there is a lot of specific code built into the Linux kernel. With each Android version release, the kernel version has also changed. The following table shows Android versions and their corresponding kernel versions:

Android version	Linux kernel version
1	2.6.25
1.5	2.6.27
1.6	2.6.29
2.2	2.6.32
2.3	2.6.35
3.0	2.6.36
4.0	3.0.1
4.1	3.0.31
4.2	3.4.0

4.2	3.4.39
4.4	3.8
5.0	3.16.1
6.0	3.18.1
7.0	4.4.1
8.0	4.10
9.0	4.4, 4.9, and 4.14
10.0	4.9, 4.14, and 4.19

The Linux kernel automatically brings some of its inherent security features, such as the following, to the Android platform:

- A user-based permissions model
- Isolation of running processes (application sandbox)
- Secure **inter-process communication (IPC)**

We shall now learn about each of these features.

The permission model

As shown in the following screenshot, any Android application must be granted permissions to access sensitive functionality—such as the internet, dialer, and so on—by the user. This provides an opportunity for the user to know in advance which functionality on the device is being accessed by the application. Simply put, it requires the user's permission to perform any kind of malicious activity (stealing data, compromising the system, and so on).

This model helps the user to prevent attacks, but if the user is unaware and gives away a lot of permissions, it leaves them in trouble (remember—when it comes to installing malware on any device, the weakest link is always the user).

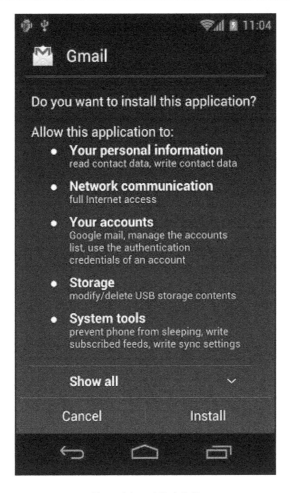

The permission model in Android

Until Android 6.0, users needed to grant the permissions during install time. Users had to either accept all the permissions or not install the application. But, starting from Android 6.0, users grant permissions to apps while the app is running. This new permission system also gives the user more control over the app's functionality by allowing the user to grant selective permissions. For example, a user can deny a particular app access to their location but provide access to the internet. The user can revoke the permissions at any time by going to the app's **Settings** screen. From a forensic perspective, what this means is that the kind of information that can be extracted from a device depends not only on the device and the installed apps but also on the permissions that are configured by the user.

Application sandbox

In Linux systems, each user is assigned a unique **user identifier** (**UID**), and users are segregated so that one user cannot access the data of another user. However, all applications under a particular user are run with the same privileges. Similarly, in Android, each application runs as a unique user. In other words, a UID is assigned to each application and is run as a separate process. This concept ensures an application sandbox at the kernel level. The kernel manages the security restrictions between the applications by making use of existing Linux concepts, such as UID and **group identifier** (**GID**). If an application attempts to do something malicious—say, to read the data of another application—this is not permitted as the application does not have user privileges. Hence, the operating system protects an application from accessing the data of another application.

Secure IPC

Android offers secure IPC, through which one activity in an application can send messages to another activity in the same or a different application. To achieve this, Android provides IPC mechanisms: Intents, Services, Content Providers, and so on. This is more relevant to developers who code third-party apps for the Android platform. Behind the scenes, forensic tools exploit some of these concepts to gain access to the device information.

Application signing

It is mandatory that all of the installed applications are digitally signed. Developers can place their applications in Google's Play Store only after signing the applications. The private key with which the application is signed is held by the developer. Using the same key, a developer can provide updates to their application, share data between the applications, and so on. Unsigned applications, if attempted to be installed, will be rejected by either Google Play or the package installer on the Android device. In Android 8.0 and above, users must navigate to the **Install unknown apps** setting in order to run unsigned apps, as shown in the following screenshot:

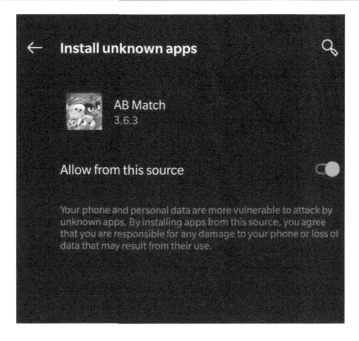

Install unknown apps screen in Android

Now that we have some basic knowledge about digitally signed applications, let's look at one of the security features in Android.

Security-Enhanced Linux (SELinux)

SELinux is a security feature that was introduced in Android 4.3 and fully enforced in Android 5.0. Until this addition, Android security was based on **Discretionary Access Control (DAC)**, which means applications can ask for permissions, and users can grant or deny those permissions. Thus, malware can create havoc on phones by gaining those permissions. But SE Android uses **Mandatory Access Control (MAC)**, which ensures that applications work in isolated environments. Hence, even if a user installs a malware app, the malware cannot access the operating system and corrupt the device. SELinux is used to enforce MAC over all the processes, including the ones running with root privileges. In SELinux, anything that is not explicitly allowed is, by default, denied. SELinux can operate in one of the two global modes: **Permissive** mode, which logs the permission denials but does not enforce them; and **Enforcing** mode, which logs and also enforces the permission denials. More details about SELinux can be found at https://source.android.com/security/selinux/concepts.

FDE

With Android 6.0 Marshmallow, Google has mandated FDE for most devices, provided that the hardware meets certain minimum standards. Encryption is the process of converting data into ciphertext using a secret key. On Android devices, FDE refers to the process of encrypting all user data using a secret key. This key is in turn encrypted by the device's **personal identification number (PIN)**/pattern/password that is set by the user. Once a device is encrypted, all user-created data is automatically encrypted before writing it to disk, and all reads automatically decrypt data before returning it to the calling process. FDE in Android works only with an **Embedded Multimedia Card (eMMC)** and similar flash devices that present themselves to the kernel as block devices.

Staring from Android 7.x, Google decided to shift the encryption feature from FDE to **file-based encryption (FBE)**. In FBE, different files are encrypted with different keys. By doing so, those files can be accessed independently, without the need to decrypt the complete partition. As a result of this, the system can now display open notifications or access boot-related files without having to wait until the user unlocks the phone.

Android Keystore

Android Keystore is used to protect sensitive cryptographic keys from unauthorized access. Keys stored within a Keystore can be used to perform cryptographic operations, but they can never be extracted outside of the Keystore. The hardware-backed Keystores provide security at hardware level—that is, even if the operating system is compromised, the keys in the hardware module would still be secure.

TEE

A TEE is an isolated area (typically, a separate microprocessor) intended to guarantee the security of data stored inside it, and also to execute code with integrity. The main processor on mobile devices is considered untrusted and cannot be used to store secret data (such as cryptographic keys). Hence, a TEE is used specifically to perform such operations, and the software running on the main processor delegates any operations that require the use of secret data to the TEE processor.

Verified Boot

Verified Boot tries to ensure that all code that is executed on an Android device comes from a legitimate source rather than from an attacker or a fraud. It establishes a full chain of trust and prevents side-loading of any other operating system. During device boot-up, each stage validates the integrity and authenticity of the next stage before handing over execution.

We shall now look into the various partitions and filesystems available on an Android device.

The Android file hierarchy

In order to perform forensic analysis on any system (desktop or mobile), it's important to understand the underlying file hierarchy. A basic understanding of how Android organizes its data in files and folders helps a forensic analyst narrow down their research to specific issues. Just as with any other operating system, Android uses several partitions. This chapter provides an insight into some of the most significant partitions and the content stored in them.

It's worth mentioning again that Android uses the Linux kernel. Hence, if you are familiar with Unix-like systems, you will understand the file hierarchy in Android very well. For those who are not very well acquainted with the Linux model, here is some basic information: in Linux, the file hierarchy is a single tree, with the top of the tree being denoted as / (called the *root*). This is different from the concept of organizing files in drives (as with Windows). Whether the filesystem is local or remote, it will be present under the root.

The Android file hierarchy is a customized version of this existing Linux hierarchy. Based on the device manufacturer and the underlying Linux version, the structure of this hierarchy may have a few insignificant changes. The following is a list of important folders that are common to most Android devices. Some of the folders listed are only visible through root access. Rooting is the process of gaining privileged access on an Android device. More details about rooting and executing the `adb` commands (which are shown in the following list) are covered in detail in `Chapter 8`, *Android Forensic Setup and Pre-Data Extraction Techniques*:

- `/boot`: As the name suggests, this partition has the information and files required for the phone to boot. It contains the kernel and **Random Access Memory (RAM)** disk, so without this partition, the phone cannot start its processes. Data residing in RAM is rich in value and should be captured during a forensic acquisition.

- `/system`: This partition contains system-related files other than the kernel and RAM disk. This folder should never be deleted as that will make the device unbootable. The contents of this partition can be viewed using the following command:

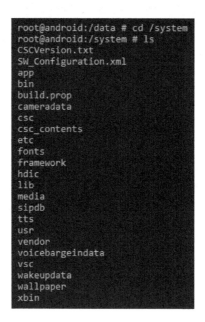

```
root@android:/data # cd /system
root@android:/system # ls
CSCVersion.txt
SW_Configuration.xml
app
bin
build.prop
cameradata
csc
csc_contents
etc
fonts
framework
hdic
lib
media
sipdb
tts
usr
vendor
voicebargeindata
vsc
wakeupdata
wallpaper
xbin
```

/system partition

- * /recovery: This is designed for backup purposes and allows the device to boot into recovery mode. In recovery mode, you can find tools to repair your phone installation.
- /data: This is the partition that contains the data of each application. Most of the data belonging to the user—such as the contacts, SMS, and dialed numbers—is stored in this folder. This folder has significant importance from a forensic point of view as it holds valuable data. The contents of the data folder can be viewed using the following command:

```
root@android:/ # cd /data
root@android:/data # ls
ISP_CV
TMAudioSocketClient
TMAudioSocketServer
anr
app
app-asec
app-private
backup
baro.dat
cfw
clipboard
dalvik-cache
data
dontpanic
drm
fota_test
gldata.sto
gps
hidden_volume.txt
lbsdata-000.sto
local
log
lost+found
media
misc
```

/data partition

- * /cache: This is the folder used to store the frequently accessed data and some of the logs for faster retrieval. The /cache partition is also important to a forensic investigation as the data residing here may no longer be present in the /data partition.

- * /misc: As the name suggests, this folder contains information about miscellaneous settings. These settings mostly define the state of the device—that is, on/off. Information about hardware settings, USB settings, and so on can be accessed from this folder.
- /sdcard: This is the partition that holds all the information present on the **Secure Digital (SD)** card. It is valuable as it can contain information such as pictures, videos, files, documents, and so on.

Now that we have understood the Android file hierarchy and looked at the important folders in it, let's have a look at the filesystem in the next section.

The Android filesystem

Understanding the filesystem is one essential part of forensic methodologies. Knowledge about the properties and the structure of a filesystem proves to be useful during forensic analysis. The filesystem refers to the way data is stored, organized, and retrieved from a volume. A basic installation may be based on one volume split into several partitions; here, each partition can be managed by a different filesystem. As is true in Linux, Android utilizes mount points, and not drives (that is, C: or E:).

 In Linux, mounting is an act of attaching an additional filesystem to the currently accessible filesystem of a computer. The filesystems in Linux are not accessed by drive names but instead are organized into a multi-level hierarchy with a directory called root at the top. Each new filesystem is added into this single filesystem tree when it is mounted.

It does not make any difference whether the filesystem exists on the local device or on a remote device. Everything is in a single hierarchy that begins with root. Each filesystem defines its own rules for managing the files in the volume. Depending on these rules, each filesystem offers a different speed for file retrieval, security, size, and so on. Linux uses several filesystems, and so does Android. From a forensic point of view, it's important to understand which filesystems are used by Android and to identify the filesystems that are of significance to the investigation. For example, the filesystem that stores the user's data is of primary concern to us, as opposed to a filesystem used to boot the device.

Viewing filesystems on an Android device

The filesystems supported by the Android kernel can be determined by checking the contents of the `filesystems` file in the `proc` folder. The content of this file can be viewed using the `# cat /proc/filesystems` command:

```
root@android:/ # cat /proc/filesystems
nodev   sysfs
nodev   rootfs
nodev   bdev
nodev   proc
nodev   cgroup
nodev   tmpfs
nodev   binfmt_misc
nodev   debugfs
nodev   sockfs
nodev   usbfs
nodev   pipefs
nodev   anon_inodefs
nodev   devpts
        ext2
        ext3
        ext4
nodev   ramfs
        vfat
        msdos
nodev   ecryptfs
nodev   fuse
        fuseblk
nodev   fusectl
        exfat
```

Filesystems on an Android device

In the preceding output, the first column tells us whether the filesystem is mounted on the device. The ones with the `nodev` property are not mounted on the device.

The second column lists all the filesystems present on the device. A simple `mount` command displays different partitions available on the device, as follows:

```
root@android:/ # mount
rootfs / rootfs ro,relatime 0 0
tmpfs /dev tmpfs rw,nosuid,relatime,mode=755 0 0
devpts /dev/pts devpts rw,relatime,mode=600 0 0
proc /proc proc rw,relatime 0 0
sysfs /sys sysfs rw,relatime 0 0
none /acct cgroup rw,relatime,cpuacct 0 0
tmpfs /mnt/asec tmpfs rw,relatime,mode=755,gid=1000 0 0
tmpfs /mnt/obb tmpfs rw,relatime,mode=755,gid=1000 0 0
none /dev/cpuctl cgroup rw,relatime,cpu 0 0
/dev/block/mmcblk0p9 /system ext4 ro,noatime,barrier=1,data=ordered 0 0
/dev/block/mmcblk0p3 /efs ext4 rw,nosuid,nodev,noatime,barrier=1,journal_async_commit,data=ordered 0 0
/dev/block/mmcblk0p8 /cache ext4 rw,nosuid,nodev,noatime,errors=panic,barrier=1,journal_async_commit,data=ordered 0 0
/dev/block/mmcblk0p12 /data ext4 rw,nosuid,nodev,noatime,barrier=1,journal_async_commit,data=ordered,noauto_da_alloc,discard 0 0
/sys/kernel/debug /sys/kernel/debug debugfs rw,relatime 0 0
/dev/fuse /storage/sdcard0 fuse rw,nosuid,nodev,noexec,relatime,user_id=1023,group_id=1023,default_permissions,allow_other 0 0
```

Partitions on the Android device

Next, let's look at the common filesystems on Android.

Common filesystems found on Android

The filesystems present in Android can be organized primarily into three main categories, as follows:

- Flash memory filesystems
- Media-based filesystems
- Pseudo filesystems

Let's look at each of them in detail.

Flash memory filesystems

Flash memory is a type of constantly powered **nonvolatile memory** (**NVM**) that retains data in the absence of a power supply. Flash memory can be erased and reprogrammed in units of memory called blocks. While the supported filesystems vary based on the device and underlying Linux kernel, the common flash memory filesystems are as follows:

- **Extended File Allocation Table** (**exFAT**) is a Microsoft proprietary filesystem that was created to be used on flash drives such as USB memory sticks and SD cards. Because of the license requirements, it isn't part of the standard Linux kernel. But still, a few manufacturers provide support for this filesystem.

- **Flash Friendly File System** (**F2FS**) was released in February 2013 to support Samsung devices running the Linux 3.8 kernel. F2FS relies on log-structured methods that optimize the NAND flash memory. The offline support features are a highlight of this filesystem, though it is still transient and being updated.

- **Yet Another Flash File System 2** (**YAFFS2**) is an open source, single-threaded filesystem released in 2002. It is mainly designed to be fast when dealing with the NAND flash. YAFFS2 utilizes **Out-of-band** (**OOB**), and this is often not captured or decoded correctly during forensic acquisition, which makes analysis difficult. We will discuss this further in `Chapter 9`, *Android Data Extraction Techniques*. YAFFS2 was the most popular release at one point and is still widely used in Android devices. YAFFS2 is a log-structured filesystem. Data integrity is guaranteed, even in the case of a sudden power outage. In 2010, there was an announcement stating that in releases after Gingerbread, devices were going to move from YAFFS2 to **fourth extended file system** (**EXT4**). Currently, YAFFS2 is not supported by newer kernel versions, but certain mobile manufacturers might still continue to support it.

- **Robust File System** (**RFS**) supports NAND flash memory on Samsung devices. RFS can be summarized as a **File Allocation Table 16** (**FAT16**) or FAT32 filesystem, whereby journaling is enabled through a transaction log. Many users complain that Samsung should stick with EXT4. RFS has been known to have lag times that slow down the features of Android.

Next in line is media-based filesystems.

Media-based filesystems

The following are some of the media-based filesystems supported by Android devices.

The **Extended File System** (**EXT**), which was introduced in 1992 specifically for the Linux kernel, was one of the first filesystems, and it used a virtual filesystem. EXT2, EXT3, and EXT4 are the subsequent versions. Journaling is the main advantage of EXT3 over EXT2. With EXT3, if there is an unexpected shutdown, there is no need to verify the filesystem. The EXT4 filesystem has gained significance with mobile devices implementing dual-core processors. The YAFFS2 filesystem is known to have a bottleneck on dual-core systems. With the Gingerbread version of Android, the YAFFS filesystem was swapped for EXT4.

The following are the mount points that use EXT4 on the Samsung Galaxy mobile:

```
/dev/block/mmcblk0p9 /system ext4 ro,noatime,barrier=1,data=ordered 0    0
/dev/block/mmcblk0p3 /efs ext4
rw,nosuid,nodev,noatime,barrier=1,journal_async_commit,data=ordered 0 0
/dev/block/mmcblk0p8 /cache ext4
```

```
rw,nosuid,nodev,noatime,barrier=1,journal_async_commit,data=ordered 0 0
/dev/block/mmcblk0p12 /data ext4
rw,nosuid,nodev,noatime,barrier=1,journal_async_commit,data=ordered,n
oauto_da_alloc,discard 0 0
```

Virtual File Allocation Table (VFAT) is an extension to the FAT16 and FAT32 filesystems. Microsoft's FAT32 filesystem is supported by most Android devices. It is supported by almost all the major operating systems, including Windows, Linux, and macOS. This enables these systems to easily read, modify, and delete the files present on the FAT32 portion of the Android device. Most of the external SD cards are formatted using the FAT32 filesystem.

Observe the following output, which shows that the /sdcard and /secure/asec mount points use the VFAT filesystem:

```
root@android:/ # cd sdcard
root@android:/sdcard # mount
rootfs / rootfs ro,relatime 0 0
tmpfs /dev tmpfs rw,nosuid,relatime,mode=755 0 0
devpts /dev/pts devpts rw,relatime,mode=600 0 0
proc /proc proc rw,relatime 0 0
sysfs /sys sysfs rw,relatime 0 0
none /acct cgroup rw,relatime,cpuacct 0 0
tmpfs /mnt/asec tmpfs rw,relatime,mode=755,gid=1000 0 0
tmpfs /mnt/obb tmpfs rw,relatime,mode=755,gid=1000 0 0
none /dev/cpuctl cgroup rw,relatime,cpu 0 0
/dev/block/mmcblk0p9 /system ext4 ro,noatime,barrier=1,data=ordered 0 0
/dev/block/mmcblk0p3 /efs ext4 rw,nosuid,nodev,noatime,barrier=1,journal_async_commit,data=ordered 0 0
/dev/block/mmcblk0p8 /cache ext4 rw,nosuid,nodev,noatime,errors=panic,barrier=1,journal_async_commit,data=ordered 0 0
/dev/block/mmcblk0p12 /data ext4 rw,nosuid,nodev,noatime,barrier=1,journal_async_commit,data=ordered,noauto_da_alloc,discard 0 0
/sys/kernel/debug /sys/kernel/debug debugfs rw,relatime 0 0
/dev/fuse /storage/sdcard0 fuse rw,nosuid,nodev,noexec,relatime,user_id=1023,group_id=1023,default_permissions,allow_other 0 0
```

mount command output in Android

The final category is pseudo filesystems.

Pseudo filesystems

Pseudo filesystems, as the name suggests, are not actual files but a logical grouping of files. The following are some of the important pseudo filesystems in Android:

- The root filesystem (rootfs) is one of the main components of Android and contains all the information required to boot the device. When the device starts the boot process, it needs access to many core files, and thus, it mounts the root filesystem. As shown in the preceding mount command-line output, this filesystem is mounted at / (root folder). Hence, this is the filesystem on which all the other filesystems are slowly mounted. If this filesystem is corrupt, the device cannot be booted.

- The `sysfs` filesystem mounts the `/sys` folder, which contains information about the configuration of the device. The following output shows various folders under the `sys` directory in an Android device:

```
root@android:/ # cd /sys
root@android:/sys # ls
block
bus
class
dev
devices
firmware
fs
kernel
module
power
```

Folders under /sys directory in Android

Since the data present in these folders is mostly related to configuration, this is not usually of much significance to a forensic investigator. But there can be some circumstances where we might want to check whether a particular setting was enabled on the phone, and analyzing this folder could be useful under such conditions.

 Note that each folder consists of a large number of files. Capturing this data through forensic acquisition is the best method to ensure that this data is not changed during an examination.

- The `devpts` filesystem presents an interface to the Terminal session on an Android device. It is mounted at `/dev/pts`. Whenever a Terminal connection is established—for instance, when an `adb` shell is connected to an Android device—a new node is created under `/dev/pts`. The following is the output showing this when the `adb` shell is connected to the device:

```
shell@Android:/ $ ls -l /dev/pts ls -l /dev/pts
crw------- shell shell 136, 0 2013-10-26 16:56 0
```

- The `cgroup` filesystem stands for **control groups**. Android devices use this filesystem to track their job. They are responsible for aggregating the tasks and keeping track of them. This data is generally not very useful during forensic analysis.

- The `proc` filesystem contains information about kernel data structures, processes, and other system-related information in the `/proc` directory. For instance, the `/sys` directory contains files related to kernel parameters. Similarly, `/proc/filesystems` displays the list of available filesystems on the device. The following command shows all the information about the **central processing unit (CPU)** of the device:

```
root@android:/ # cat /proc/cpuinfo
Processor       : ARMv7 Processor rev 0 (v7l)
processor       : 0
BogoMIPS        : 1592.52

processor       : 2
BogoMIPS        : 1990.65

processor       : 3
BogoMIPS        : 1990.65

Features        : swp half thumb fastmult vfp edsp neon vfpv3 tls
CPU implementer : 0x41
CPU architecture: 7
CPU variant     : 0x3
CPU part        : 0xc09
CPU revision    : 0

Chip revision   : 0011
Hardware        : SMDK4x12
Revision        : 000c
Serial          :
```

Output of the cpuinfo command on an Android device

Similarly, there are many other useful files that provide valuable information when you traverse them.

- The `tmpfs` filesystem is a temporary storage facility on the device that stores the files in RAM (volatile memory). The main advantage of using RAM is faster access and retrieval. But once the device is restarted or switched off, this data will not be accessible anymore. Hence, it's important for a forensic investigator to examine the data in RAM before a device reboot happens, or to extract the data via RAM acquisition methods.

Today's forensic tools can easily mount these filesystems and display the contents in a **graphical user interface** (GUI) screen, thereby enabling forensic investigators to easily navigate and parse through the files. In the initial days of Android forensics, an investigator had to typically run a set of Linux or Windows commands to format and view these filesystems.

Summary

In this chapter, we covered the Android operating system's underlying features, filesystems, and other details that are useful in a forensic investigation. We learned about interesting security capabilities that are built into Android. Unlike iOS, several variants of Android exist as many devices run the Android operating system, and each may have different filesystems and unique features. The fact that Android is open and customizable also changes the playing field of digital forensics. This knowledge will be helpful to understand forensic acquisition techniques.

In the next chapter, we will discuss how to set up a forensic workstation before performing the analysis.

8
Android Forensic Setup and Pre-Data Extraction Techniques

In the previous chapter, we covered the fundamentals of the Android architecture, security features, filesystems, and other capabilities. Having an established forensic environment before the start of an examination is important, as it ensures that the data is protected while you, as the examiner, maintain control of the workstation. This chapter will explain the process of—and what to consider when—setting up a digital forensic examination environment. It is paramount that you maintain control of the forensic environment at all times; this prevents the introduction of contaminants that could affect the forensic investigation.

We will cover the following topics in this chapter:

- Setting up a forensic environment for Android
- Connecting an Android device to a workstation
- Screen lock bypassing techniques
- Gaining root access

Setting up a forensic environment for Android

As a forensic examiner, you may encounter a wide range of mobiles over the course of your investigation. Therefore, it is necessary to have a basic environment set up on top of which you can build based on requirements. It is also very important that you maintain complete control over the environment at all times to avoid any unexpected situations. Setting up a proper lab environment is an essential part of the forensic process. The Android forensic setup usually involves the following steps:

1. Start with a fresh or forensically sterile computer environment. This means that other data is either not present on the system or is contained in a manner that prevents it from contaminating the present investigation.
2. Install the basic software necessary to connect to the device. Android forensic tools and methodologies will work on the Windows, Linux, and macOS platforms.
3. Obtain access to the device. You must be able to enable settings or bypass them in order to allow the data to be extracted from the Android device.
4. Issue commands to the device using the methods defined in this chapter and in `Chapter 9`, *Android Data Extraction Techniques*.

The following sections provide guidance on setting up a basic Android forensic workstation.

Installing the software

The Android **Software Development Kit (SDK)** helps the development world to build, test, and debug applications to run on Android. The Android SDK comes with Android Studio, the official **integrated development environment (IDE)** for developing Android apps. Android Studio provides valuable documentation and other tools that can be of great help during the investigation of an Android device. Alternatively, you can download just the platform tools, which are components of the Android SDK and include tools that can interact with the Android platform, such as the ADB, fast boot, and so on; these will be described in more detail in the following sections.

A good understanding of the Android SDK will help you to get to grips with the particulars of a device and its data on the device.

Android Studio consists of software libraries, APIs, tools, emulators, and other reference material. It can be downloaded for free from `https://developer.android.com/studio/index.html`. The platform tools can be downloaded from `https://developer.android.com/studio/releases/platform-tools`.

During a forensic investigation, having these tools helps you connect to and access data on Android devices. The Android SDK is updated very frequently, so it's important to verify that your workstation also remains up to date. The Android SDK can run on Windows, Linux, and macOS.

Installing the Android platform tools

A working installation of the Android SDK or Android platform tools is a must during the investigation of a forensic device. The Windows version of Android Studio is around 718 MB, and rather heavy compared to the software for the platform tools, which is just 20 MB.

The following is the step-by-step procedure to install the Android platform tools on a Windows 10 machine:

1. Before you install Android Studio or the platform tools, make sure that your system has **Java Development Kit** (JDK) installed, because the Android SDK relies on Java SE Development Kit.

 JDK can be downloaded from `http://www.oracle.com/technetwork/java/javase/downloads/index.html`.

2. Download the latest version of the platform tools from `https://developer.android.com/studio/releases/platform-tools`.

3. Right-click and extract the ZIP files to a folder. The installation location is your choice and must be remembered for future access. In this example, we will extract it to the `C:\` folder.

4. Open the directory (C:\platform-tools) and note that the following tools are listed:

Name	Date modified	Type	Size
api	12/24/2019 6:56 PM	File folder	
lib64	12/24/2019 6:56 PM	File folder	
systrace	12/24/2019 6:56 PM	File folder	
adb.exe	10/18/2019 6:50 A...	Application	2,523 KB
AdbWinApi.dll	10/18/2019 6:50 A...	Application extens...	96 KB
AdbWinUsbApi.dll	10/18/2019 6:50 A...	Application extens...	62 KB
dmtracedump.exe	10/18/2019 6:50 A...	Application	234 KB
etc1tool.exe	10/18/2019 6:50 A...	Application	409 KB
fastboot.exe	10/18/2019 6:50 A...	Application	1,284 KB
hprof-conv.exe	10/18/2019 6:50 A...	Application	41 KB
libwinpthread-1.dll	10/18/2019 6:50 A...	Application extens...	226 KB
make_f2fs.exe	10/18/2019 6:50 A...	Application	460 KB
mke2fs.conf	10/18/2019 6:50 A...	CONF File	2 KB
mke2fs.exe	10/18/2019 6:50 A...	Application	709 KB
NOTICE.txt	10/18/2019 6:50 A...	Text Document	292 KB
source.properties	10/18/2019 6:50 A...	PROPERTIES File	1 KB
sqlite3.exe	10/18/2019 6:50 A...	Application	1,177 KB

Android platform tools

This completes the basic Android tool installation. If you're installing the full-blown Android Studio version, you should still see the platform tools folder under the newly installed Android directory.

Creating an Android virtual device

With Android Studio you can create an **Android virtual device** (**AVD**), also called an emulator, which is often used by developers when creating new applications; however, an emulator has significance from a forensic perspective, too. Emulators are useful when trying to understand how applications behave and execute on a device. This could be helpful in confirming certain findings that are unearthed during a forensic investigation.

Also, while working on a device that is running on an older platform, you can design an emulator for the same platform. Furthermore, before installing a forensic tool on a real device, the emulator can be used to find out how a forensic tool works and changes the content on an Android device. To create a new AVD (on the Windows workstation), go through the following steps:

1. Open Android Studio and navigate to **Tools** | **AVD Manager**. The **Android Virtual Device Manager** window is shown in the following screenshot:

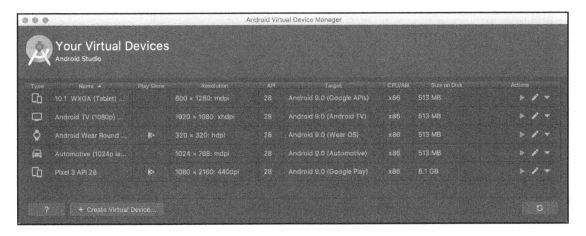

Android Virtual Device Manager

2. Click on **Create Virtual Device** to create a new virtual device. In the screens that follow, select the appropriate hardware, system image, API level, AVD name, and so on, and proceed further. For example, the following screenshot shows Android Pie being selected:

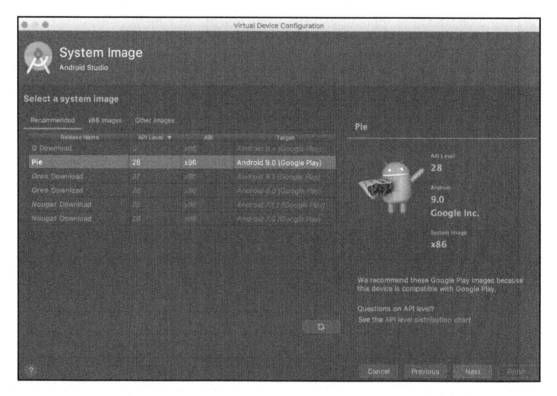

Virtual device configuration

3. A confirmation message is shown once the device is successfully created. Now, select the AVD and click on the **Play** button.

4. This should launch the emulator. Note that this could take a few minutes, or even longer, depending on the workstation's CPU and RAM. The emulator does consume a significant amount of resources on the system. After a successful launch, the AVD will run, as shown in the following screenshot:

The Android emulator

From a forensic perspective, analysts and security researchers can leverage the functionality of an emulator to understand the file system, data storage, and so on. The data created when working on an emulator is stored in your home directory in a folder named `android`. For instance, in our example, the details about the Pixel_XL_API_28 emulator that we created earlier are stored under
`C:\Users\Rohit\.android\avd\Pixel_XL_API_28.avd`.

Among the various files present under this directory, the following are those that are of interest to a forensic analyst:

- `cache.img`: This is the disk image of the `/cache` partition (remember that we discussed the `/cache` partition of an Android device in *Chapter 7, Understanding Android*).
- `sdcard.img`: This is the disk image of the SD card partition.
- `Userdata-qemu.img`: This is the disk image of the `/data` partition. The `/data` partition contains valuable information about the device user.

Now that we have understood the steps to set up the environment, let's connect the Android device to a forensic workstation.

Connecting an Android device to a workstation

Forensic acquisition of an Android device using open source tools requires you to connect the device to a forensic workstation. Forensic acquisition of any device should be conducted on a forensically sterile workstation. This means that the workstation is strictly used for forensics and not for personal use.

 Note that any time a device is plugged into a computer, changes can be made to the device; you must have full control of all interactions with the Android device at all times.

The following steps should be performed by you in order to successfully connect the device to a workstation. Note that write protection may prevent the successful acquisition of the device, since commands may need to be pushed to the device in order to pull information. All the following steps should be validated on a test device prior to attempting them on real evidence.

Identifying the device cable

The physical USB interface of an Android device allows it to connect to a computer to share data, such as songs, videos, and photos. This USB interface might change from manufacturer to manufacturer and also from device to device. For example, some devices use mini-USB while some others use micro-USB and USB Type C. Apart from this, some manufacturers use their own proprietary formats, such as EXT-USB, EXT micro-USB, and so on. The first step in acquiring an Android device is to determine what kind of device cable is required.

There are different types, such as mini-USB, micro-USB, and other proprietary formats. The following is a brief description of the most widely used connector types:

Connector type	Description
Mini - A USB	It is approximately 7 x 3 mm in size, with two of the corners on one long side lifted out.
Micro - B USB	It is approximately 6 x 1.5 mm in size, with two corners cut off to form a trapezoid.
Co-axial	It has a circular hole with a pin sticking up in the middle. There are different sizes in this category, varying from 2 to 5 mm in diameter. Widely used with Nokia models.
D Sub-miniature	It has the shape of a rectangle with two rounded corners. The length of the rectangle varies, but the height is always 1.5 to 2 mm. Used mostly by Samsung and LG devices.

Next, let's have a quick look at how to install device drivers.

Installing device drivers

In order to identify the device properly, the computer may need certain drivers to be installed. Without the necessary drivers, the computer may not identify and work with the connected device. The issue is that, since Android is allowed to be modified and customized by manufacturers, there is no single generic driver that works for all Android devices. Each manufacturer writes its own proprietary drivers and distributes them over the internet, so it's important to identify the specific device drivers that need to be installed. Of course, some Android forensic toolkits (which we will discuss in the following chapters) do come with some generic drivers or a set of the most widely used drivers; they may not work with all models of the Android phone.

Some Windows operating systems are able to autodetect and install drivers once the device is plugged in, but more often than not they fail. The device drivers for all manufacturers can be found on their respective websites.

Accessing the connected device

If you haven't done so already, connect the unlocked Android device to the computer directly using the USB cable. The Android device will appear as a new drive and you will be able to access the files on the external storage. If the device is locked, then at this point, you will not be able to access any files and may need to use the **Turn on USB storage** option, which can be enabled on the phone, as shown in the following screenshot:

USB mass storage in Android 4.1 version

With some Android phones (especially with HTC), the device may expose more than one functionality when connected with a USB cable. For instance, as shown in the following screenshot, when an HTC device is connected it presents a menu with four options. The default selection is **Charge only**. When the **Disk drive** option is selected, it is mounted as a disk drive:

HTC mobile USB options

When the device is mounted as a disk drive, you will be able to access the SD card present on the device. From a forensic point of view, the SD card has significant value as it may contain files that are important to an investigation; however, the core application data stored under /data/data will remain on the device and cannot be accessed with these methods.

The Android debug bridge

Considered to be one of the most crucial components in Android forensics, the **Android debug bridge** (**ADB**) is a command-line tool that allows you to communicate with the Android device and control it. We will learn about the ADB in detail in upcoming chapters; for now, we will focus on a basic introduction to the ADB. You can access the ADB tool under /platform-tools/.

Before we discuss anything about the ADB, we need to have an understanding of the **USB debugging** option.

USB debugging

The primary function of this option is to enable communication between the Android device and the workstation on which the Android SDK is installed. On a Samsung phone, you can access this under **Settings** | **Developer Options**, as shown in the following screenshot:

The USB debugging option in a Samsung S8 device

Other Android phones may have different environments and configuration features. You may have to force the **Developer Options** option by accessing build mode.

However, starting from Android 4.2, the **Developer Options** menu is hidden to make sure that users do not enable it by accident. To enable it, go to **Settings** | **About Phone** and then tap the **Build Number** field seven times. After this, **Developer Options** will be available in the **Settings** menu. Prior to Android 4.2.2, enabling this option was the only requirement for communicating with the device over ADB; however, starting from Android 4.2.2, Google has introduced the secure USB debugging option. This feature only allows hosts that are explicitly authorized by the user to connect to the device using ADB.

Thus, when you connect the device to a new workstation via USB in order to access ADB, you need to first unlock the device and authorize access by pressing **OK** in the confirmation window, as shown in the following screenshot. If **Always allow from this computer** is checked, the device will not prompt for authorization in the future:

Secure USB debugging

When the **USB debugging** option is selected, the device will run the **adb daemon** (adbd) in the background and will continuously look for a USB connection. The daemon will usually run under a nonprivileged shell user account and thus will not provide access to the complete data; however, on rooted phones, adbd will run under the root account and therefore provide access to all the data. It is not recommended that you root a device to gain full access unless all other forensic methods fail. Should you elect to root an Android device, the methods must be well-documented and tested prior to attempting it on real evidence. Rooting will be discussed at the end of this chapter.

On the workstation where the Android SDK is installed, adbd will run as a background process. Also, on the same workstation, a client program, which can be invoked from a shell by issuing the adb command, will run. When the adb client is started, it first checks whether an adb daemon is already running. If the response is negative, it initiates a new process to start the adb daemon. The adb client program communicates with local adbd over port 5037.

Accessing the device using adb

Once the environment setup is complete and the Android device is in USB debugging mode, connect the Android device to the forensic workstation with a USB cable and start using adb.

Detecting connected devices

The following adb command provides a list of all the devices connected to the forensic workstation. This will also list the emulator if it is running at the time of issuing the command. Also remember that, if the necessary drivers are not installed, then the following command will show a blank message. If you encounter this situation, download the necessary drivers from the manufacturer and install them:

```
C:\android-sdk\platform-tools>adb.exe devices
List of devices attached
4df16ac3115e5f05          device
```

We now have a list of devices connected to the workstation. Next, we will see how to kill the local ADB server.

Killing the local ADB server

The following command kills the local adb service:

```
C:\android-sdk\platform-tools>adb.exe kill-server
```

After killing the local adb service, issue the adb devices command. You will see that the server is started, as shown in the following screenshot:

```
C:\android-sdk\platform-tools>adb.exe devices
List of devices attached
* daemon not running. starting it now on port 5037 *
* daemon started successfully *
4df16ac3115e5f05          device
```

We will now access the ADB shell on the Android device.

Accessing the adb shell

The ADB shell command allows you to access the shell on an Android device and interact with the device.

The following is the command to access the `adb` shell and execute a basic `ls` command to see the contents of the current directory:

```
C:\android-sdk\platform-tools>adb.exe shell shell@android:/ $ ls
ls acct cache
config d
data default.prop dev
efs etc
factory fstab.smdk4x12 init
init.bt.rc init.goldfish.rc init.rc init.smdk4x12.rc init.smdk4x12.usb.rc
....
```

The Android emulator can be used by you to execute and understand `adb` commands before using them on the device. In `Chapter 9`, *Android Data Extraction Techniques*, we will explain more about leveraging adb to install applications, copy files and folders from the device, view device logs, and so on.

Basic Linux commands

We will now take a quick look at some commonly used Linux commands and their usage with respect to an Android device:

- `ls`: The `ls` command (with no option) lists the files and directories present in the current directory. With the `-l` option, this command shows files and directories and also their size, modified date and time, the owner of the file and its permission, and so on, as shown in the following command-line output:

```
shell@android:/ $ ls -l
ls -l
drwxr-xr-x root      root               2015-01-17 10:13 acct
drwxrwx--- system    cache              2014-05-31 14:55 cache
dr-x------ root      root               2015-01-17 10:13 config
lrwxrwxrwx root      root               2015-01-17 10:13 d ->
/sys/kernel/debug
drwxrwx--x system    system             2015-01-17 10:13 data
-rw-r--r-- root      root           116 1970-01-01 05:30 default.prop
drwxr-xr-x root      root               2015-01-17 10:13 dev
drwxrwx--x radio     system             2013-08-13 09:34 efs
lrwxrwxrwx root      root               2015-01-17 10:13 etc ->
/system/etc
...
```

Similarly, the following are a few options that can be used along with the `ls` command:

Option	Description
a	Lists hidden files
c	Displays files by timestamp
d	Displays only directories
n	Displays the long-format listing, with GID and UID numbers.
R	Displays subdirectories as well
t	Displays files based on timestamp
u	Displays the file access time

Depending on the requirements, one or more of the following options can be used by the investigator to view the details:

- cat: The `cat` command reads one or more files and prints them to standard output, as shown in the following command lines:

```
shell@android:/ $ cat default.prop
cat default.prop
#
# ADDITIONAL_DEFAULT_PROPERTIES
#
ro.secure=1
ro.allow.mock.location=0
ro.debuggable=0
persist.sys.usb.config=mtp
```

To combine multiple files into one, we can use the > operator. To append to an existing file, we can use the >> operator.

- cd: The `cd` command is used to change from one directory to another. This is more frequently used while navigating from one folder to another. The following example shows the commands used to change to the `system` folder:

```
shell@android:/ $ cd /system
cd /system
shell@android:/system $
```

- cp: The `cp` command can be used to copy a file from one location to another. The syntax for this command is as follows:

```
$ cp [options] <source><destination>
```

- chmod: The chmod command is used to change the access permissions to filesystem objects (files and directories). It may also alter special mode flags. The syntax for this command is as follows:

  ```
  $ chmod [option] mode files
  ```

  For example, chmod 777 on a file gives read, write, and execute permissions to everyone.

- dd: The dd command is used to copy a file, converting and formatting it according to the operands. With Android, the dd command can be used to create a bit-by-bit image of the Android device. More details of imaging are covered in *Chapter 4*, *Data Acquisition from iOS Backups*. The following is the syntax that needs to be used with this command:

  ```
  dd if=/test/file of=/sdcard/sample.image
  ```

- rm: The rm command can be used to delete files or directories. The following is the syntax for this command:

  ```
  rm file_name
  ```

- grep: The grep command is used to search files or output for a particular pattern. The syntax for this command is as follows:

  ```
  grep [options] pattern [files]
  ```

- pwd: The pwd command displays the current working directory. For example, the following command-line output shows that the current working directory is /system:

  ```
  shell@android:/system $ pwd
  pwd
  /system
  ```

- mkdir: The mkdir command is used to create a new directory. The following is the syntax for this command:

  ```
  mkdir [options] directories
  ```

- exit: The exit command can be used to exit the shell you are in. Just type exit in the shell to exit from it.

Next, we will see how to handle an Android device efficiently before the investigation.

Handling an Android device

Handling an Android device in a proper manner prior to the forensic investigation is a very important task. Care should be taken to make sure that our unintentional actions don't result in data modification or any other unwanted happenings. The following sections throw light on certain issues that need to be considered while handling the device in the initial stages of a forensic investigation.

With improvements in technology, the concept of *device locking* has effectively changed over the last few years. Most users now have a passcode locking mechanism enabled on their device because of the increase in general security awareness. Before we look at some of the techniques used to bypass locked Android devices, it is important for us not to miss an opportunity to disable the passcode when there is a chance.

When an Android device that is to be analyzed is first accessed, check whether the device is still active (unlocked). If so, change the settings of the device to enable greater access to the device. When the device is still active, consider performing the following tasks:

- **Enabling USB debugging**: Once the USB debugging option is enabled, it gives greater access to the device through the adb connection. This is of great significance when it comes to extracting data from the device. The location of the option to enable USB debugging might change from device to device, but it's usually under **Developer Options** in **Settings**. Most methods for physically acquiring Android devices require USB debugging to be enabled.
- **Enabling the Stay awake setting**: If the **Stay awake** option is selected and the device is connected for charging, then the device never locks. Again, if the device locks, the acquisition can be halted.
- **Increasing screen timeout**: This is the time for which the device will be effectively active once it is unlocked. The location to access this setting varies depending upon the model of the device. On a Samsung Galaxy S3 phone, you can access this setting by navigating to **Settings** | **Display** | **ScreenTimeout**.

Apart from these, as mentioned in Chapter 1, *Introduction to Mobile Forensics*, the device needs to be isolated from the network to make sure that remote wipe options do not work on the device. The Android Device Manager allows the phone to be remotely wiped or locked. This can be done by signing in to the Google account, which is configured on the mobile. More details about this are supplied in the following section. If the Android device is not set up to allow remote wiping, the device can only be locked using the Android Device Manager. There are also several **mobile device management (MDM)** software products available on the market, which allow users to remotely lock or wipe the Android device. Some of these may not require specific settings to be enabled on the device.

Using the available remote wipe software, it is possible to delete all the data, including emails, applications, photos, contacts, and other files, as well as those found on the SD card. To isolate the device from the network, you can put the device in airplane mode and disable Wi-Fi as an extra precaution. Enabling airplane mode and disabling Wi-Fi works well, as the device will not be able to communicate over a cellular network and cannot be accessed via Wi-Fi. Removing the SIM card from the phone is also an option, but that does not effectively stop the device from communicating over Wi-Fi or other cellular networks. To place the device in airplane mode, press and hold the Power Off button and select **Airplane mode**.

All these steps can be done when the Android device is not locked; however, during the investigation, we commonly encounter devices that are locked. Therefore, it's important to understand how to bypass the lock code if it is enabled on an Android device.

Screen lock bypassing techniques

Because of the increase in user awareness and the ease of functionality, there has been an exponential increase in the usage of passcode options to lock Android devices. This means that bypassing the device's screen lock during a forensic investigation becomes increasingly important. The applicability of the screen lock bypass techniques discussed so far is based on the situation. Note that some of these methods may result in us making changes to the device. Make sure that you test and validate all the steps listed on non-evidentiary Android devices. You must have authorization to make the required changes to the device, document all steps taken, and be able to describe the steps taken if courtroom testimony is required.

Currently, there are three types of screen lock mechanisms offered by Android. Although there are some devices that have voice-lock, face-lock, and fingerprint-lock options, we will limit our discussion to the following three options, since these are the most widely used on all Android devices:

- **Pattern lock**: The user sets a pattern or design on the phone and the same pattern must be drawn to unlock the device. Android was the first smartphone to introduce a pattern lock.
- **PIN code**: This is the most common lock option and is found on many mobile phones. The PIN code is a four-digit number that needs to be entered to unlock the device.
- **Passcode**: This is an alphanumeric passcode. Unlike the PIN, which takes four digits, the alphanumeric passcode includes letters as well as digits.

The following section details some techniques you can use to bypass these Android lock mechanisms. Depending on the situation, these techniques might help an investigator to bypass the screen lock.

Using ADB to bypass the screen lock

If USB debugging appears to be enabled on the Android device, it is wise to take advantage of it by connecting with adb using a USB connection, as discussed in the earlier sections of this chapter. You should connect the device to the forensic workstation and issue the adb devices command. If the device shows up, it implies that USB debugging is enabled. If the Android device is locked, you must attempt to bypass the screen lock. The following two methods may allow you to bypass the screen lock when USB debugging is enabled.

Deleting the gesture.key file

Deleting the gesture.key file will remove the pattern lock on the device; however, it's important to note that this will permanently change the device, as the pattern lock is gone. This should be considered if you are conducting covert operations. The following shows how the process is done:

1. Connect the device to the forensic workstation (a Windows machine, in our example) using a USB cable.

2. Open the command prompt and execute the following instructions:

   ```
   adb.exe shell
   cd /data/system rm gesture.key
   ```

3. Reboot the device. If the pattern lock still appears, just draw any random design and the device should unlock without any trouble.

 This method works when the device is rooted. This method may not be successful on unrooted devices. Rooting an Android device should not be performed without proper authorization, as the device is altered.

Updating the settings.db file

To update the `settings.db` file, go through the following steps:

1. Connect the device to the forensic workstation using a USB cable.
2. Open the command prompt and execute the
   following: `/data/data/com.android.providers.settings/databases`
   `sqlite3 settings.db`:

```
                        :/ $ cd /data/data/com.android.providers.settings/databases
    sqlite3 settings.db
    update system set value=0 where name='lock_pattern_autolock';
c     update secure set value=0 where name='lock_pattern_autolock';
d /data/data/com.android.providers.settings/databases
    update system set value=0 where name='lockscreen.lockedoutpermanently';
    update secure set value=0 where name='lockscreen.lockedoutpermanently';
  sqlite3 settings.db
  .quit
  exit
```

3. Exit and reboot the device.
4. The Android device should be unlocked. If it is not, attempt to remove
   the `gesture.key` as explained earlier.

We will have a look at the recovery mode and ADB connection in the following section.

Checking for the modified recovery mode and ADB connection

In Android, recovery refers to the dedicated partition where the recovery console is present. The two main functions of recovery are deleting all user data and installing updates. For instance, when you factory-reset your phone, recovery boots up and deletes all the data. Similarly, when updates are to be installed on the phone, it is done in recovery mode.

There are many enthusiastic Android users who install custom ROM through a modified recovery module. This modified recovery module is mainly used to make the process of installing custom ROM easy. Recovery mode can be accessed in different ways, depending on the manufacturer of the device; information on which method is right for which manufacturer's devices is easily available on the internet. Usually, this is done by holding different keys together, such as the Volume button and Power button. Once in recovery mode, connect the device to the workstation and try to access the adb connection. If the device has a recovery mode that is not modified, you may not be able to access the adb connection. Modified recovery versions of the device present the user with different options as shown in the following screenshot:

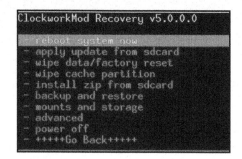

Next, we will see how to flash the recovery partition.

Flashing a new recovery partition

There are mechanisms available to flash the recovery partition of an Android device with a modified image. The fastboot utility facilitates this process. Fastboot is a diagnostic protocol that comes with the SDK package and is used primarily to modify the flash filesystem through a USB connection from a host computer. For this, you need to start the device in boot loader mode, in which only the most basic hardware initialization is performed.

Once the protocol is enabled on the device, it will accept a specific set of commands that are sent to it via the USB cable using a command line. Flashing or rewriting a partition with a binary image stored on the computer is one such command that is allowed. Once the recovery is flashed, boot the device in recovery mode, mount the /data and /system partitions, and use adb to remove the gesture.key file. Reboot the phone and you should be able to bypass the screen lock; however, this works only if the device bootloader is unlocked. Also, flashing permanently alters the device. Instead of flashing, you could use the fastboot boot command to boot to a recovery image temporarily to delete the key file without permanently changing the recovery partition.

Using automated tools

There are several automated solutions available on the market for unlocking Android devices. Commercial tools, such as Cellebrite and XRY, are capable of bypassing the screen locks, but most of them require USB debugging to be enabled. We will now examine how to unlock an Android device using the UFED user lock code recovery tool. This tool only works on those devices that support USB OTG. This process also requires a UFED camera, Cable No. 500-Bypass lock, and Cable No. 501-Bypass lock. Once the tool is installed on the workstation, go through the following steps to unlock the Android device:

1. Run the tool on the workstation and press 1, as shown in the following screenshot:

```
UFED User Lock Code Recovery Tool

Disclaimer: All actions are subject to the full responsibility of the user, and
Cellebrite is not liable for any damage to the device.

Follow the instructions to recover the lock code.

Before you begin, check your computer's power options to make sure it won't go
into sleep mode. The process could take from a few minutes up to 21 hours. You
can still use the computer during this time.


What type of device is it?

[1] Android
[2] iOS (Apple)
[0] Exit
```

UFED user lock code recovery tool

2. Now, connect side A of Cable No. 500-Bypasslock to a USB port of the workstation. Also, connect side B of Cable No. 500-Bypasslock to Cable No. 501-OTG and then connect the other end to the device.
3. Once connected, the tool prompts you to select the recovery profile. Select [1] Manually select the recovery profile..
4. Now, select the lock type used on the device and the recovery profile, and proceed by following the instructions on the screen.

5. After this, make sure that the keypad appears on the device screen and that it's ready to accept the PIN code.

6. Close any message windows that may appear. Press 1 and hit *Enter*. Now, make five incorrect login attempts by entering random input, and click on **Forgot pattern** at the bottom of the device.

7. Follow the instructions on the screen, wait for the camera window to open, and then click on the camera window.

8. Use the cursor to select any nonempty area on the device's screen by placing the green square over it—for example, select any number on the screen. This is used by the tool to detect whether the device is unlocked. Press *Enter* to start the process.

9. The tool will try a number of combinations to unlock the device. Once unlocked, it will prompt you to end the process.

We will now learn about the Android Device Manager and how to unlock a device using it.

Using Android Device Manager

Most of the latest Android phones come with a service called Android Device Manager, which helps the owner of a device to locate their lost phone. This service can also be used to unlock a device; however, this is possible only when you know the Google account credentials that are configured on the device. If you have access to the account credentials, then follow these steps to unlock the device:

1. Visit `http://google.com/android/devicemanager` on your workstation.

2. Sign in using the Google account that is configured on the device.

3. Select the device you need to unlock and click on **Lock**, as shown in the following screenshot:

Android Device Manager

4. Enter a temporary password and click on **Lock** again.
5. Once it's successful, enter the temporary password on the device to unlock it.

This can be done without knowing the credentials of the computer that the login is saved on (that is, the suspect's PC).

Bypass using Find My Mobile (for Samsung phones only)

Using Find My Mobile is a technique that's worth attempting if you're handling a Samsung device; however, it only works if the device owner is already logged into the Samsung account on the device and you know the Samsung credentials that are configured on the device.

To start the process, access the Find My Mobile service from the web browser and then log in using the Samsung account credentials registered on the device, as follows:

1. Tap on the **Lock My Screen** option located on the left side.:

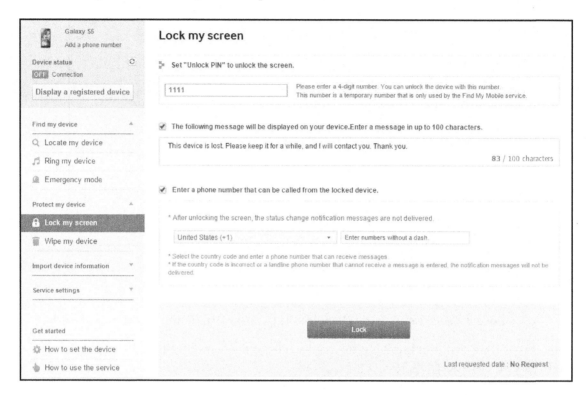

2. Now, enter any temporary PIN and then tap on the **Lock** button. (You may also see the **unlock my screen** option for some devices, which also serves the same purpose). The phone can now be unlocked with the temporary PIN that was set earlier.

Next, let's take a look at a smudge attack.

Smudge attack

In rare cases, a smudge attack may be used to deduce the password of a touchscreen mobile device. This attack relies on identifying the smudges left behind by the user's fingers. While this may present a bypass method, it must be said that a smudge attack is unlikely to work since most Android devices are touchscreen and smudges will also be present from using the device; however, it has been demonstrated that, under proper lighting, the smudges that are left behind can be easily detected, as shown in the following screenshot.

By analyzing the smudge marks, we can discern the pattern that is used to unlock the screen. This attack is more likely to work while discerning the pattern lock on the Android device. In some cases, PIN codes can also be recovered depending upon the cleanliness of the screen. So, during a forensic investigation, care should be taken when the device is first handled to make sure that the screen is not touched:

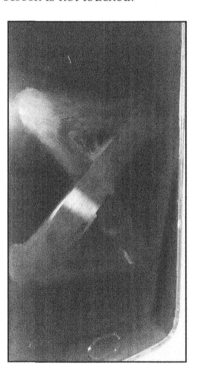

Smudges visible on a device under proper lighting

We will now be looking at the next method, which is the forgot password option.

Using the forgot password/forgot pattern option

If you know the username and password of the primary Gmail address that is configured on the device, you can change the PIN, password, or swipe on the device. After making a certain number of failed attempts to unlock the screen, Android provides an option called **Forgot pattern?** or **Forgot password?**, as shown in the following screenshot:

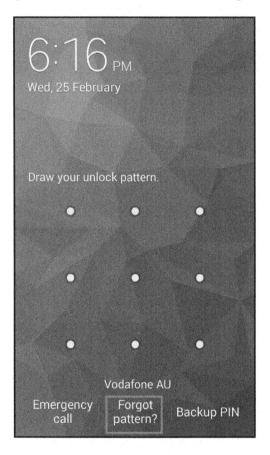

Forgot pattern option on an Android device

Tap on that link and sign in using the Gmail username and password. This will allow you to create a new pattern lock or passcode for the device.

 Note that this works only on devices running Android 4.4 or earlier.

Bypassing third-party lock screens by booting into safe mode

If the screen lock is a third-party app, rather than the in-built lock, it can be bypassed by booting into safe mode and disabling it. To boot into safe mode on an Android device 4.1 or later, press and hold the *Power* button until the Power options menu appears. Then, press and hold the *Power* button and you'll be prompted to reboot your Android device into safe mode. Tap the **OK** button, as shown in the following screenshot:

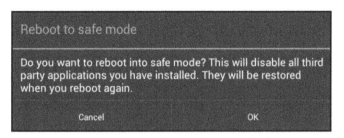

Safe mode in Android

Once you're in safe mode, you can disable the third-party lock screen app or uninstall it completely. After this, reboot the device and you should be able to access it without any lock screen.

Secure USB debugging bypass using ADB keys

As mentioned earlier, while using USB debugging, if the **Always allow from this computer** option is checked, the device will not prompt for authorization in the future. This is done by storing certain keys, namely adbkey and adbkey.pub, on the computer. Any attempt to connect to adb from an untrusted computer is denied. In this case, the adbkey and the adbkey.pub files can be pulled from the suspect's computer and copied to the investigator's workstation. The device will then assume that it is communicating with a known, authorized computer. The adbkey and adbkey.pub files can be found at C:Users<username>.android on Windows machines.

Secure USB debugging bypass in Android 4.4.2

As explained in earlier sections, the secure USB debugging feature introduced in Android 4.4.2 allows only authorized workstations to connect to the device; however, there's a bug in this feature, as reported at `https://labs.mwrinfosecurity.com/`, which allows a user to bypass the Secure USB debugging feature and connect the device to any workstation. Here are the steps to follow to bypass Secure USB debugging on an Android device:

1. On an unlocked device, attempt to use `adb`. An error message will be shown by the device.

2. Now, navigate to either the emergency dialer or the lock-screen camera and execute the following commands:

```
$ adb kill-server
$ adb shell
```

3. The confirmation dialog will be triggered and the workstation can now be authorized without unlocking the device. The confirmation dialog box will be displayed on the emergency dialer, as shown in the following screenshot:

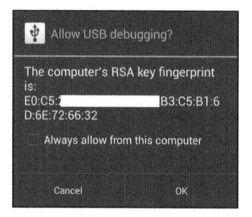

Secure USB debugging in Android 4.2.2

4. Once connected to the device through `adb`, try to bypass the lock screen using the following command:

```
$ adb shell pm clear com.android.keyguard
```

Next, let's see how to bypass the screen lock by crashing the lock screen.

Crashing the lock screen UI in Android 5.x

On devices running Android 5.0 to 5.1.1, the password lock screen (not the PIN or pattern locks) can be bypassed by crashing the screen UI. This can be accomplished by performing the following steps, as explained at `https://android.gadgethacks.com/`:

1. Click on the **Emergency Call** option on the lock screen and then enter any random input (for example, 10 asterisks) on the dialer screen.
2. Double-tap the field to highlight the entered text, as shown in the following screenshot, and select **Copy**. Now, paste it into the same field:

Crashing lock screen UI

3. Repeat this process to add more characters. Do this until the field no longer highlights the characters on double-tapping.
4. Go back to the lock screen and open the camera shortcut. Now, pull down the notifications screen and tap the **Settings** icon. You will then be prompted to enter a password.

5. Press and hold the input field and select **Paste**, repeat this process multiple times. Once enough characters are pasted into the field, the lock screen will crash, allowing you to access the device.

Now, let's look at some more techniques.

Other techniques

All of the aforementioned techniques and available commercial tools are useful to any forensic examiner, like you, trying to get access to the data on an Android device; however, there could be situations where none of these techniques work. To obtain a complete physical image of the device, techniques such as chip-off and JTAG may be required when commercial and open source solutions fail. A short description of these techniques is included here.

While the chip-off technique removes the memory chip from a circuit and tries to read it, the JTAG technique involves probing the JTAG **test access ports** (**TAPs**) and soldering connectors to the JTAG ports in order to read data from the device memory. The chip-off technique is more destructive because, once the chip is removed from a device, it is difficult to restore the device to its original functional state. Also, expertise is needed to carefully remove the chip from the device by desoldering the chip from the circuit board. The heat required to remove the chip can also damage or destroy the data stored on that chip, which means that this technique should be used only when the data is not retrievable by open source or commercial tools or the device is damaged beyond repair. When using the JTAG technique, JTAG ports help you to access the memory chip to retrieve a physical image of the data without needing to remove the chip. To turn off screen lock on a device, you can identify where the lock code is stored in the physical memory dump, turn off the locking, and copy that data back to the device. Commercial tools, such as Cellebrite Physical Analyzer, can accept .bin files from chip-off and JTAG acquisitions and crack the lock code for you. Once the code is either manually removed or cracked, you can analyze the device using normal techniques.

 Both the chip-off and JTAG techniques require extensive research and experience to be attempted on a real device. A great resource for JTAG and chip-off on devices can be found at https://forensicswiki.xyz/page/Main_Page.

In this section, we looked into various ways to bypass a screen lock on Android device. We will now learn what Android rooting is all about.

Gaining root access

As a mobile device forensic examiner, it is essential for you to know everything that relates to twisting and tweaking the device. This will help you to understand the internal workings of the device in detail and understand many issues that you may face during your investigation. Rooting Android phones has become a common phenomenon, and you can expect to encounter rooted phones during forensic examinations. Where applicable, you may also need to root the device in order to acquire data for forensic examination. This means that it's important to know the ins and outs of rooted devices and how they are different from other phones. The following sections cover information about Android rooting and other related concepts.

What is rooting?

The default administrative account in Unix-like operating systems is called **root**. In Linux, the root user has the power to start/stop any system service, edit/delete any file, change the privileges of other users, and so on. We have already learned that Android uses the Linux kernel, and so most Linux concepts are applicable to Android as well; however, most Android phones do not let you log in as a root user by default.

Rooting an Android phone is all about gaining access to the device to perform actions that are not normally allowed on the device. Manufacturers want devices to function in a certain manner for normal users. Rooting a device may void a warranty, since using root opens the system to vulnerabilities and provides the user with superuser capabilities.

Imagine a malicious application gaining access to an entire Android system with root access. Remember that, in Android, each application is treated as a separate user and is issued a UID. This means that applications have access to limited resources and the concept of application isolation is enforced. Essentially, rooting an Android device allows superuser capabilities and provides open access to the Android device.

Superuser capabilities are similar to the admin capability on a Windows machine, and give privileged access to perform actions that may not be done by a normal user. In mobiles, this superuser access is disabled by design, but rooting a phone allows you to gain this privilege.

Understanding the rooting process

Even though hardware manufacturers try to impose enough restrictions to restrict access to the root, hackers have always found different ways to get access to the root. The process of rooting varies depending on the underlying device manufacturer; however, rooting any device usually involves exploiting a security bug in the device's firmware, then copying the su (superuser) binary to a location in the current process's path (/system/xbin/su), and granting it executable permissions with the chmod command.

For the sake of simplicity, imagine that an Android device has three to four partitions, which run programs not entirely related to Android (Android being one among them).

The boot loader is present in the first partition and is the first program that runs when the phone is powered on. The primary job of this boot loader is to boot other partitions and load the Android partition, commonly referred to as ROM by default. To see the boot loader menu, a specific key combination is required, such as holding the power button and pressing the volume up button. This menu provides options for you to boot into other partitions, such as the recovery partition.

The recovery partition deals with installing upgrades to the phone, which are written directly to the Android ROM partition. This is the mode that you see when you install any official update on the device. Device manufacturers make sure that only official updates are installed through the recovery partition. This means that bypassing this restriction would allow you to install/flash any unlocked Android ROM. Modified recovery programs are those that not only allow an easier rooting process, but also provide various options that are not seen in the normal recovery mode. The following screenshot shows the normal recovery mode:

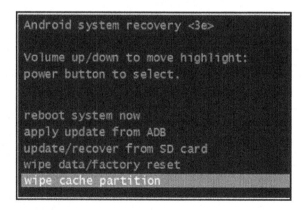

Normal Android system recovery mode

The following screenshot shows the modified recovery mode:

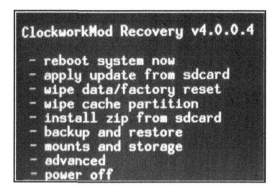

The modified recovery mode

The most commonly used recovery program in the Android world is Clockwork recovery, also called **ClockworkMod**. Most rooting methods begin by flashing a modified recovery to the recovery partition. After that, you can issue an update, which can root the device; however, you don't need to perform all the actions manually, as software is available for most models that can root your phone with a single click.

Starting from Android 7.x, Google started strictly enforcing **verified boot** on devices. Verified boot guarantees that the software on the device is not modified before booting into the normal mode. This is implemented in such a way that each stage verifies the integrity and authenticity of the next stage before executing it. If a particular partition or segment is modified, the integrity check fails and the mobile may not boot into normal mode. More information about verified boot can be found
at https://source.android.com/security/verifiedboot/verified-boot.

This also means that rooting such Android devices is going to be extremely difficult because rooting involves tweaking the Android OS. Marshmallow was the first Android version to provide alerts on system integrity, but since Android 7.x, this has been made mandatory.

Rooting an Android device

We will now look at the different methods available to root an Android device. The primary factor that influences your choice of method is whether the underlying boot loader is locked or unlocked. Gaining root access on a device with an unlocked boot loader is very easy, while gaining root access to a device with a locked boot loader is not so straightforward, which means that unlocking your Android phone's bootloader is often the first step to rooting and flashing custom ROMs. This can be done either through fastboot mode (discussed in earlier sections) or by following a vendor-specific boot loader unlock procedure. Once the device bootloader is unlocked, the next step is to copy the su binary and grant it executable permissions. This can be done in many ways.

The following is how to root a Samsung Galaxy S7 (International SM-G930F/FD/X, Korean SM-G930K/L/S, and Canadian SM-G930W8 Exynos models):

1. Make sure OEM unlock is enabled in the **Developer** options.
2. Download ODIN (available at `https://build.nethunter.com/samsung-tools/Odin_3.12.3.zip`) and extract the contents of the archive to the directory of your choice.
3. Download the TWRP image (available at `https://twrp.me/samsung/samsunggalaxys7.html`).
4. Reboot your device into download mode. To do this, hold the Volume down + Home buttons while your device reboots. Once you see the download mode warning screen, press Volume up to continue.
   Start Odin and put the TWRP image in the AP slot; don't forget to disable **Auto-Reboot**. Start flashing the recovery.
5. To exit download mode, hold Volume down + Home + Power; when the screen blanks, immediately change Volume down to Volume up.
6. Allow system modifications by swiping right.
7. Download SuperSU (available at `https://download.chainfire.eu/supersu`).
8. Transfer the archive with SuperSU to the device via MTP and install it via the corresponding TWRP option.

Rooting is a highly device-specific process and hence the forensic investigator needs to be cautious before applying these techniques on any Android device. Rooting a device has both advantages and disadvantages associated with it. The following are the advantages of rooting:

- Rooting allows modification of the software on the device to the deepest level—for example, you can overclock or underclock the device's CPU.

- It allows restrictions imposed on the device by carriers, manufacturers, and so on, to be bypassed.
- For extreme customization, new customized ROMs can be downloaded and installed.

The following are the disadvantages of rooting:

- Rooting a device must be done with extreme care as errors may result in irreparable damage to the software on the phone, turning the device into a useless brick.
- Rooting might void the warranty of a device.
- Rooting results in increased exposure to malware and other attacks. Malware with access to the entire Android system can create havoc.

Once the device is rooted, applications such as the **Superuser app** are available to provide and deny root privileges. This app helps you to grant and manage superuser rights on the device, as shown in the following screenshot:

Application requesting root access

We will now look at root access.

Root access - ADB shell

A normal Android phone does not allow you to access certain directories and files on the device. For example, try to access the /data/data folder on an Android device that is not rooted. You will see the following message:

```
C:\android-sdk\platform-tools>adb.exe shell
shell@android:/ $ cd /data/data
shell@android:/data/data $ ls
opendir failed, Permission denied
255|shell@android:/data/data $
```

Permission denial without root access

On a rooted phone, you can run the adb shell as root by issuing the following command:

```
C:\android-sdk\platform-tools>adb.exe root
```

The following screenshot shows the output of the preceding command:

```
C:\android-sdk\platform-tools>adb.exe shell
root@android:/ # cd /data/data
root@android:/data/data # ls
android.googleSearch.googleSearchWidget
com.android.MtpApplication
com.android.Preconfig
com.android.apps.tag
com.android.backupconfirm
com.android.bluetooth
com.android.browser
```

Successful execution of shell command on a rooted device

Thus, rooting a phone enables you to access folders and data that are otherwise not accessible. Also note that # symbolizes root or superuser access, while $ reflects a normal user, as shown in the preceding command lines.

Android 7.0 (Nougat) and later versions support **file-based encryption (FBE)**, which allows the encryption of different files with different keys. For a forensic investigator like you, it is important to note that it is not possible to apply a permanent root to an FBE-enabled device for acquisition purposes. Instead, it is recommended that you use a custom recovery methodology, because the recovery partition runs with root privileges.

Summary

In this chapter, we learned how to set up a proper forensic workstation before conducting investigations on an Android device. Start with a sterile forensic workstation that has the necessary basic software and device drivers installed on it. If the method of forensic acquisition requires the Android device to be unlocked, you need to determine the best method by which to gain access to the device. If the device has the USB debugging feature enabled, then bypassing the screen-lock is just a cakewalk. We learned about the various screen lock bypass techniques and helped you to determine which one to use under different circumstances. Depending on the forensic acquisition method and the scope of the investigation, rooting the device should provide complete access to the files present on the device. We also learned about rooting and how it can be used to gain complete access to the device's filesystem and perform actions that are not normally allowed.

Now that the basic concepts of gaining access to an Android device have been covered, we will cover acquisition techniques and describe how data is pulled using each method in Chapter 9, *Android Data Extraction Techniques*.

Android Data Extraction Techniques

9

Using any of the screen lock bypass techniques explained in `Chapter 8`, *Android Forensic Setup and Pre-Data Extraction Techniques*, an examiner can try to access a locked device. Once the device is accessible, the next task is to extract the information present on the device. This can be achieved by applying various data extraction techniques to the Android device.

This chapter will help you to identify the sensitive locations present on an Android device and explain various logical and physical techniques that can be applied to the device to extract the necessary information.

In this chapter, we will cover the following topics:

- Understanding data extraction techniques
- Manual data extraction
- Logical data extraction
- Physical data extraction, which covers imaging an Android device and SD card, JTAG, and chip-off techniques

Understanding data extraction techniques

Data residing on an Android device may be an integral part of civil, criminal, or internal investigations done as part of a corporate company's internal probe. While dealing with investigations involving Android devices, you, as the forensic examiner, need to be mindful of the issues that need to be taken care of during the forensic process; this includes determining whether root access is permitted (via consent or legal authority) and what data can be extracted and analyzed during the investigation. For example, in a criminal case involving stalking, the court may only allow SMS, call logs, and photos to be extracted and analyzed on the Android device belonging to the suspect. In this case, it may make the most sense to logically capture only those specific items. However, it is best to obtain a full physical data extraction from the device and only examine the areas admissible by the court. You never know where your investigation may lead and it is best to obtain as much data from the device as possible immediately, rather than wishing you had a full image should the scope of consent change. Data extraction techniques on an Android device can be classified into three types:

- Manual data extraction
- Logical data extraction
- Physical data extraction

As described in `Chapter 1`, *Introduction to Mobile Forensics*, manual extraction involves browsing through the device normally and capturing any valuable information, while logical extraction deals with accessing the filesystem, and physical extraction is about extracting a bit-by-bit image of the device. The extraction methods for each of these types will be described in detail in the following sections.

 Some methods may require the device to be rooted to fully access the data. Each method has different implications and their success rates will depend on the tool and method used as well as the device's make and model.

Manual data extraction

This method of extraction involves you utilizing the normal user interface of the mobile device to access content present in the memory. You will browse through the device normally by accessing different menus to view details such as call logs, text messages, and IM chats. The content of each screen is captured by taking pictures and can be presented as evidence.

The main drawback of this type of examination is that only the files that are accessible via the operating system (in UI mode) can be investigated. Care must be taken when manually examining the device, as it's easy to press the wrong button and erase or add data. Manual extraction should be used as the last resort to verify findings extracted using one of the other methods. Certain circumstances may warrant you to conduct a manual examination as the first step. This may include cases of life or death situations or missing persons where a quick scan of the device may lead the police to the individual.

Logical data extraction

Logical data extraction techniques extract the data present on the device by interacting with the operating system and accessing the filesystem. These techniques are significant because they provide valuable data, work on most devices, and are easy to use. Once again, the concept of rooting comes into the picture while extracting the data. Logical techniques do not actually require root access for data extraction. However, having root access on a device allows you to access all of the files present on a device. This means that some data may be extracted on a non-rooted device while root access will open the device and provide access to all of the files present on the device. Hence, having root access to a device would greatly influence the amount and kind of data that could be extracted through logical techniques. The following sections explain various techniques that can be used to extract data logically from an Android device.

ADB pull data extraction

As seen earlier, `adb` is a command-line tool that helps you to communicate with a device to retrieve information. Using `adb`, you can extract data from all of the files on the device or just the relevant files in which you are interested. This is the most widely used technique as part of logical extraction.

To access an Android device through `adb`, the USB debugging option must be enabled. From Android 4.2.2, due to secure USB debugging, the host connecting to the device should also be authorized. If the device is locked and USB debugging is not enabled, try to bypass the screen lock using the techniques explained in `Chapter 8`, *Android Forensic Setup and Pre-Data Extraction Techniques*.

As a forensic examiner, it's important for you to know how the data is stored on the Android device and to understand where important and sensitive information is stored so that the data can be extracted accordingly. Application data often contains a wealth of user data that may be relevant to the investigation. All files pertaining to applications of interest should be examined for relevance, as will be explained in Chapter 10, *Android Data Analysis and Recovery*. The application data can be stored in one of the following locations:

- **Shared preferences**: This stores data in key-value pairs in a lightweight XML format. Shared preference files are stored in the `shared_pref` folder of the application `/data` directory.

- **Internal storage**: This stores data that is private and is present in the device's internal memory. Files saved to the internal storage are private and cannot be accessed by other applications.

- **External storage**: This stores data that is public in the device's external memory, which does not usually enforce security mechanisms. This data is available in the `/sdcard` directory.

- **SQLite database**: This data is available in the `/data/data/PackageName/` database. It is usually stored with the `.db` file extension. The data present in a SQLite file can be viewed using the SQLite browser (`https://sourceforge.net/projects/sqlitebrowser/`) or by executing the necessary SQLite commands on the respective files.

Every Android application stores data on the device using one or more of the preceding data storage options. So, the Contacts application would store all of the information about the contact details in the `/data/data` folder under its package name. Note that `/data/data` is a part of your device's internal storage, where all of the apps are installed under normal circumstances. Some application data will reside on the SD card and in the `/data/data` partition. Using `adb`, we can pull the data present in this partition for further analysis using the `adb pull` command. Once again, it's important to note that this directory is only accessible on a rooted phone.

In Android 7.0 (Nougat), a new storage type called device encrypted storage has been introduced to allow apps to store certain kinds of data in this storage. As a result of this, you will notice new file paths such as `misc_de`, `misc_ce`, `system_de`, and `system_ce` under the `/data` folder. From a forensic perspective, this is a very important change because what this also means is that, on devices running Android Nougat, `/data/data` is *not* the only location where artifacts are stored, for example, SMS data location on old devices:

`/data/com.android.providers.telephony/databases/smsmms.db`
and SMS data location on Nougat devices:
`/user_de/0/com.android.providers.telephony/databases/smsm ms.db`.

On a rooted phone, the `adb pull` command on the `databases` folder of the Dropbox app can be executed as follows:

```
C:\android-sdk\platform-tools>adb.exe pull /data/data/com.dropbox.android/databases C:\temp
pull: building file list...
pull: /data/data/com.dropbox.android/databases/prefs.db-journal -> C:\temp/prefs.db-journal
pull: /data/data/com.dropbox.android/databases/prefs.db -> C:\temp/prefs.db
pull: /data/data/com.dropbox.android/databases/db.db-journal -> C:\temp/db.db-journal
pull: /data/data/com.dropbox.android/databases/db.db -> C:\temp/db.db
4 files pulled. 0 files skipped.
1753 KB/s (140352 bytes in 0.078s)
```

The adb pull command

Similarly, on a rooted phone, the entire /data folder can be pulled in this manner. As shown in the following screenshot, the complete /data directory on the Android device can be copied to the local directory on the machine. The entire data directory was extracted in 97 seconds. The extraction time will vary depending on the amount of data residing in /data:

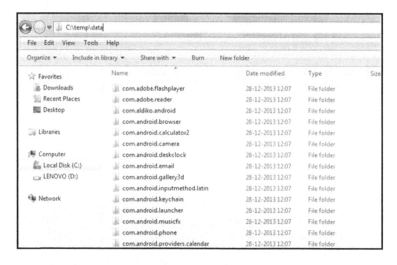

The /data directory extracted to a forensic workstation

On a non-rooted device, a pull command on the /data directory does not extract the files, as shown in the following output, since the shell user does not have permission to access those files:

```
C:\android-sdk\platform-tools>adb.exe pull /data C:\temp
pull: building file list...
0 files pulled. 0 files skipped.
```

ADB pull command on non-rooted device

The data copied from a rooted phone through the preceding process maintains its directory structure, hence allowing an investigator to browse through the necessary files to gain access to the information. By analyzing the data of the respective applications, a forensic expert can gather critical information that can influence the outcome of the investigation. Note that examining the folders natively on your forensic workstation will alter the dates and times of the content. You should make a copy of the original output to use for a date/time comparison.

Using SQLite Browser to view the data

SQLite Browser is a tool that can help during the course of analyzing extracted data. SQLite Browser allows you to explore database files with the following extensions: `.sqlite`, `.sqlite3`, `.sqlitedb`, `.db`, and `.db3`. The main advantage of using SQLite Browser is that it shows data in a table form.

Navigate to **File** | **Open Database** to open a `.db` file using SQLite Browser. As shown in the following screenshot, there are three main tabs: **Database Structure**, **Browse Data**, and **Execute SQL**. The **Browse Data** tab allows you to see the information present in different tables within the `.db` files.

We will be mostly using this tab during our analysis. Alternatively, tools such as Oxygen Forensic SQLite Viewer can also be used for the same purpose. Recovering deleted data from database files is possible and will be explained in `Chapter 10`, *Android Data Analysis and Recovery*:

SQLite Browser

The following sections throw light on identifying important data and manually extracting various details from an Android phone. Gaining access to the Terminal on Android has been covered in earlier chapters. In the following section, we will directly jump into gaining device information from there.

Extracting device information

Knowing the details of your Android device, such as the model, version, and more, will aid your investigation. For example, when the device is physically damaged and this prohibits the examination of the device information, you can grab details about the device by executing the following command under the /system folder:

```
# cat build.prop
```

This can be seen in the following screenshot:

```
root@android:/system # cat build.prop
# begin build properties
# autogenerated by buildinfo.sh
ro.build.id=JZO54K
ro.build.display.id=JZO54K.I        MH4
ro.build.version.incremental=I      MH4
ro.build.version.sdk=16
ro.build.version.codename=REL
ro.build.version.release=4.1.2
ro.build.date=Tue Sep 17 17:26:31 KST 2013
ro.build.date.utc=1379406391
ro.build.type=user
ro.build.user=dpi
ro.build.host=DELL224
ro.build.tags=release-keys
ro.product.model=GT-I9300
ro.product.brand=samsung
ro.product.name=m0xx
ro.product.device=m0
ro.product.board=smdk4x12
ro.product.cpu.abi=armeabi-v7a
ro.product.cpu.abi2=armeabi
ro.product_ship=true
ro.product.manufacturer=samsung
ro.product.locale.language=en
ro.product.locale.region=GB
ro.wifi.channels=
ro.board.platform=exynos4
```

The build.prop file

After extracting device information, we will now extract call logs.

Extracting call logs

Accessing the call logs of a phone is often required during an investigation to confirm certain events. The information about call logs is stored in the `contacts2.db` file located at `/data/data/com.android.providers.contacts/databases/`. As mentioned earlier, you can use SQLite Browser to see the data present in this file after extracting it to a local folder on the forensic workstation. Let's see how to extract call logs by following these steps:

1. As shown in the following screenshot, using the `adb pull` command, the necessary `.db` files can be extracted to a folder on the forensic workstation:

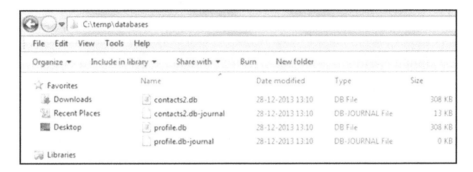

The contacts2.db file copied to a local folder

2. Note that applications used to make calls can store call log details in the respective application folder. All communication applications must be examined for call log details, as follows:

```
C:\android-sdk-windows\platform-tools>adb.exe pull
/data/data/com.android.providers.contacts C:temp
```

This will give the following output:

```
pull: /data/data/com.android.providers.contacts/databases/contacts2.db-mjFB7EA79BB -> C:\temp/databases/contacts2.db-mjFB7EA79BB
pull: /data/data/com.android.providers.contacts/databases/contacts2.db-mj7DE1FC9E3 -> C:\temp/databases/contacts2.db-mj7DE1FC9E3
pull: /data/data/com.android.providers.contacts/databases/contacts2.db-mj2151EE924 -> C:\temp/databases/contacts2.db-mj2151EE924
pull: /data/data/com.android.providers.contacts/databases/contacts2.db-mjABC96A935 -> C:\temp/databases/contacts2.db-mjABC96A935
pull: /data/data/com.android.providers.contacts/databases/profile.db-shm -> C:\temp/databases/profile.db-shm
pull: /data/data/com.android.providers.contacts/databases/profile.db-wal -> C:\temp/databases/profile.db-wal
pull: /data/data/com.android.providers.contacts/databases/profile.db -> C:\temp/databases/profile.db
pull: /data/data/com.android.providers.contacts/databases/contacts2.db-shm -> C:\temp/databases/contacts2.db-shm
pull: /data/data/com.android.providers.contacts/databases/contacts2.db-wal -> C:\temp/databases/contacts2.db-wal
pull: /data/data/com.android.providers.contacts/databases/contacts2.db -> C:\temp/databases/contacts2.db
pull: /data/data/com.android.providers.contacts/shared_prefs/com.android.providers.contacts_preferences.xml -> C:\temp/shared_prefs/com.android
rences.xml
pull: /data/data/com.android.providers.contacts/shared_prefs/ContactsUpgradeReceiver.xml -> C:\temp/shared_prefs/ContactsUpgradeReceiver.xml
pull: /data/data/com.android.providers.contacts/files/photos/2446 -> C:\temp/files/photos/2446
376 files pulled. 0 files skipped.
1820 KB/s (13795864 bytes in 7.398s)
```

3. Now, open the `contacts2.db` file using SQLite Browser (by navigating to **File** | **Open Database**) and browse through the data present in different tables. The **calls** table present in the `contacts2.db` file provides information about the call history. The following screenshot highlights the call history along with the name, number, duration, and date:

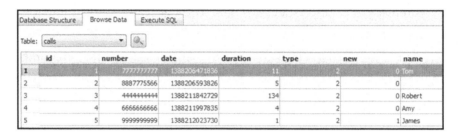

id	number	date	duration	type	new	name
1	1	7777777777	1388206471836	11	2	0 Tom
2	2	8887775566	1388206593826	5	2	0
3	3	4444444444	1388211842729	134	2	0 Robert
4	4	6666666666	1388211997835	4	2	0 Amy
5	5	9999999999	1388212023730	1	2	1 James

On devices running Android 7.0 (Nougat), call log data has been moved out of the `contacts2.db` file. On these devices, call log data can be accessed at `/data/com.android.providers.contacts/databases/calllog.db`

Extracting SMS/MMS

During the course of an investigation, you may be asked to retrieve the text messages that were sent by and delivered to a particular mobile device. Hence, it is important to understand where the details are stored and how to access the data. The `mmssms.db` file, which is present under `/data/data/com.android.providers.telephony/databases`, contains the necessary details. As with call logs, you must ensure that applications capable of messaging are examined for relevant message logs by using the following command:

```
adb.exe pull /data/data/com.android.providers.telephony C:\temp
```

This will give the following output:

```
C:\android-sdk\platform-tools>adb.exe pull /data/data/com.android.providers.telephony C:\temp
pull: building file list...
pull: /data/data/com.android.providers.telephony/databases/telephony.db-journal -> C:\temp/databases/telephony.db-journal
pull: /data/data/com.android.providers.telephony/databases/telephony.db -> C:\temp/databases/telephony.db
pull: /data/data/com.android.providers.telephony/databases/nwk_info.db-journal -> C:\temp/databases/nwk_info.db-journal
pull: /data/data/com.android.providers.telephony/databases/nwk_info.db -> C:\temp/databases/nwk_info.db
pull: /data/data/com.android.providers.telephony/databases/mmssms.db-shm -> C:\temp/databases/mmssms.db-shm
pull: /data/data/com.android.providers.telephony/databases/mmssms.db-wal -> C:\temp/databases/mmssms.db-wal
pull: /data/data/com.android.providers.telephony/databases/mmssms.db -> C:\temp/databases/mmssms.db
pull: /data/data/com.android.providers.telephony/shared_prefs/preferred-apn.xml -> C:\temp/shared_prefs/preferred-apn.xml
pull: /data/data/com.android.providers.telephony/optable.db -> C:\temp/optable.db
9 files pulled. 0 files skipped.
3096 KB/s (6193778 bytes in 1.953s)
```

Extracting SMS data

The phone number can be seen under the **address** column and the corresponding text message can be seen under the **body** column, as shown in the following screenshot:

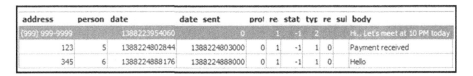

address	person	date	date sent	pro!	re	stat	tyr	re	sul	body
(999) 999-9999		1388223954060		0		1	-1		2	Hi.. Let's meet at 10 PM today
123	5	1388224802844	1388224803000	0	1	-1	1	0		Payment received
345	6	1388224888176	1388224888000	0	1	-1	1	0		Hello

The calls table in the contacts2.db file

We will now extract browser history information.

Extracting browser history information

Extracting browser history information is one task that is often required of a forensic examiner. Apart from the default Android browser, different browser applications can be used on an Android phone, such as Firefox Mobile and Google Chrome. All of these browsers store their browser history in the SQLite .db format. For our example, we are extracting data from the default Android browser to our forensic workstation. This data is located at /data/data/com.android.browser. The file named browser2.db contains the browser history details. The following screenshot shows the browser data, as represented by **Oxygen Forensic SQLite Viewer**. Note that the trial version will hide certain information:

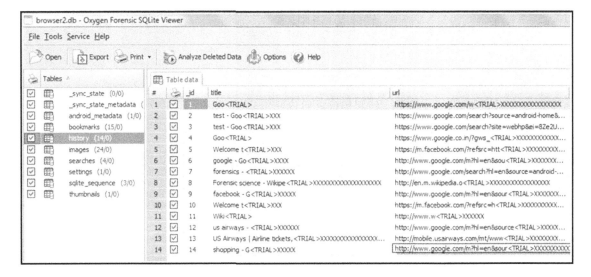

The browser2.db file in Oxygen Forensic SQLite Viewer

Please note that the aforementioned behavior might change if the browser's incognito mode is used.

Several details covered in the preceding section are not stored on the device if the browser's incognito mode is used. Next, we will be analyzing social networking and IM chats.

Analysis of social networking/IM chats

Social networking and IM chat applications such as Facebook, Twitter, and WhatsApp reveal sensitive data that could be helpful during the investigation of any case. The analysis is pretty much the same as with any other Android application. Download the data to a forensic workstation and analyze the .db files to find out whether you can unearth any sensitive information. For example, let's look at the Facebook application and try to see what data can be extracted.

First, we extract the /data/data/com.facebook.katana folder and navigate to the databases folder. The fb.db file present under this folder contains the information that is associated with the user's account. The friends_data table contains information about the user's friends' names, along with their phone numbers, email IDs, and dates of birth, as shown in the following screenshot. Similarly, other files can be analyzed to find out whether any sensitive information can be gathered:

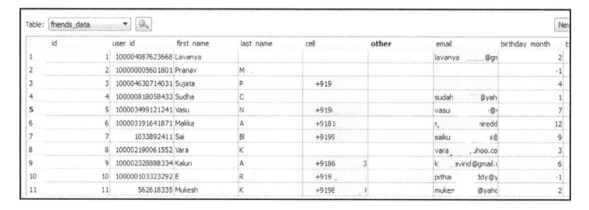

The fb.db file in SQLite Browser

Similarly, by analyzing the data present in the /data/data folder, information about the geolocation, calendar events, user notes, and more can be grabbed.

ADB backup extraction

Starting from Android 4.0, Google implemented the `adb backup` functionality, which allows users to back up application data to a computer using the `adb` tool. This process does not require root access and, hence, can be very useful during forensic examination. The main drawback is that it does not back up every application installed on the device. The backup feature is application dependent, as the owner of the application can choose to allow backups. Backups are allowed by default, but the developer can disable it if they want to. Hence, most third-party apps have this enabled and the `adb backup` command will work for them. Here is the syntax for the `adb backup` command:

```
adb backup [-f <file>] [-apk|-noapk] [-shared|-noshared] [-all] [-
system|nosystem] [<packages...>]
```

Let's discuss this in detail:

- `-f`: This is used to choose where the backup file will be stored. If not specified, it defaults to `backup.ab` in the present working directory.
- `[-apk|noapk]`: This is used to choose whether or not to back up the `.apk` file. The default is `-noapk`.
- `[-obb|-noobb]`: This is used to choose whether or not to back up the `.obb` (APK expansion) files. It defaults to `-noobb`.
- `[-shared|-noshared]`: This is used to choose whether or not to back up data from shared storage and the SD card. The default is `-noshared`.
- `[-all]`: This includes all applications for which backups are enabled.
- `[-system|-nosystem]`: This is used to choose whether or not to include system applications. It defaults to `-system`.
- `[<packages>]`: This is used to list a specific package name to be backed up.

Once the device is connected to the workstation and `adb` can access it, run the `adb backup -shared -all` command, as shown in the following screenshot:

The adb backup command

Once the command is run, the user then needs to approve the permission on the device, as shown in the following screenshot. For this reason, if the device is screen locked, it's not possible to make a backup:

Backup permission on the device

An Android backup file is stored as a .ab file and, by default, it is stored in the platform-tools folder of the Android SDK. There are free tools, such as Android Backup Extractor, that can convert the .ab file into a .tar file, which can then be viewed. Android Backup Extractor can be downloaded from https://sourceforge.net/projects/adbextractor/. This tool is a Java-based application, so ensure that Java is installed on the workstation before using the tool. To convert the backup file into .tar format, issue the following command:

```
java -jar abe.jar unpack backup.ab backup.tar
```

This will automatically create a file with the .tar extension, which can then be viewed easily using Archive tools such as WinRAR or 7Zip. However, note that if the password was entered on the device when the backup was created, the file will be encrypted and, therefore, you'll need to provide the password as an argument in the preceding command. The backup file contains two main folders—apps and shared. The apps folder contains all of the information that is present under /data/data for the applications included in the backup. The shared folder contains all of the data present on the SD card.

ADB dumpsys extraction

The `adb dumpsys` command allows you to gather information about services and applications running on the system. The `adb shell dumpsys` command gives diagnostic output for all system services. The `dumpsys` command does not require root privileges to be executed and requires only USB debugging to be enabled as with any other `adb` command. As shown in the following screenshot, to see the list of all the services that you can use with `dumpsys`, run the `adb.exe shell service list` command:

```
C:\android-sdk\platform-tools>adb.exe shell service list
found 111 services:
0       SYSSCOPE: [com.sec.android.app.sysscope.service.ISysScopeService]
1       sip: [android.net.sip.ISipService]
2       phoneext: [com.android.internal.telephony.ITelephonyExt]
3       phone: [com.android.internal.telephony.ITelephony]
4       com.orange.authentication.simcard: [com.orange.authentication.simcard.ISimCardAuthenticationService]
5       iphonesubinfo: [com.android.internal.telephony.IPhoneSubInfo]
6       simphonebook: [com.android.internal.telephony.IIccPhoneBook]
7       isms: [com.android.internal.telephony.ISms]
8       nfc: [android.nfc.INfcAdapter]
9       FMPlayer: [com.samsung.media.fmradio.internal.IFMPlayer]
10      motion_recognition: [android.hardware.motion.IMotionRecognitionService]
11      samsung.facedetection_service: [com.sec.android.facedetection.IFaceDetectionService]
12      voip: [android.os.IVoIPInterface]
13      commontime_management: []
14      mini_mode_app_manager: [com.sec.android.app.minimode.manager.IMiniModeAppManager]
15      tvoutservice: [android.os.ITvoutService]
```

The dumpsys service list command

Analyzing certain `dumpsys` services, such as Wi-Fi, user, and notification, can be helpful in certain scenarios. Here are some of the interesting cases where running the `dumpsys` command could be helpful during forensic analysis:

The `dumpsys iphonesubinfo` service can be used to get information about a device ID or the IMEI number, as shown in the following screenshot:

```
C:\android-sdk\platform-tools>adb.exe shell dumpsys iphonesubinfo
Phone Subscriber Info:
  Phone Type = GSM
  Device ID = 353        6486
```

The dumpsys command showing the IMEI number

The `dumpsys wifi` service gives information about Wi-Fi points accessed by the user. It shows the SSIDs of the connections that have been saved. This information can be used to pin down the user to a particular location. Here is the `adb dumpsys` command, which gives this information:

```
C:\android-sdk\platform-tools>adb.exe shell dumpsys wifi
Wi-Fi is enabled
Stay-awake conditions: 0

Internal state:
current HSM state: ConnectedState
mLinkProperties InterfaceName: wlan0 LinkAddresses: [192.168.0.106/24,]
mWifiInfo , MAC: 88:30:8a:f3:f1:d5, Supplicant state: COMPLETED, RSSI: -
mDhcpInfoInternal addr: 192.168.0.106/24 mRoutes: 0.0.0.0/0 -> 192.168.0
mNetworkInfo NetworkInfo: type: WIFI[], state: CONNECTED/CONNECTED, reas
mLastSignalLevel 2
mLastBssid 60:e3:27:be:d5:30
mLastNetworkId 1
mReconnectCount 0
mIsScanMode false
Supplicant status
bssid=60:e3:27:be:d5:30
ssid=Roro
id=1
```

The dumpsys command showing the last connected Wi-Fi details

The `dumpsys usagestats` service gives information about recently used applications, along with their date of usage. For example, the following screenshot shows that no apps were used on February 1, 2016, but on January 31, 2016, the Google Chrome browser was used and there was an attempt to back up the phone data:

```
C:\android-sdk\platform-tools>adb.exe shell dumpsys usagestats
Date: 20160129 (old data version)
Date: 20160131
  android: 1 times, 7 ms
    com.android.server.ShutdownActivity: 1 starts
  com.android.chrome: 1 times, 172801 ms
    com.google.android.apps.chrome.Main: 1 starts
    org.chromium.chrome.browser.ChromeTabbedActivity: 1 starts, 500-750ms=1
  com.sec.android.app.launcher: 4 times, 509170 ms
    com.android.launcher2.Launcher: 4 starts, 2000-3000ms=1
  com.android.backupconfirm: 2 times, 77425 ms
    com.android.backupconfirm.BackupRestoreConfirmation: 2 starts, 500-750ms=1
Date: 20160201
  android: 0 times, 3052 ms
```

The dumpsys command showing recently used apps

Observe that against `Date 20160201, android: 0` times denotes that no apps were used. But for `Date: 20160131, android: 1 times` confirms that one app was used and the later sections provide more details on what app was used and so on. Depending on the case being investigated, the forensic analyst needs to figure out whether any of the `dumpsys` commands can be of use. Running a `dumpsys` command immediately after a device seizure can be extremely helpful later on. By running the `adb shell dumpsys` command, you can record all of the `dumpsys` service information.

Using content providers

In Android, the data of one application cannot be accessed by another application under normal circumstances. However, Android provides a mechanism through which data can be shared with other applications. This is precisely achieved through the use of content providers. Content providers present data to external applications in the form of one or more tables. These tables are no different from the tables found in a relational database. They can be used by applications to share data, usually through the URI addressing scheme. They are used by other applications that access the provider using a provider-client object. During the installation of an app, the user determines whether or not the app can gain access to the requested data (content providers). For instance, contacts, SMS/MMS, and a calendar are examples of content providers.

Hence, by taking advantage of this, we can create an app that can grab all of the information from all of the available content providers. This is precisely how most commercial forensic tools work. The advantage of this method is that it can be used on both rooted and non-rooted devices. For our example, we use AFLogical, which takes advantage of the content provider mechanism to gain access to the information. This tool extracts the data and saves it to an SD card in CSV format. The following steps extract the information from an Android device using AFLogical Open Source Edition 1.5.2:

1. Download AFLogical OSE 1.5.2
   from `https://github.com/nowsecure/android-forensics/downloads`.

 The AFLogical LE edition is capable of extracting a large amount of information and requires registration via forensics using an active law enforcement or government agency email address. AFLogical OSE can pull all available MMSes, SMSes, contacts, and call logs.

2. Ensure that USB debugging mode is enabled and connect the device to the workstation.

3. Verify that the device is identified by issuing the `adb.exe devices` command:

Identify connected device

4. Save the AFLogical OSE app in the home directory and issue the `adb.exe install AFLogical-OSE_1.5.2.apk` command to install it on the device:

```
C:\android-sdk\platform-tools>adb.exe install AFLogical-OSE_1.5.2.apk
1798 KB/s (28794 bytes in 0.015s)
        pkg: /data/local/tmp/AFLogical-OSE_1.5.2.apk
Success
```

Installing AFLogical app

5. Once the application is installed, you can run it directly from the device and click on the **Capture** button present at the bottom of the app, as shown in the following screenshot:

The AFLogical OSE app

6. The app starts extracting data from the respective content providers and, once the process is complete, a message will be displayed, as shown in the following screenshot:

Message displayed after the extraction is complete

7. The extracted data is saved to the SD card of the device in a directory named `forensics`. The extracted information is stored in CSV files, as shown in the following screenshot. The CSV files can be viewed using any editor:

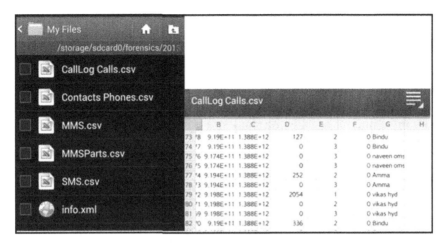

Files extracted using AFLogical OSE

8. The `info.xml` file present in the same directory provides information about the device, including the IMEI number, IMSI number, Android version, information about installed applications, and so on.

However, note that third-party app installation should be allowed (by selecting the **Unknown Sources** option) on the device for this to work. Other tools that can help during an investigation to logically extract data will be covered in `Chapter 11`, *Android App Analysis, Malware, and Reverse Engineering*.

This section covered various logical acquisition techniques. We will now look into physical data extraction techniques.

Physical data extraction

Physical extraction refers to the process of obtaining an exact bit-by-bit image of a device. It is important to understand that a bit-by-bit image is not the same as copying and pasting the contents of a device. If we copy and paste the contents of a device, it will only copy the available files, such as visible files, hidden files, and system-related files. This method is considered a logical image. With this method, deleted files and files that are not accessible are not copied by the `copy` command. Deleted files can be recovered (based on the circumstances) using certain techniques, which we will see in the following chapters. Unlike logical extraction, physical extraction is an exact copy of the device's memory and includes more information, such as the slack space and unallocated space.

Android data extraction through physical techniques is commonly performed using the `dd` command, while other advanced techniques such as JTAG and chip-off are also available, but are usually hard to implement and require great precision and experience to try them on real devices during the course of an investigation. As with any other technique, if an individual performs these procedures incorrectly, data on the device can be corrupted or become irretrievable, thereby making it non-admissible in a court of law. JTAG and chip-off techniques are covered in detail in the following sections. However, extracting data through the `dd` command requires root access. The following sections provide an overview of various techniques that can be used to perform physical extraction.

Imaging an Android phone

Imaging a device is one of the most important steps in mobile device forensics. When possible, it's imperative to obtain a physical image of an Android device before performing any techniques to extract the data directly from the device. In forensics, this process of obtaining a physical acquisition is commonly called *imaging the device*. The terms physical image, forensic image, and raw image are often used to refer to the image captured through this process. Let's first revisit how imaging is done on a desktop computer as it helps us to correlate and realize the problems associated with imaging Android devices. Let's assume that a desktop computer, which is not powered on, is seized from a suspect and sent for forensic examination. In this case, a typical forensic examiner would remove the hard disk, connect it to a write blocker, and obtain a bit-by-bit forensic image using any of the available tools. The original hard disk is then safely protected during the forensic imaging of the data.

With an Android device, all of the areas that contain data cannot be easily removed. Also, if the device is active at the time of receiving it for examination, it is not possible to analyze the device without making any changes to it, because any interaction would change the state of the device.

An Android device may have two file storage areas: internal and external storage. Internal storage refers to the built-in non-volatile memory. External storage refers to the removable storage medium, such as a micro SD card. However, it's important to note that some devices do not have a removable storage medium such as an SD card, but they divide the available permanent storage space into internal and external storage. Hence, it's not always true that external storage is removable. When a removable SD card is present, a forensic image of the memory card has to be obtained. As discussed in `Chapter 7`, *Understanding Android*, these removable cards are generally formatted with the FAT32 filesystem. Some mobile device acquisition methods will acquire the SD card through the Android device. This process, while useful, will be slow due to the speed limitations of USB phone cables.

Android, by default, does not provide access to internal directories and system-related files. This restricted access is to ensure the security of the device. For instance, the `/data/data` folder is not accessible on a non-rooted device. This folder is especially of interest to us because it stores most of the user-created data and many applications write valuable data into this folder. Hence, to obtain an image of the device, we need to root the Android device. Rooting a device gives us superuser privileges and access to all of the data. It is important to realize that this book has been stressing that all of the steps taken should be forensically sound and should not make changes to the device whenever possible. Rooting an Android device will make changes to it and should be tested on any device that you have not previously investigated. Rooting is common for Android devices, but getting root access could alter the device in a manner that renders the data changed or—worse yet—wiped. Some Android devices, such as the Nexus 4 and 5, may force the data partition to be wiped before allowing root access. This negates the need to root the device to gain access because all of the user data is lost during the process. Just remember that, while rooting provides access to more data when successfully done, it can also wipe data or destroy the phone. Hence, you must ensure that you have consent or legal rights to manipulate an Android device before proceeding with the root. As rooting techniques have been discussed in `Chapter 8`, *Android Forensic Setup and Pre-Data Extraction Techniques*, we will proceed with the example assuming that the device is rooted.

The following is a step-by-step process to obtain a forensic image of a rooted Android device:

1. Connect the Android device to the workstation and verify that the device is identified by issuing the `adb devices` command, as shown here:

```
C:\android-sdk\platform-tools>adb.exe devices
List of devices attached
4df16ac31▇▇▇▇▇▇        device
```

Identify connected devices

2. Once the `adb` access is ready, the partitions can be acquired from the Android device using the following steps:

   - **Using the** `dd` **command**: The `dd` command can be used to create a raw image of the device. This command helps us to create a bit-by-bit image of the Android device by copying low-level data.
   - **Inserting a new SD card**: Insert a new SD card into the device to copy the image file to this card. Make sure that this SD card is wiped and does not contain any other data. You might also need to testify that no additional data is present on the drive.
   - **Executing the command**: The filesystem of an Android device is stored in different locations within the `/dev` partition. A simple `mount` command on a Samsung Galaxy S3 phone returns the following output:

```
root@android:/ # mount
rootfs / rootfs ro,relatime 0 0
tmpfs /dev tmpfs rw,nosuid,relatime,mode=755 0 0
devpts /dev/pts devpts rw,relatime,mode=600 0 0
proc /proc proc rw,relatime 0 0
sysfs /sys sysfs rw,relatime 0 0
none /acct cgroup rw,relatime,cpuacct 0 0
tmpfs /mnt/asec tmpfs rw,relatime,mode=755,gid=1000 0 0
tmpfs /mnt/obb tmpfs rw,relatime,mode=755,gid=1000 0 0
none /dev/cpuctl cgroup rw,relatime,cpu 0 0
/dev/block/mmcblk0p9 /system ext4 ro,noatime,barrier=1,data=ordered 0 0
/dev/block/mmcblk0p3 /efs ext4 rw,nosuid,nodev,noatime,barrier=1,journal_asy
/dev/block/mmcblk0p8 /cache ext4 rw,nosuid,nodev,noatime,errors=panic,barrie
/dev/block/mmcblk0p12 /data ext4 rw,nosuid,nodev,noatime,barrier=1,journal_a
/sys/kernel/debug /sys/kernel/debug debugfs rw,relatime 0 0
/dev/fuse /storage/sdcard0 fuse rw,nosuid,nodev,noexec,relatime,user_id=1023
```

mount command output on an Android device

3. From the preceding output, we can identify the blocks where the /system, /data, and /cache partitions are mounted. Although it's important to image all of the files, most of the data is present in the /data and /system partitions. When time allows, all partitions should be acquired for completeness. Once this is done, execute the following command to image the device:

dd if=/dev/block/mmcblk0p12 of=/sdcard/tmp.image

In the preceding example, the data partition of a Samsung Galaxy S3 was used (where if is the input file and of is the output file).

The preceding command will make a bit-by-bit image of the mmcblk0p12 file (data partition) and copy the image file to an SD card. Once this is done, the dd image file can be analyzed using the available forensic software.

 You must ensure that the SD card has enough storage space to contain the data partition image. Other methods are available to acquire data from rooted devices.

If the image cannot be written to the SD card directly, you can use the netcat command to write the output directly to the machine. The netcat tool is a Linux-based tool used for transferring data over a network connection. Android devices do not usually come with netcat installed. Let's see how to use this command in the following steps:

1. To check whether netcat is installed, simply open the ADB shell and type nc. If it returns saying **nc is not found**, netcat will have to be installed manually on the device. You can download netcat compiled for Android at https://sourceforge.net/projects/androidforensics-netcat/files/.

2. Push netcat on to the device using the following command on your computer:

adb push nc /dev/Case_Folder/nc

The command should have created Case_Folder in /dev and nc should be in it.

3. Now, we need to give it permission to execute from the ADB shell. This can be done as follows:

chomd +x /dev/Case_Folder/nc

4. Open two Terminal windows with the ADB shell open in one of them. The other will be used to listen to the data being sent from the device. Now, we need to enable port forwarding over ADB from your computer:

```
adb forward tcp:9999 tcp:9999
```

9999 is the port we chose to use for netcat; it can be any arbitrary port number between 1023 and 65535 on a Linux or Mac system (1023 and below are reserved for system processes and require root permission to use them). In the other Terminal window, run the following:

```
nc 127.0.0.1 9999 > data_partition.img
```

The data_partition.img file should now be created in the current directory of your computer. When the data is finished transferring, netcat will terminate in both terminals and return to Command Prompt. The process can take a significant amount of time depending on the size of the image.

Imaging a memory (SD) card

There are many tools available that can image a memory card. The following example uses WinHex to create a raw disk image of the SD card. The following is the step-by-step process with which to image a memory card using WinHex:

1. **Connecting the memory card**: Remove the SD card from the memory slot and use a card reader to connect the memory card to the forensic workstation.

2. **Write-protect the card**: Open the disk using WinHex. Navigate to **Options | Edit Mode** and select **Read-only Mode (=write-protected mode)**, as shown in the following screenshot. This is to make sure that the device is write-protected and no data can be written on it:

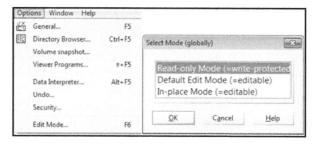

WinHex view of Edit Mode (left) and WinHex Read-only Mode enabled (right)

3. **Calculating the hash value**: Calculate the hash value of the memory card to make sure that no changes are made at any point during the investigation. Navigate to **Tools | Compute hash** and choose any hashing algorithm.

4. **Creating the image of the disk**: Navigate to **File | Create Disk Image**, as shown in the following screenshot. Select the raw image option (.dd) to create an image. This completes the imaging of the memory card:

The WinHex disk image option

Once a forensic image is obtained using any of the methods described previously, it needs to be analyzed to extract the relevant information. There are several commercial tools, such as Cellebrite and XRY, that can analyze image files. Analyzing Android images is covered in detail in Chapter 10, *Android Data Analysis and Recovery*.

Joint Test Action Group

Joint Test Action Group (JTAG) involves using advanced data acquisition methods, which involve connecting to specific ports on the device and instructing the processor to transfer the data stored on the device. Using this method, a full physical image of a device can be acquired. It is always recommended to first try out the other techniques mentioned earlier, as they are easy to implement and require less effort. An analyst must be experienced and properly trained before attempting JTAG as the device may be damaged if not handled properly.

The JTAG process usually involves the following forensic steps:

1. In JTAG, the device **Test Access Ports (TAPs)** are used to access the CPU of the device. Identifying the TAPs is the primary and most important step. TAPs are identified and the connection is traced to the CPU to find out which pad is responsible for each function. Although device manufacturers document resources about the JTAG schematics of a particular device, they are not released for general viewing. A good site for JTAG on an Android device is `https://forensicswiki.xyz/wiki/index.php?title=JTAG_Forensics`.

2. Wire leads are then soldered to appropriate connector pins and the other end is connected to the device that can control the CPU, as shown in the following photograph (published by Jim Swauger at `http://www.binaryintel.com/services/jtag-chip-off-forensics/jtag-forensics/`). JTAG jigs can be used to forgo soldering for certain devices. The use of a jig or JTAG adapter negates the need to solder, as it connects the TAPs to the CPU:

The JTAG setup

- Once the preceding steps are complete, power must be applied to boot the CPU. The voltage that must be applied depends on the specifications released by the hardware manufacturer. Do not apply a voltage beyond the number given in the specification.

- After applying the power, a full binary memory dump of the NAND flash can be extracted.
- Analyze the extracted data using the forensic techniques and tools learned in this book. A raw .bin file will be obtained during the acquisition; most forensic tools support the ingestion and analysis of this image format.

JTAG may sound complicated (perhaps it is), but it serves many useful purposes and three advantages are listed here:

- The main advantage of this technique is that it works even if the device is not powered on.
- It does not require root, ADB, or USB debugging.
- It can be used to recover device PINs/passwords and so can image the entire flash memory and recover/crack password files.

It is also important to understand that the JTAG technique should not result in the loss of functionality of the device. If reassembled properly, the device should function without any problems. Although the JTAG technique is effective in extracting data, only experienced and qualified personnel should attempt it. Any error in soldering the JTAG pads or applying the wrong voltage could severely damage the device.

The chip-off technique

Chip-off, as the name suggests, is a technique where the NAND flash chips are removed from the device and examined to extract information. Hence, this technique will work even when the device is passcode-protected and USB debugging is not enabled. Unlike the JTAG technique, where the device functions normally after examination, the chip-off technique usually results in the destruction of the device, that is, it is more difficult to reattach the NAND flash to the device after examination. The process of reattaching the NAND flash to the device is called re-balling and requires training and practice.

Chip-off techniques usually involve the following forensic steps:

1. All of the chips on the device must be researched to determine which chip contains user data.

2. Once determined, the NAND flash is physically removed from the device. This can be done by applying heat to desolder the chip:

Chip-off technique
Source: http://www.binaryintel.com/services/jtag-chip-off-forensics/chip-off_forensics/

3. This is a very delicate process and must be done with great care, as it may result in damaging the NAND flash.

4. The chip is then cleaned and repaired to make sure that the connectors are present and functioning.

5. Using specialized hardware device adapters, the chip can now be read. This is done by inserting the chip into the hardware device, that supports the specific NAND flash chip. In this process, raw data is acquired from the chip, resulting in a `.bin` file.

6. The data acquired can now be analyzed using forensic techniques and the tools described earlier.

The chip-off technique is most helpful when a device is damaged severely, locked, or otherwise inaccessible. However, the application of this technique requires not only expertise but also costly equipment and tools. There is always a risk of damaging the NAND flash while removing it and, hence, it is recommended to try out the logical techniques first to extract any data.

While root access is a must to perform any of the techniques discussed earlier, it must be noted here that, at the time of writing this book, none of these techniques would work on devices that have **Full Disk Encryption (FDE)** enabled. As discussed in `Chapter 7`, *Understanding Android*, Google has mandated the use of FDE for most devices starting from Android 6.0. Although some techniques were demonstrated and published for decrypting full disk encryption, they are device-specific and are not widely applicable.

Summary

This chapter covered various manual, logical, and physical data extraction techniques. We learned when and how to apply these techniques during the course of an investigation. Logical techniques extract data by interacting with the device using tools such as ADB. Physical techniques, on the other hand, access a larger set of data; they are complex and require a great deal of expertise to perform. Imaging a device produces a bit-by-bit image of the device, which is later analyzed using tools. Imaging a device is one of the primary steps to ensure that the data on the device is not modified. Android 7.0 and above poses a new challenge to forensic investigators by bringing in new security features and file paths that may limit acquisition. With this knowledge, you can perform device acquisition to extract relevant data from an Android device.

In the next chapter, we will see how to extract relevant data such as call logs, text messages, and browsing history from an image file. We will also cover data recovery techniques, using which we can recover data deleted from a device.

10
Android Data Analysis and Recovery

In the previous chapter, we covered various logical and physical extraction techniques. In physical extraction, a bit-by-bit image of the Android device is obtained, which contains valuable information. In this chapter, we will learn how to analyze and extract relevant data, such as call logs and text messages, from an image file. While the data extraction and analysis techniques provide information about various details, not all techniques can provide information about the deleted data. Data recovery is a crucial aspect of mobile forensics, as it helps to unearth the deleted items.

This chapter aims at covering various techniques, that can be used by a forensic analyst to recover the data from an Android device.

In this chapter, we will cover the following two major topics:

- Analyzing and extracting data from Android image files using the Autopsy tool
- Understanding techniques to recover deleted files from an SD card and the internal memory

Analyzing and extracting data from Android image files using the Autopsy tool

The term **Android image** refers to the physical image (also called a forensic image or raw image) that is obtained by performing any of the physical data extraction techniques. Using the techniques explained in Chapter 9, *Android Data Extraction Techniques*, you can image the entire /data/data block or any particular block that is of relevance to the investigation. Once the image is obtained, an investigator like you can manually go through the contents of the file or take advantage of the available tools to parse through the contents. Commercial tools, such as Cellebrite and XRY, can drill into the data and present a comprehensive picture of the contents. Autopsy is one of the very widely used open source tools in the forensics world that performs an excellent job of analyzing an Android image.

The Autopsy platform

Autopsy is a forensic platform and acts as a GUI for the Sleuth Kit. It is available for free; you can download it at http://www.sleuthkit.org/. The Sleuth Kit is a collection of Unix and Windows-based tools and utilities, which are used to perform forensic analysis. Autopsy displays the results by forensically analyzing a given volume, and thereby helps investigators to focus on relevant sections of the data. Autopsy is free and extensible and has several modules that can be plugged in. Autopsy can be used to load and analyze an Android image that is obtained after physical extraction.

Adding an image to Autopsy

Once you have downloaded and installed Autopsy, follow these steps to add an image to Autopsy:

1. Open the Autopsy tool and select the **Create New Case** option, as shown in the following screenshot:

Creating a new case in Autopsy

2. Enter all of the necessary case details, including the name of the case, the location where data needs to be stored, and so on, as shown in the following screenshot:

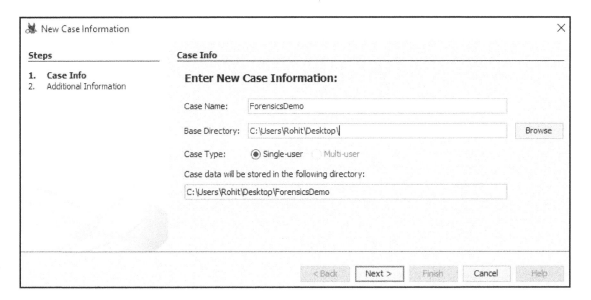

Entering case information in Autopsy

3. Enter the case number and examiner details, and click on **Finish**.

4. Now, click on the **Add Data Source** button, add the image file to be analyzed, and click on **Next**:

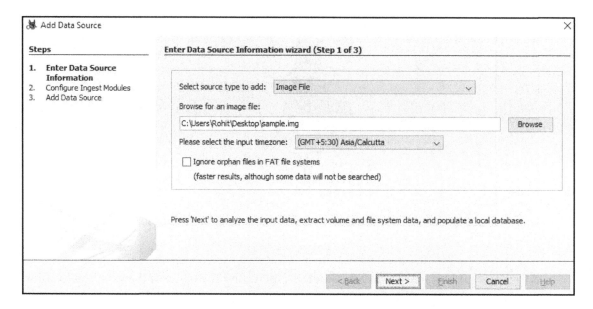

Entering data source information in Autopsy

5. On the next screen, you can configure what modules have to be run on the images, as shown in the following screenshot. It is recommended to select the **Recent Activity**, **Exif Parser**, **Keyword Search**, and **Android Analyzer** modules. In the next step, click on **Finish**:

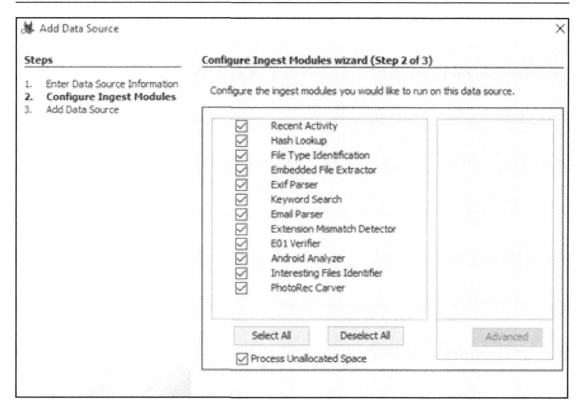

Configuring modules in Autopsy

Once this is done, the tool usually takes a few minutes to parse through the image depending on its size. During this time, you might see some errors or warning messages if any are encountered by the tool. However, Autopsy provides the fastest access to the artifacts and the filesystem when compared to other tools.

Analyzing an image using Autopsy

Once the image is loaded, expand the file present under **Data Sources** to see data present in the image. For example, the following screenshot shows the contents of the /data/ folder:

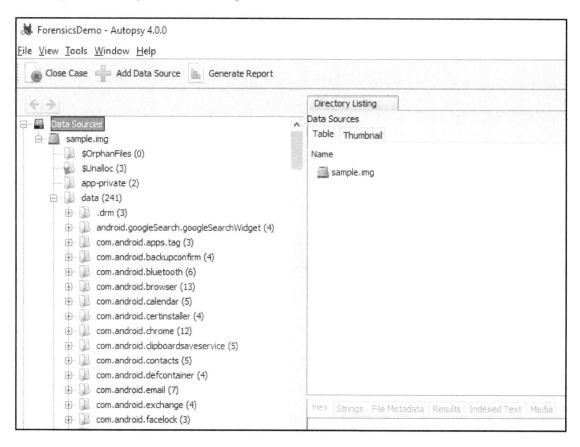

Analyzing an image in Autopsy

In the preceding example, only the `/data` portion of the device has been imaged. If the entire device had been imaged, then the tool would show more volumes. Depending on the underlying details of the investigation, relevant portions need to be analyzed. In the following example, by examining the folders present under `com.android.browser`, we can extract the list of various sites visited by the user along with their access dates:

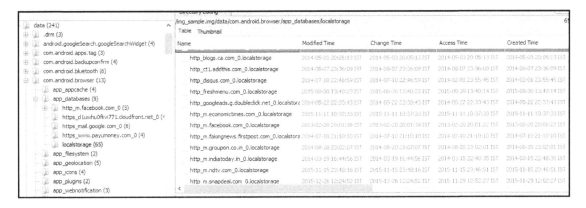

Analyzing browsing details in Autopsy

Valuable data, such as text messages, browsing history, chats, call history, pictures, videos, and location details, could be unearthed by analyzing the data present under various sections. In the next section, we shall look into data recovery from an SD card and the internal memory.

Understanding techniques to recover deleted files from the SD card and the internal memory

Data recovery is one of the most significant and powerful aspects of forensic analysis. The ability to recover deleted data can be crucial to crack many civil and criminal cases. From a normal user's point of view, recovering data that has been deleted would usually refer to the operating system's built-in solutions, such as the Recycle Bin in Windows. While it's true that data can be recovered from these locations, due to an increase in user awareness, these options don't often work. For instance, on a desktop computer, people now use *Shift + Delete* as a way to delete a file completely from their desktop.

Data recovery is the process of retrieving deleted data from a device when it cannot be accessed normally. Consider the scenario where a mobile phone has been seized from a terrorist. Wouldn't it be of the greatest importance to know which items were deleted by the terrorist? Access to any deleted SMS messages, pictures, dialed numbers, application data, and more can be of critical importance, as they often reveal sensitive information. With Android, it is possible to recover most of the deleted data if the device files are properly acquired. However, if proper care is not taken while handling the device, the deleted data could be lost forever. To ensure that the deleted data is not overwritten, it is recommended to keep the following points in mind:

- Do not use the phone for any activity after seizing it. The deleted data exists on the device until space is needed by some other incoming data. Hence, the phone must not be used for any sort of activity to prevent the data from being overwritten.
- Even when the phone is not used, without any intervention from our end, data can be overwritten. For instance, an incoming SMS would automatically occupy space, which could overwrite the data marked for deletion. To prevent the occurrence of such events, you should follow the forensic handling methods described in the previous chapters. The easiest solution is to place the device in airplane mode or disable all connectivity options on the device. This prevents the delivery of any new messages.

All Android filesystems have metadata that contains information about the hierarchy of files, filenames, and so on. Deletion will not really erase this data but remove the filesystem metadata. When text messages or any other files are deleted from the device, they are just made invisible to the user, but the files are still present on the device. Essentially, the files are simply marked for deletion, but they reside on the filesystem until being overwritten. Recovering deleted data from an Android device involves two scenarios: recovering data that is deleted from the SD card, such as pictures, videos, application data, and more, and recovering data that is deleted from the internal memory of the device. The following sections cover the techniques that can be used to recover deleted data from both the SD card and the internal memory of the Android device.

Recovering deleted data from an external SD card

Data present on SD cards can reveal a lot of information to forensic investigators. SD cards are capable of storing pictures and videos taken by the phone's camera, voice recordings, application data, cached files, and more. Essentially, anything that can be stored on a computer hard drive can be stored on an SD card as much as the available space allows.

Recovering the deleted data from an external SD card is a straightforward process. SD cards can be mounted as an external mass storage device and forensically acquired using standard digital forensic methods, as discussed in Chapter 9, *Android Data Extraction Techniques*. As mentioned in the previous chapters, SD cards in Android devices often use the FAT32 filesystem. The main reason for this is that the FAT32 filesystem is widely supported in most operating systems, including Windows, Linux, and macOS X. The maximum file size on a FAT32 formatted drive is around 4 GB. With increasingly high-resolution formats now available, this limit is commonly reached. Apart from this, FAT32 can only be used on partitions that are less than 32 GB in size. Hence, the exFAT filesystem, which overcomes these problems, is now being used in some of the devices.

Recovering the deleted data from an external SD card can be easily accomplished if it can be mounted as a drive. Hence, if the SD card is removable, connect it to a workstation using a write blocker for acquisition. However, the latest Android devices do not usually mount as a mass storage. This is because these devices use the **Media Transfer Protocol** (**MTP**) or **Picture Transfer Protocol** (**PTP**) protocols instead of USB mass storage. The problem with USB mass storage is that the computer would need exclusive access to the storage. In other words, the external storage needs to be completely disconnected from the Android OS when it is connected to a workstation. This has led to several other complications for mobile apps. When an Android device uses MTP, it appears to the computer as a media device and not as **Removable Storage**, as shown in the following screenshot:

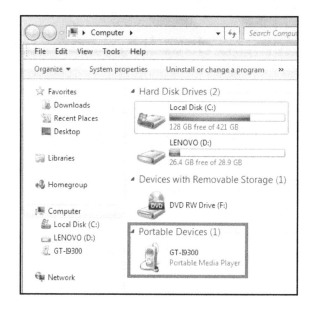

Android device connection using MTP

But the normal data recovery tools would need a mount drive to perform a scan. Hence, most of the latest devices that use MTP/PTP are not treated as a mount drive, and so the traditional data recovery tools that work for computers do not work on them.

For this reason, when the device uses MTP/PTP and is not mounted as a drive, the recovery can be done by certain Android-specific data recovery tools that need the USB debugging option to be turned on. Almost all Android data recovery tools in the market need you to enable USB debugging so that your device and the SD card can be recognized before starting Android data recovery.

You must understand that Android devices might use space on the SD card to cache application data; therefore, it is important to make sure that as much data as possible is obtained from the device prior to removing the SD card. Some older devices automatically mount the device as a drive when connected through USB. It is a sound forensic practice to not work directly on the device for data extraction, data recovery, and so on. Hence, a physical image of the SD card needs to be taken and all required analysis is performed on the image itself. It is recommended to acquire the SD card through the device as well as separately to ensure that all data is obtained. To achieve the SD card image, dd through adb can be used while the device is running to obtain an image of the SD card of the device if the device cannot be powered off due to possible evidence running in the memory. If the SD card is removed and connected to the workstation through a card reader, it appears as external mass storage, which can then be imaged using the standard forensic techniques described in earlier chapters.

Once the image is obtained, it can be analyzed using any standard forensic tools, such as FTK Imager. FTK Imager is a simple tool that can be used to create and analyze disk images. It is available for download at https://accessdata.com/product-download/ftk-imager-version-3.2.0.

The following is a step-by-step process to recover the deleted files from an SD card image using FTK Imager:

1. Start FTK Imager and click on **File**, then click on **Add Evidence Item...** in the menu:

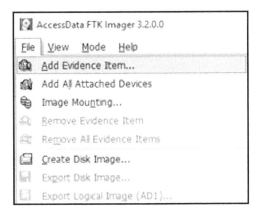

Adding evidence in FTK Imager

2. Select **Image File** as the evidence type in the **Select Source** dialog, and click on **Next**:

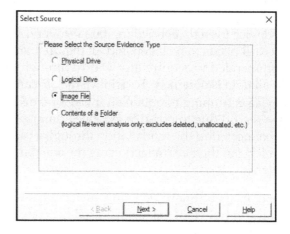

Selecting file type in FTK Imager

3. In the **Select File** dialog, go to the location where the SDCARD.dd SD card image file is present, select it, and click on **Finish**:

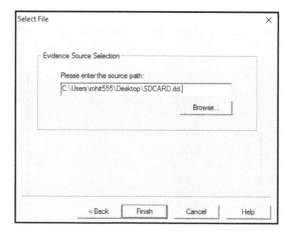

Selecting the image file for analysis in FTK Imager

4. The contents of the SD card image are then shown in the **View** pane. You can browse through the folders by clicking on the + sign. When a folder is highlighted, the contents are shown on the right pane. When a file is selected, its contents can be seen in the bottom pane. As shown in the following screenshot, the deleted files are also shown with a red cross mark over the icon:

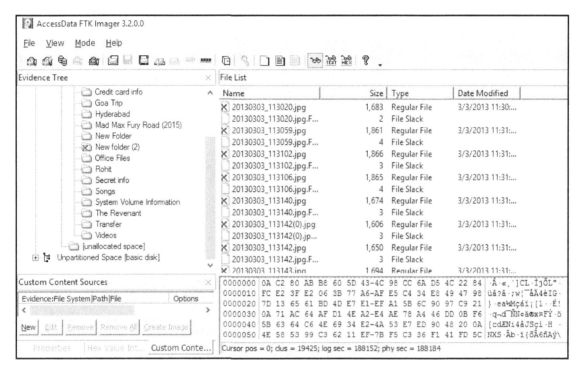

Deleted files shown with a red cross over the icons in FTK Imager

5. To copy the deleted files to the workstation, right-click on the marked file and select **Export Files...**, as shown in the following screenshot:

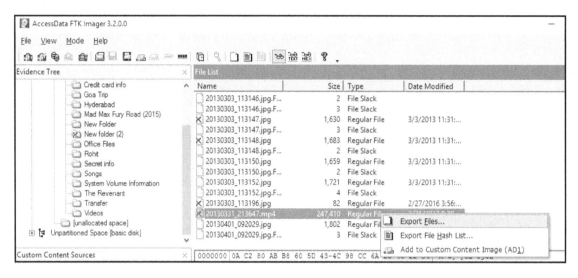

Recovering deleted images in FTK Imager

It is also recommended to check whether the device has any backup applications or files installed. The initial release of Android did not include a mechanism for users to back up their personal data. Hence, several backup applications were used extensively by users. Using these apps, users can back up their data either to the SD card or to the cloud. For example, the **Super Backup** app contains the options to back up call logs, contacts, SMS, and more, as shown in the following screenshot:

The Super Backup Android app

Upon detection of a backup application, you must attempt to determine where the data is stored. Usually, the backup folder path is the internal SD card. The folder path is also present in the backup app's settings. The data saved in a backup may contain important information, and hence, looking for any third-party backup app on the device would be very helpful.

Recovering data deleted from the internal memory

Recovering files that are deleted from an Android device's internal memory (such as SMS, contacts, and app data) is not supported by all analytical tools and may require manual carving. Unlike some media containing common filesystems, such as SD cards, the filesystem may not be recognized and mounted by forensic tools. Also, you cannot get access to the raw partitions of the internal memory of an Android phone unless the phone is rooted. It is recommended to image the device before and after the rooting process happens. The following are some of the other issues that you may face when attempting to recover data from the internal memory on Android devices:

- To get access to the internal memory, you can try to root the phone. However, the rooting process might involve writing some data to the /data partition, and this process could overwrite the data of value on the device.
- Unlike SD cards, the internal filesystem here is not FAT32 (which is widely supported by forensic tools). The internal filesystem could be YAFFS2 (on older devices), EXT3, EXT4, RFS, or something proprietary built to run on Android. Therefore, many of the recovery tools designed for use with Windows filesystems won't work.
- Application data on Android devices is commonly stored in the SQLite format. While most forensic tools provide access to the database files, they may have to be exported and viewed in a native browser. You must examine the raw data to ensure that the deleted data is not overlooked by the forensic tool.

The discussed reasons make it difficult, but not impossible, to recover the deleted data from the internal memory. The internal memory of Android devices holds the bulk of the user data and the possible keys to your investigation. As previously mentioned, the device must be rooted to access the raw partitions. Most of the Android recovery tools on the market do not highlight the fact that they only work on rooted phones. Let's now take a look at how we can recover deleted data from an Android phone.

Recovering deleted files by parsing SQLite files

Android uses SQLite files to store most data. Data related to text messages, emails, and certain app data is stored in SQLite files. SQLite databases can store deleted data within the database itself. Files marked for deletion by the user no longer appear in the active SQLite database files. Therefore, it is possible to recover the deleted data, such as text messages and contacts. There are two areas within a SQLite page that can contain deleted data—unallocated blocks and free blocks.

Most of the commercial tools that recover deleted data scan the unallocated blocks and free blocks of the SQLite pages. Parsing the deleted data can be done using the available forensic tools, such as **Oxygen Forensics SQLite Viewer**. The trial version of the SQLite Viewer can be used for this purpose; however, there are certain limitations on the amount of data that you can recover. You can write your own script to parse the files for deleted content, and for this, you need to have a good understanding of the SQLite file format. The `http://www.sqlite.org/fileformat.html` page is a good place to start. If you do not want to reinvent the wheel and want to reuse the existing scripts, you can try the available open source Python scripts (`http://az4n6.blogspot.in/2013/11/python-parser-to-recover-deleted-sqlite.html`) to parse the SQLite files for deleted records.

For our example, we will recover deleted SMSes from an Android device. Recovering deleted SMSs from an Android phone is quite often requested as part of the forensic analysis of a device, mainly because text messages contain data, which can reveal a lot of information. There are different ways to recover deleted text messages on an Android device. First, we need to understand where the messages are being stored on the device. In `Chapter 9`, *Android Data Extraction Techniques*, we explained the important locations on the Android device where user data is stored. Here is a quick recap of this:

- Every application stores its data under the `/data/data` folder (again, this requires root access to acquire data).
- The files under the location, `/data/data/com.android.providers.telephony/databases`, contain details about the SMS/MMS.

Under the mentioned locations, text messages are stored in an SQLite database file, which is named `mmssms.db`. Deleted text messages can be recovered by examining this file. Here are the steps to recover deleted SMSes using the `mmssms.db` file:

1. On the Android device, enable the USB debugging mode and connect the device to the forensic workstation. Using the `adb` command-line tool, extract the databases folder present at `/data/data/` by issuing the following command:

   adb.exe pull /data/data/com.android.providers.telephony/databases C:\temp

   The output can be seen as follows:

```
C:\android-sdk\platform-tools>adb.exe pull /data/data/com.android.providers.telephony/databases C:\temp
pull: building file list...
pull: /data/data/com.android.providers.telephony/databases/telephony.db-journal -> C:\temp/telephony.db-journal
pull: /data/data/com.android.providers.telephony/databases/telephony.db -> C:\temp/telephony.db
pull: /data/data/com.android.providers.telephony/databases/nwk_info.db-journal -> C:\temp/nwk_info.db-journal
pull: /data/data/com.android.providers.telephony/databases/nwk_info.db -> C:\temp/nwk_info.db
pull: /data/data/com.android.providers.telephony/databases/mmssms.db-shm -> C:\temp/mmssms.db-shm
pull: /data/data/com.android.providers.telephony/databases/mmssms.db-wal -> C:\temp/mmssms.db-wal
pull: /data/data/com.android.providers.telephony/databases/mmssms.db -> C:\temp/mmssms.db
7 files pulled. 0 files skipped.
3242 KB/s (6177288 bytes in 1.860s)
```

ADB pull command

Once the files are extracted to the local machine, use the Oxygen Forensics SQLite Viewer tool to open the `mmssms.db` file.

2. Click on the table named `sms` and observe the current message under the **Tables** data tab in the tool.

3. One way to view the deleted data is by clicking on the **Blocks containing deleted data** tab, as shown in the following screenshot:

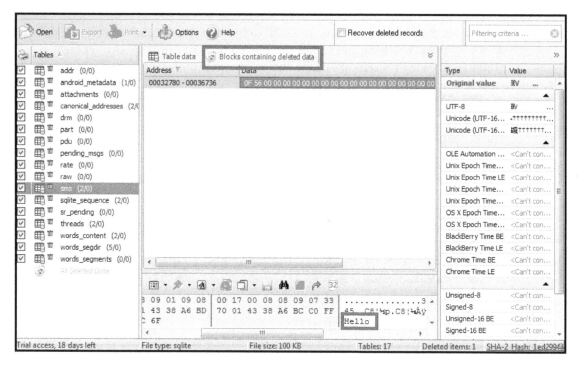

Recovering deleted SMS messages

Similarly, other data residing on Android devices that is stored in SQLite files can be recovered by parsing for deleted content. When the preceding method doesn't provide access to the deleted data, you should look at the file in raw hex file for data marked as deleted, which can be manually carved and reported.

Recovering files using file-carving techniques

File carving is an extremely useful method in forensics because it allows data that has been deleted or hidden to be recovered for analysis. In simple terms, file carving is the process of reassembling computer files from fragments in the absence of filesystem metadata. In file carving, specified file types are searched for and extracted across the binary data to create a forensic image of a partition or an entire disk. File carving recovers files from the unallocated space in a drive based merely on file structure and content without any matching filesystem metadata. Unallocated space refers to the part of the drive that no longer holds any file information indicated by the filesystem structures, such as the file table.

Files can be recovered or reconstructed by scanning the raw bytes of the disk and reassembling them. This can be done by examining the header (the first few bytes) and footer (the last few bytes) of a file.

File-carving methods are categorized based on the underlying technique in use. The header-footer carving method relies on recovering the files based on their header and footer information. For instance, for JPEG files, these start with `0xffd8` and end with `0xffd9`.

The locations of the header and footer are identified and everything between those two endpoints is carved. Similarly, the carving method based on the file structure uses the internal layout of a file to reconstruct the file. However, the traditional file-carving techniques, such as the ones that we've already explained, may not work if the data is fragmented. To overcome this, new techniques, such as smart carving, use the fragmentation characteristics of several popular filesystems to recover the data.

Once the phone is imaged, it can be analyzed using tools such as **Scalpel**. Scalpel is a powerful open source utility to carve files. This tool analyzes the block database storage, identifies the deleted files, and recovers them. Scalpel is filesystem-independent and is known to work on various filesystems, including FAT, NTFS, EXT2, EXT3, HFS, and more. More details about Scalpel can be found at `https://github.com/sleuthkit/scalpel`. The following steps explain how to use Scalpel on an Ubuntu workstation:

1. Install Scalpel on the Ubuntu workstation using the `sudo apt-get install scalpel` command.

2. The `scalpel.conf` file present under the `/etc/scalpel` directory contains information about the supported file types, as shown in the following screenshot:

```
scalpel.conf ✖

# GRAPHICS FILES
#- - - - - - - - - - - - - - - - - - - - - - - - - - - - - - - - - - - - - - - - - - - - - - - - - - - - - - - - - - - - - - - - - - - - -
#
#
# AOL ART files
#       art      y      150000   \x4a\x47\x04\x0e          \xcf\xc7\xcb
#       art      y      150000   \x4a\x47\x03\x0e          \xd0\xcb\x00\x00
#
# GIF and JPG files (very common)
#|      gif      y      5000000  \x47\x49\x46\x38\x37\x61         \x00\x3b
#       gif      y      5000000  \x47\x49\x46\x38\x39\x61         \x00\x3b
# ⏢     jpg      y      200000000 \xff\xd8\xff\xe0\x00\x10        \xff\xd9
#
#
# PNG
#       png      y      20000000         \x50\x4e\x47?   \xff\xfc\xfd\xfe
#
#
# BMP    (used by MSWindows, use only if you have reason to think there are
#        BMP files worth digging for. This often kicks back a lot of false
#        positives
```

The scalpel configuration file

This file needs to be modified to mention the files that are related to Android. A sample `scalpel.conf` file can be downloaded from https://www.nowsecure.com/tools-and-trainings/#viaforensics. You can also uncomment the files and save the `conf` file to select file types of your choice. Once this is done, replace the original `conf` file with the one that is downloaded.

3. Scalpel needs to be run along with the preceding configuration file on the `dd` image being examined. You can run the tool using the following command by inputting the configuration file and the `dd` file:

```
$ scalpel -c /home/unigeek/Desktop/scalpel-android.conf
/home/unigeek/Desktop/userdata.dd -o /home/unigeek/Desktop/rohit
```

Once this command is run, the tool starts to carve the files and build them accordingly as shown in the following screenshot:

```
File Edit View Search Terminal Help
unigeek@ubuntu:~$ scalpel -c /home/unigeek/Desktop/scalpel-android.conf /home/un
igeek/Desktop/userdata.dd -o /home/unigeek/Desktop/rohit
Scalpel version 1.60
Written by Golden G. Richard III, based on Foremost 0.69.

Opening target "/home/unigeek/Desktop/userdata.dd"

Image file pass 1/2.
/home/unigeek/Desktop/userdata.dd: 100.0% |*************|    3.9 MB    00:00 ETA
Allocating work queues...
Work queues allocation complete. Building carve lists...
Carve lists built.  Workload:
gif with header "\x47\x49\x46\x38\x37\x61" and footer "\x00\x3b" --> 0 files
gif with header "\x47\x49\x46\x38\x39\x61" and footer "\x00\x3b" --> 2 files
jpg with header "\xff\xd8\xff\xe0\x00\x10" and footer "\xff\xd9" --> 71 files
jpg with header "\xff\xd8\xff\xe1" and footer "\x7f\xff\xd9" --> 1 files
png with header "\x50\x4e\x47\x3f" and footer "\xff\xfc\xfd\xfe" --> 0 files
png with header "\x89\x50\x4e\x47" and footer "" --> 71 files
sqlitedb with header "\x53\x51\x4c\x69\x74\x65\x20\x66\x6f\x72\x6d\x61\x74" and
footer "" --> 0 files
email with header "\x46\x72\x6f\x6d\x3a" and footer "" --> 0 files
doc with header "\xd0\xcf\x11\xe0\xa1\xb1\x1a\xe1\x00\x00" and footer "\xd0\xcf\
x11\xe0\xa1\xb1\x1a\xe1\x00\x00" --> 0 files
doc with header "\xd0\xcf\x11\xe0\xa1\xb1" and footer "" --> 0 files
htm with header "\x3c\x68\x74\x6d\x6c" and footer "\x3c\x2f\x68\x74\x6d\x6c\x3e"
 --> 1 files
pdf with header "\x25\x50\x44\x46" and footer "\x25\x45\x4f\x46\x0d" --> 0 files
pdf with header "\x25\x50\x44\x46" and footer "\x25\x45\x4f\x46\x0a" --> 0 files
wav with header "\x52\x49\x46\x3f\x3f\x3f\x3f\x57\x41\x56\x45" and footer ""
 --> 0 files
amr with header "\x23\x21\x41\x4d\x52" and footer "" --> 0 files
```

Running the Scalpel tool on a dd file

4. The `output` folder that was specified in the preceding command now contains lists of folders that are based on the file types, as shown in the following screenshot. Each of these folders contains data that is based on the folder name. For instance, `jpg 2-0` contains files related to the `.jpg` extension that have been recovered:

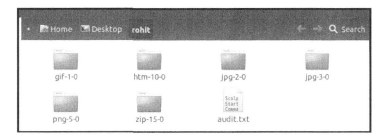

Output folder after running the Scalpel tool

5. As shown in the preceding screenshot, each folder contains recovered data from the Android device, such as images, PDF files, ZIP files, and more. While some pictures are recovered completely, some are not recovered fully, as shown in the following screenshot:

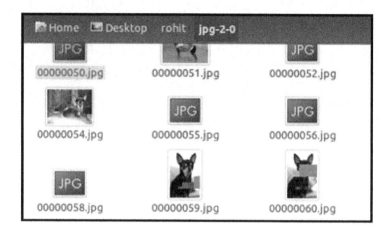

Recovered data using the Scalpel tool

Applications such as **DiskDigger** can be installed on Android devices to recover different types of files from both the internal memory and SD cards. DiskDigger includes support for JPG files, MP3 and WAV audio, MP4 and 3GP video, raw camera formats, Microsoft Office files (DOC, XLS, and PPT), and more. However, as mentioned earlier, the application requires root privileges on the Android device to recover the content from the internal memory. These changes should be clearly documented by you. The DiskDigger Android app operates in two different modes, basic scan mode and full scan mode.

The full scan mode works only on rooted devices, whereas the basic scan mode works on any device. As shown in the following screenshot, on a rooted phone, the app automatically locates and displays the available partitions:

The DiskDigger app

After you select the memory partition, the tool now prompts you to select the types of files that you would like to recover. Proceed by selecting the file types of interest:

The DiskDigger app file selection screen

Once the scanning begins, the DiskDigger app will automatically show you the files that are available for recovery. The recovered files can be either saved to the app or to the device directly. Hence, file-carving techniques play a very important role in recovering important deleted files from the device's internal memory.

Recovering contacts using your Google account

You can also restore the contacts on the device using the Contacts app through the Google account that is configured on the device. This would work if the user of the device has previously synced their contacts using the **Sync Settings** option available in Android. This option synchronizes the contacts and other details and stores them in the cloud. A forensic examiner like you with legal authority or proper consent can restore the deleted contacts if you can get access to the Google account configured on the device. Once the account is accessed, perform the following steps to restore the data:

1. Log in to your Google Contacts app on the Android device using the configured Google account. The following example is attempt on a OnePlus 5 device running the Android Pie version.
2. Click on **Settings** and then look for **Restore**, as shown in the following screenshot:

The Restore menu in the Contacts app

3. Click on **Restore**, and the following screen will appear:

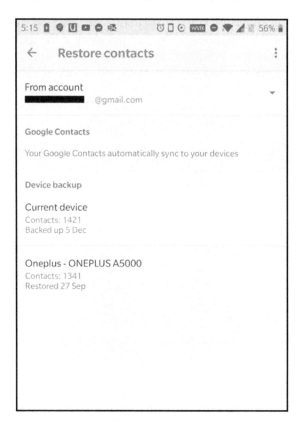

The Restore contacts dialog box

As you can see, you can restore the contact list to a previous state when the backup was taken at various points in time. You can also use the **Undo changes** option under the **Settings** menu to restore the contacts to any state in the past 30 days:

Restore deleted contacts in Google account

Hence, using any one of the preceding techniques, a forensic examiner like you can attempt to easily recover deleted data.

Summary

In this chapter, we learned various techniques to recover deleted data from an Android device. This process depends on various factors, which heavily rely on access to the data residing in the internal memory and SD card. We saw various techniques to recover deleted data from both SD card as well as internal memory. While the recovery of deleted items from external storage, such as an SD card, is easy, the recovery of deleted items from the internal memory takes considerable effort. We have also learned SQLite file-parsing and file-carving techniques, using which deleted data can be extracted from an Android device. With this knowledge, you can now perform data recovery during a forensic investigation.

The next chapter discusses the forensic analysis of Android apps and malware and the reverse engineering of Android apps.

11
Android App Analysis, Malware, and Reverse Engineering

Third-party applications are commonly used by smartphone users. Android users download and install several apps from app stores such as Google Play. During forensic investigations, it is often helpful to perform an analysis of these apps to retrieve valuable data and to detect any malware. For instance, a photo vault app might lock sensitive images present on a device. Hence, it would be of great significance to have the knowledge to identify the passcode for the photo vault app.

Also, apps such as Facebook, WhatsApp, Skype, and so on are widely used these days, and they are often the source of valuable data that aids in cracking a case. Hence, it is important to know what kind of data these apps store and the location of this data. While the data extraction and data recovery techniques we discussed in earlier chapters provide access to valuable data, app analysis helps us gain information about the specifics of an application, such as preferences and permissions.

In this chapter, we will cover the following topics:

- Analyzing widely used Android apps to retrieve valuable data
- Techniques to reverse engineer an Android application
- Android malware

Analyzing widely used Android apps to retrieve valuable data

On Android, everything the user interacts with is an application. While some apps are preinstalled by the device manufacturer, others are downloaded and installed by the user. For example, even routine functions, such as contacts, calls, SMS, and so on, are performed through their respective apps. Thus, Android app analysis is crucial during the course of an investigation. Several third-party apps, such as WhatsApp, Facebook, Skype, Chrome browser, and so on, are used widely, and they handle a lot of valuable information. Depending on the type of application, most of these apps store sensitive information on the device's internal memory or SD card. Analyzing them may provide information about the location details of the user, their communication with others, and more. Using the forensic techniques we described earlier, it is possible to get access to the data stored by these applications. However, you, as a forensic examiner, need to develop the necessary skills to convert the available data into useful data. This is achieved when you have a comprehensive understanding of how the application handles data.

As we discussed in previous chapters, all applications store their data in the /data/data folder by default. Apps also store certain other data on the SD card, if they want to, by asking permission at the time of installation. Information about applications present on the device can be gathered by inspecting the contents of the /data/data folder, but this is not straightforward as it requires analyzing each individual app folder under this path. As an alternative, you can inspect the packages.list file present under /data/system. This file contains information about all the apps, along with their package names and data paths.

This can be performed using the following command:

```
# cat packages.list
```

The following is the output of the preceding command:

```
C:\android-sdk\platform-tools>adb.exe shell
root@android:/ # cd /data/system
root@android:/data/system # cat packages.list
com.google.android.location 10021 0 /data/data/com.google.android.location
com.android.defcontainer 10026 0 /data/data/com.android.defcontainer
com.sec.android.gallery3d 10092 0 /data/data/com.sec.android.gallery3d
com.sec.android.fotaclient 10041 0 /data/data/com.sec.android.fotaclient
com.monotype.android.font.helvneuelt 10052 0 /data/data/com.monotype.android.font
com.sec.android.motions.settings.panningtutorial 10067 0 /data/data/com.sec.andro
com.fmm.dm 10128 0 /data/data/com.fmm.dm
android.googleSearch.googleSearchWidget 10049 0 /data/data/android.googleSearch.
com.android.providers.calendar 10087 0 /data/data/com.android.providers.calendar
com.android.bluetooth 10083 0 /data/data/com.android.bluetooth
```

Content of the packages.list file

Now, let's look specifically at some third-party apps that are widely used and handle valuable data.

> The following apps are only being covered to make you familiar with the kind of data that can be extracted and the possible locations where the data can be obtained. You will need to take appropriate permissions and should abide by the legal rules before performing these tasks on a device. As we explained in `Chapter 8`, *Android Forensic Setup and Pre-Data Extraction Techniques*, the following techniques only work after the device has been rooted.

Facebook Android app analysis

The Facebook Android app is one of the most widely used social networking applications. It stores its information in the `/data/data` folder, within the `com.facebook.katana` package. The following details provide an overview of the kind of information that can be gathered across various files:

- **Facebook contacts**: Information about the user's Facebook contacts can be retrieved by analyzing the `contacts_db2` database, which is present under the following path:
    - **Path**: `/data/data/com.facebook.katana/databases/contacts_db2`.
    - The `contacts_db2` database (SQLite file) contains a table named contacts, which contains most of the user's information, such as their first name, last name, display name, and URL for display picture.

- **Facebook notifications**: Information about a user's notifications can be gathered by analyzing the `notification_db` database, which is present under the following path:
  - **Path**: `/data/data/com.facebook.katana/databases/notificatio ns_db`.
  - The `gql_notifications` table present under the preceding path holds the user's information. The `seen_state` column confirms whether a notification has been seen or not. The `updated` column points to the time when the notification was updated. The `gql_payload` column contains the notification and the sender information.
- **Facebook messages**: A Facebook message conversation may be of crucial importance in several cases and can be viewed by analyzing the `threads_db2` database:
  - **Path**: `/data/data/com.facebook.katana/databases/threads_db2`
- **Videos from newsfeed**: The `/video-cache` folder contains videos that have been downloaded from the user's newsfeed. Note that these are not the videos posted by the user, but rather they are the videos that appeared on their newsfeed:
  - **Path**: `/data/data/com.facebook.katana/files/video-cache`
- **Images from newsfeed**: The `/images` folder contains various images that appear on the user's profile, such as the ones from their newsfeed and contact profile pictures. Several directories are present within this folder and images may be stored in formats other than `.jpg`, such as `.cnt`:
- **Path**: `/data/data/com.facebook.katana/cache/images`
- **Newsfeed data**: The `newfeed_db` database contains data shown to the user on their newsfeed. As shown in the following screenshot, analyzing this database would provide valuable information, such as when a particular story was loaded by the device (the `fetched_at` column), if a particular story was seen by the user (the `seen_state` column), and where the corresponding files of a story are stored on the device (the `cache_file_path` column):
- **Path**: `/data/data/com.facebook.katana/databases/newsfeed_db`:

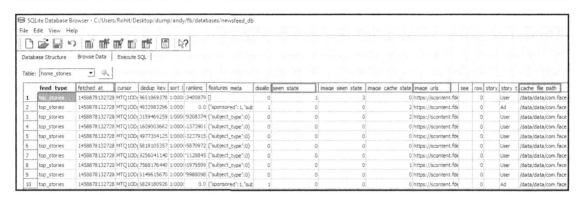

The Facebook newsfeed.db file analyzed in SQLite browser

In the preceding screenshot, `fetched_at` specifies the date and time when this information is fetched. Notice that the app uses Linux epoch time, also known as Unix time or Posix time, to store this information. This format is often used by multiple apps and, hence, is worth taking a look at. Linux epoch time is stored as the number of seconds (or milliseconds) since midnight on January 1, 1970. There are several online sites, such as `https://www.epochconverter.com/`, that can readily convert the Linux epoch time into a normal format. For example, the following screenshot shows Linux epoch time 1,577,881,839 converted into a normal format:

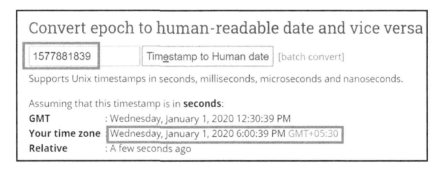

Example of time format

Now that we have performed an analysis of the Facebook app, let's perform a similar analysis with our next application, which is WhatsApp.

WhatsApp Android app analysis

WhatsApp is the most popular chat (audio and video) messaging service and is used by more than a billion people across the globe. It stores its information under the /data/data folder, with the package name, com.whatsapp. The following is an overview of the important files that are of interest from a forensic perspective:

- **User's profile pic**: The user's profile picture is saved with the me.jpg filename and is present under the following path:
  - **Path**: /data/data/com.whatsapp/me.jpg

- **User's phone number (associated with WhatsApp)**: The me file that's present under the main folder contains the phone number that is associated with the user's WhatsApp account. Note that this may or may not be the phone number that is associated with the SIM:
  - **Path**: /data/data/com.whatsapp/me

- **Contacts profile pic**: The /avatars directory contains thumbnails of the profile pictures of the user's contacts (who use WhatsApp):
  - **Path**: /data/data/com.whatsapp/files/Avatars

- **Chat messages**: All message-related information, including chats and sender details, is present in the msgstore.db file, which is present at the following location:
  - **Path**: /data/data/com.whatsapp/databases/msgstore.db

- **WhatsApp files**: Most of the files shared with WhatsApp, such as images, videos, and audio messages, are stored on the SD card in the following location:
  - **Path**: /sdcard/WhatsApp/Media

Both sent and received files are stored separately here in their respective folder names.

Next, we will look at another application that is used for telecommunication and specializes in providing video chat and voice calls: Skype.

Skype Android app analysis

Skype is an app that offers video chat and voice call services. The application's data is stored under the `/data/data` folder, with the package name `com.skype.raider`. The following are some important artifacts that can be extracted by analyzing the Skype app:

- **Username and IP address**: The `shared.xml` file present under the following path contains information about the username and the last IP address that connected to Skype:
    - **Path**: `/data/data/com.skype.raider/files/shared.xml`

- **Profile picture**: The user's profile picture is present in the `/thumbnails` directory, whose path is as follows:
    - **Path**: `/data/data/com.skype.raider/files/<username>/thumbnails/`

- **Call logs**: Information about call logs made from Skype is available in the `main.db` file. Analyzing this file gives us a lot of information:
    - **Path**: `/data/data/com.skype.raider/files/<username>/main.db/`.
    - For example, the `duration` table provides information about call duration, the `start_timestamp` field gives the start time of a call, and the `creation_timestamp` field indicates when the call is initiated (this includes unanswered calls). The `type` column indicates whether the call was incoming (value= 1) or outgoing (value= 2).

- **Chat messages**: The `messages` table present in the `main.db` file contains all the chat messages. The `author` and `from_dispname` columns provide information about who wrote the message. The `timestamp` column shows the date/time of the message. The `body_xml` column contains the content of the message:
    - **Path**: `/data/data/com.skype.raider/files/<username>/main.db/`

- **Files transferred**: The `Transfers` table contains information about transferred files, such as the filename, the size of the file, and their location on the device:
    - **Path**:
      `/data/data/com.skype.raider/files/<username>/main.db/`.
    - The actual images or files that are received will be stored on an SD card. If a file is downloaded, it will be in the `Downloads` folder in the root of the SD.
- **Group chats**: The `ChatMembers` table shows a list of users who are present in a particular chat. The `adder` column shows the user who initiated the conversation:
    - **Path**:
      `/data/data/com.skype.raider/files/<username>/main.db/`

Now, we will perform an analysis on the Gmail application.

Gmail Android app analysis

Gmail is a widely used email service offered by Google. The application data is saved under the `/data/data` folder, with the package name `com.google.android.gm`. The following are the important artifacts that can be extracted by analyzing the Gmail app:

- **Account details**: The XML files present under `/shared_prefs` confirm the email account details. Details of other accounts, which are linked to the current email, can be identified from the `Gmail.xml` file:
    - **Path**:
      `/data/data/com.google.android.gm/cache/<username>@gmail.com`
- **Attachments**: Attachments that are recently used in both sending and receiving emails are saved to the `/cache` directory. This is valuable because it gives us access to items that have been deleted from the email service too. Each row also contains a `messages_conversation` value. This value can be compared with the `conversations` table of the email attachment. The `filename` column identifies the path on the device where the file is located. The following is the exact path for this folder:
    - **Path**:
      `/data/data/com.google.android.gm/cache/<username>@gmail.com`:

```
127|root@android:/data/data/com.google.android.gm/cache/           @gmail.com # ls
04 Vulnerabilities-1.pptx
04 Vulnerabilities-2.pptx
05 XSS-1.pptx
05 XSS.pptx
06 SQLi.pptx
07 CSRF & Others.pptx
83110S_08_Final_AJ-1.docx
83110S_08_Final_AJ.docx
B05387_04_16-1.png
B05387_04_16-2.png
B05387_04_16-3.png
B05387_04_16-4.png
```

List of attachments present under Gmail's cache directory

- **Email subject**: The subject of this email can be recovered by analyzing the `conversations` table present in the `mailstore.<username>@gmail.com.db` file:
    - **Path**: `/data/data/com.google.android.gm/databases/mailstore.<username>@gmail.com.db`
- **Search history**: Any text searches that were made within the app are stored in the `suggestions.db` file, which is present at the following location:
    - **Path**: `/data/data/com.google.android.gm/databases/suggestions.db`

Let's wrap up this section by performing a final analysis on the Google Chrome application.

Google Chrome Android app analysis

Google Chrome is the default web browser on Google Pixel and many other devices, and it is used widely to browse the internet. The application data is present under the `/data/data` folder, with the package name, `com.android.chrome`. The following are the important artifacts that can be extracted by analyzing the Gmail app:

- **Profile picture**: The profile picture of the user is stored with the `Google Profile Picture.png` filename in the following location:
    - **Path**: `/data/data/com.android.chrome/app_chrome/Default/Google Profile Picture.png`

- **Bookmarks**: The `Bookmarks` file contains information about all the bookmarks synced with the account. Details such as the site name, URL, and the time when it was bookmarked can be gathered by analyzing this file:
  - **Path**:
    `/data/data/com.android.chrome/app_chrome/Default/Boo kmarks`
- **Browsing history**: The `History.db` file contains the user's web history stored in various tables. For example, as shown in the following screenshot, the `keyword_search_terms` table contains information about the searches that were made using the Chrome browser:

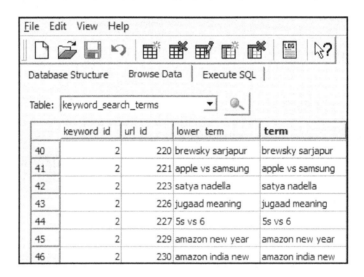

Google Chrome browsing history

- The `segments` table contains a list of sites visited by the user (but not all of the sites). It's interesting to note that Chrome stores the data belonging to not just the device, but the account in general. In other words, information about sites that have been visited from other devices using the same account is also stored on the device; for example, the `URLs` table contains the browsing history for a Google account across several devices.
- **Path**:
  `/data/data/com.android.chrome/app_chrome/Default/His tory.`

- **Login Data**: The `Login Data` database contains the login information of different sites saved in the browser. The site URL, along with the username and password, is stored in the respective tables:
  - **Path**:
    `/data/data/com.android.chrome/app_chrome/Default/Log in Data`

- **Frequently visited sites**: The `Top Sites` database contains a list of frequently visited sites:
  - **Path**:
    `/data/data/com.android.chrome/app_chrome/Default/Top Sites`

- **Other data**: Other information, such as the phone numbers or email addresses entered by the user during form fills across different sites, is stored in the `Web Data` database. Any tables that are present within this database contain autofill data:
  - **Path**:
    `/data/data/com.android.chrome/app_chrome/Default/Web Data`

Now that we have analyzed the different third-party apps, we will look at the techniques we can use to reverse engineer Android apps.

Techniques to reverse engineer an Android application

You may need to deal with applications that stand as a barrier to accessing the required information. For instance, take the case of the gallery on a phone that is locked by an *AppLock* application. In this case, in order to access the pictures and videos stored in the gallery, you first need to enter the passcode to the *AppLock*. Hence, it would be interesting to know how the *AppLock* app stores the password on the device. You might look into the SQLite database files. However, if they are encrypted, then it's hard to even tell that it's a password. Reverse engineering applications would be helpful in such cases where you want to better understand the application and how the application stores the data.

To state it in simple terms, reverse engineering is the process of retrieving source code from an executable. Reverse engineering an Android app is done in order to understand the functionality of the app, the data storage, the security mechanisms in place, and more. Before we proceed to learn how to reverse engineer an Android app, here is a quick recap of the Android apps:

- All the applications that are installed on the Android device are written in the Java programming language.
- When a Java program is compiled, we get bytecode. This is sent to a dex compiler, which converts it into Dalvik bytecode.
- Thus, the class files are converted into dex files using a dx tool. Android uses something called **Dalvik virtual machine (DVM)** to run its applications.
- JVM's bytecode consists of one or more class files, depending on the number of Java files that are present in an application. Regardless, a Dalvik bytecode is composed of only one dex file.

Thus, the dex files, XML files, and other resources that are required to run an application are packaged into an Android package file (an APK file). These APK files are simply collections of items within ZIP files. Therefore, if you rename an APK extension file to a `.zip` file, then you will be able to see the contents of the file. However, before you can do this, you need to get access to the APK file of the application that is installed on the phone. Here is how the APK file corresponding to an application can be accessed.

Extracting an APK file from an Android device

Apps that come preinstalled with the phone are stored in the `/system/app` directory. Third-party applications that are downloaded by the user are stored in the `/data/app` folder. The following method helps you gain access to the APK files on the device; it works on both rooted and non-rooted devices:

1. Identify the package name of the app by issuing the `# adb.exe shell pm list packages` command.

   The following is the output of the preceding command:

```
C:\android-sdk\platform-tools>adb.exe shell pm list packages
package:android
package:android.googleSearch.googleSearchWidget
package:com.android.MtpApplication
package:com.android.Preconfig
package:com.android.apps.tag
package:com.android.backupconfirm
package:com.android.bluetooth
package:com.android.browser
package:com.android.calendar
package:com.android.certinstaller
package:com.android.chrome
package:com.android.clipboardsaveservice
package:com.android.contacts
package:com.android.defcontainer
package:com.android.email
package:com.android.exchange
package:com.android.facelock
```

List of package names present on the device

As shown in the preceding command-line output, the list of package names is displayed. Try to find a match between the app in question and the package name. Usually, the package names are very much related to the app names. Alternatively, you can use the Android Market or Google Play to identify the package name easily. The URL for an app in Google Play contains the package name, as shown in the following screenshot:

Facebook App in the Google Play Store

2. Identify the full pathname of the APK file for the desired package by issuing the `adb shell pm path` command, as follows:

```
C:\android-sdk\platform-tools>adb.exe shell pm path com.android.chrome
package:/data/app/com.android.chrome-1.apk
```

Identifying full pathname of APK

3. Pull the APK file from the Android device to the forensic workstation using the `adb pull` command:

```
C:\android-sdk\platform-tools>adb.exe pull /data/app/com.android.chrome-1.apk C:\temp
3706 KB/s (42168820 bytes in 11.110s)
```

adp pull command

Now, let's analyze the contents of an APK file. An Android package is a container for an Android app's resources and executables. It's a zipped file that contains the following files:

- `AndroidManifest.xml`: This contains information about the permissions and more.
- `classes.dex`: This is the class file that's been converted into a dex file by the dex compiler.
- `Res`: The application's resources, such as the image files, sound files, and more, are present in this directory.
- `Lib`: This contains native libraries that the application may use.
- `META-INF`: This contains information about the application's signature and signed checksums for all the other files in the package.

Once the APK file has been obtained, you can proceed to reverse engineer the Android application.

Steps to reverse engineer Android apps

APK files can be reverse-engineered in different ways to get the original code. The following is one method that uses the `dex2jar` and JD-GUI tools to gain access to the application code. For our example, we will examine the `com.twitter.android-1.apk` file. The following are the steps to successfully reverse engineer the APK file:

1. Rename the APK extension to ZIP to see the contents of the file. Rename the `com.twitter.android-1.apk` file to `twitter.android-1.zip` and extract the contents of this file using any file archiver application. The following screenshot shows the files that were extracted from the original file, `twitter.android-1.zip`:

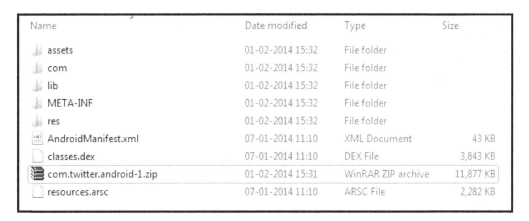

Name	Date modified	Type	Size
assets	01-02-2014 15:32	File folder	
com	01-02-2014 15:32	File folder	
lib	01-02-2014 15:32	File folder	
META-INF	01-02-2014 15:32	File folder	
res	01-02-2014 15:32	File folder	
AndroidManifest.xml	07-01-2014 11:10	XML Document	43 KB
classes.dex	07-01-2014 11:10	DEX File	3,843 KB
com.twitter.android-1.zip	01-02-2014 15:31	WinRAR ZIP archive	11,877 KB
resources.arsc	07-01-2014 11:10	ARSC File	2,282 KB

Extracted files of an APK file

2. The `classes.dex` file that we discussed previously can be accessed after extracting the contents of the APK file. This dex file needs to be converted into a class file in Java. This can be done using the `dex2jar` tool.

3. Download the `dex2jar` tool from `https://github.com/pxb1988/dex2jar`, drop the `classes.dex` file into the `dex2jar` tools directory, and issue the following command:

```
C:\Users\Rohit\Desktop\Training\Android\dex2jar-0.0.9.15>d2j-
dex2jar.bat classes.dex dex2jar classes.dex -> classes-dex2jar.jar
```

4. When the preceding command is successfully run, it creates a new `classes -dex2jar.jar` file in the same directory, as shown in the following screenshot:

Name	Date modified	Type	Size
lib	05-06-2013 10:24	File folder	
classes.dex	07-01-2014 11:10	DEX File	3,843 KB
classes-dex2jar.jar	01-02-2014 15:43	Executable Jar File	3,699 KB
d2j-apk-sign.bat	05-06-2013 10:21	Windows Batch File	1 KB
d2j-apk-sign.sh	05-06-2013 10:21	SH File	2 KB
d2j-asm-verify.bat	05-06-2013 10:21	Windows Batch File	1 KB
d2j-asm-verify.sh	05-06-2013 10:21	SH File	2 KB
d2j-decrpyt-string.bat	05-06-2013 10:21	Windows Batch File	1 KB
d2j-decrpyt-string.sh	05-06-2013 10:21	SH File	2 KB
d2j-dex2jar.bat	05-06-2013 10:21	Windows Batch File	1 KB

The classes-dex2jar.jar file created by the dex2jar tool

5. To view the contents of this JAR file, you can use a tool such as JD-GUI. As shown in the following screenshot, the files present in an Android application and the corresponding code can be seen:

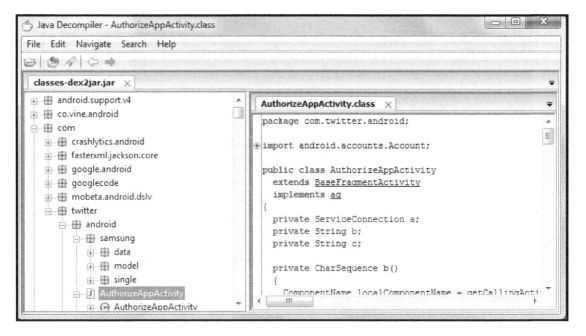

The JD-GUI tool

Once we get access to the code, it is easy to analyze how the application stores the values, permissions, and more information that may be helpful to bypass certain restrictions. When malware is found on a device, this method to decompile and analyze the application may prove useful, as it will show what is being accessed by the malware and provide clues to where the data is being sent. The following sections focus on Android malware in detail.

Android malware

As Android's market share continues to increase, so do attacks or malware targeted at Android users. Mobile malware is a broad term that refers to a piece of software that performs unintended actions and includes Trojans, spyware, adware, ransomware, and others. According to pandasecurity, Android devices are 50 times more infected with malware compared to iOS devices (`https://www.pandasecurity.com/mediacenter/ mobile-security/android-more-infected-than-ios/`). In 2019, the famous Agent Smith malware alone infected almost 25 million Android devices, as per a Cybersecurity Hub news report (`https://www.cshub.com/malware/articles/incident-of-the-week- malware-infects-25m-android-phones`).

One of the primary reasons for this situation is that, unlike Apple's App Store, which is tightly controlled by the company, Google's Play Store is an open ecosystem without any detailed upfront security reviews. Malware developers can easily move their apps to the Play Store and thereby distribute their apps. Google now has a malware-detecting software named Google Bouncer, which will automatically scan an uploaded app for malware, but attackers have figured out several ways to remain undetected. Moreover, Android officially allows us to load apps that have been downloaded over the internet (side-loading), unlike iOS, which does not allow unsigned apps.

For example, as shown in the following screenshot, when the **Unknown sources** option is selected on an Android device, it allows the user to install apps that have been downloaded from any site over the internet:

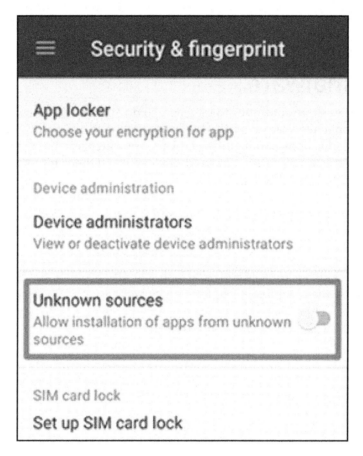

Side-loading option in Android

The third-party app stores that host Android apps are known to be hubs of malware. This prompted Google to roll out the *Verify Apps* feature starting from Android 4.2, which scans apps locally on Android devices to look for malicious activities, such as SMS abuse. As shown in the following screenshot, the Verify apps feature may warn the user, or in some cases may even block the installation. However, this is an opt-in service, so users can disable this feature if they wish to:

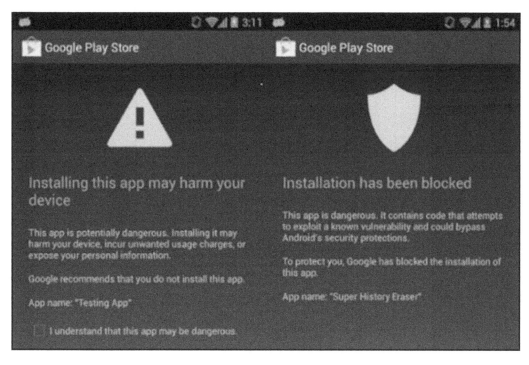

Verify apps feature in Android

Starting with Android Oreo, Google has rolled out a new feature called Play Protect, which is a better version of the verifying apps feature. The primary job of Play Protect is to block or warn the users of malicious or harmful apps that have been installed on the Android device. For example, as shown in the following screenshot, the Play Protect feature may show a warning message during the app's installation:

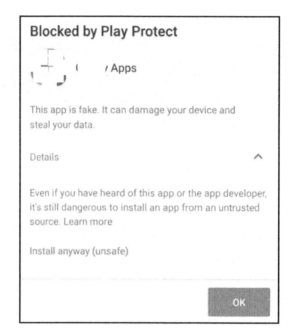

Play Protect feature

Next, let's have a look at the types of malware.

Types of Android malware

There are different kinds of malware types that can infect an Android device. The following are some of the most common ones:

- **Banking malware**: It can be distributed as fake banking applications to steal banking credentials typed by the users, or steal any other sensitive personal information from the user's account. Banking Trojans can intercept or modify banking transactions and perform dangerous actions such as sending, deleting, and intercepting SMS messages, as well as keylogging.

- **Spyware**: Spyware monitors, logs, and sends important information from the target device to the attacker's server. This information might comprise SMS messages, recorded phone calls, screenshots, keylogs, emails, or any other application data that may be of interest to the attacker. BusyGasper, a spyware identified by Kaspersky Lab experts in early 2018, not only possesses common spyware capabilities, such as collecting information from popular messaging applications, such as WhatsApp, Viber, and Facebook, but it also has device sensor listeners, including motion detectors.

- **Adware**: Adware is another popular malicious or unwanted application type that is very common on Android devices. It is relatively easy to detect, as the victim will receive continuous popups and ads on their device's screen. Such unwanted programs are not always harmless, since popups may result in downloading another piece of malware, including the types already mentioned – spyware and banking Trojans.

- **Ransomware**: The main targets of ransomware are Windows-based desktop computers and servers, but it also exists on mobile platforms, and on Android in particular. Usually, it only locks the device screen with a ransom note, but sometimes it encrypts users' data as well.

- **Crypto-mining malware**: Cryptocurrencies are extremely popular nowadays, so this type of malicious program is available even for mobile platforms, such as Android. The goal of such applications is to mine cryptocurrency, using a victim's device computation capacity. Occasionally, this type of malware can even put smartphone hardware at risk.

Advanced malware is also capable of rooting the device and installing new apps. For example, the Android Mazar malware, which was discovered in Feb 2016, spreads via text messages and is capable of gaining administrator rights on phones, allowing it to wipe handsets, make calls, or read texts.

 A full list of Android malware families and their capabilities is available at https://forensics.spreitzenbarth.de/android-malware/.

Once malware gets into a device, it can perform dangerous actions, some of which are as follows:

- Send and read your text messages
- Steal sensitive data, such as pictures, videos, and credit card numbers
- Manipulate files or data present on the device
- Send SMS to a premium-rated number

- Infect your browser and steal any data typed into its **Change device** settings
- Wipe all data present on the device
- Lock the device until a ransom is paid
- Display advertisements continuously

Now that we have understood the different types of malware, we will see how the malware spreads in your device.

How does Android malware spread?

An Android device can be infected with malware in several different ways. The following are some of the possible ways:

- **Repackaging legitimate application**: This is the most common method used by attackers. First, the attacker downloads a legitimate application and disassembles it. Then, they add their malicious code and reassemble the application. The new malicious application now functions exactly as the legitimate application does, but it also performs malicious activity in the background. This kind of application is commonly found in third-party Android app stores and is downloaded by many people.
- **Exploiting Android vulnerabilities**: In this scenario, an attacker exploits the bugs or the vulnerabilities that are discovered in the Android platform to install their malicious application or to perform any unwanted actions. For example, installer hijacking, which was identified in 2015, has been exploited by attackers to replace an Android application with malware during installation.
- **Bluetooth and MMS propagation**: Malware is also spread via Bluetooth and MMS. The victim receives the malware when the device is in discoverable mode, for example, when it can be seen by other Bluetooth-enabled devices. In the case of MMS, the malware is attached to the message, just like how computer viruses are sent through email attachments. However, in both these methods, the user has to agree, at least once, to run the file.
- **App downloading a malicious update**: In this case, the app that was originally installed does not contain any malicious code, but a function present within the code will download malicious commands at runtime. This can be done via a stealthy update or user update. For example, the Plankton malware uses stealthy updates that directly download a JAR file from a remote server and do not need any user permission. In the case of user updates, the user has to allow the app to download the new version of the app.

- **Remote install**: The attacker may compromise the credentials of the user's account on the device and thereby remotely install apps on the device. This generally happens in targeted scenarios and is less frequent compared to the previous two methods we just described.

Now that we've looked at the possible ways in which the Android malware can spread, let's try to identify the presence of malware in your device.

Identifying Android malware

From a forensic perspective, it's important to identify the presence of any malware on the device prior to performing any analysis. This is because malware can alter the state of the device or contents on the device, thereby making the analysis or the results inconsistent. There are tools available on the market that can analyze the physical extraction to identify malware. For example, Cellebrite UFED Physical Analyzer has BitDefender's anti-malware technology, which scans for malware. As shown in the following screenshot, once the physical image has been loaded into the tool, the file can be scanned for malware:

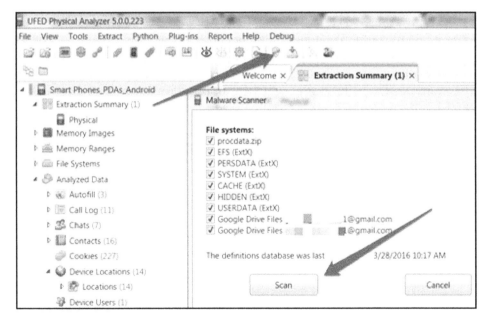

Scanning for malware in UFED Physical Analyzer

Once the scan starts, the BitDefender software tries to unpack the `.apk` files and looks for infected or malicious files. This process is automatic and the tool points to the malicious apps, as shown in the following screenshot:

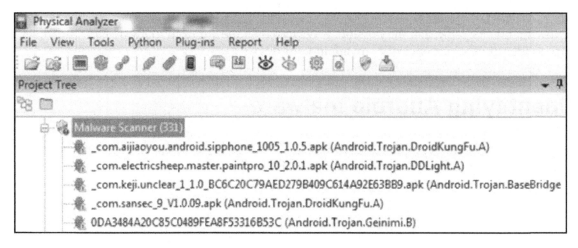

Malware scanner results in UFED Physical Analyzer

The tool simply points out that something malicious is present on the device. The forensic investigator has to then manually confirm whether this is a valid issue by analyzing the respective application. This is where the reverse engineering skills that we discussed in the previous sections need to be leveraged. Once the application has been reverse-engineered and the code has been obtained, it is recommended that you take a look at the `AndroidManifest.xml` file to find out the app permissions. This will be helpful for understanding where the app stores the data, what resources it is trying to access, and more. For example, a Flashlight application does not need read/write access to your SD card data, or to make a phone call:

```
<uses-permission android:name="android.permission.ACCESS_COARSE_LOCATION">
</uses-permission>
<uses-permission android:name="android.permission.ACCESS_FINE_LOCATION">
</uses-permission>
<uses-permission android:name="android.permission.ACCESS_NETWORK_STATE">
</uses-permission>
<uses-permission android:name="android.permission.ACCESS_WIFI_STATE">
</uses-permission>
<uses-permission android:name="android.permission.CALL_PHONE">
</uses-permission>
<uses-permission android:name="android.permission.CAMERA">
</uses-permission>
<uses-permission android:name="android.permission.GET_ACCOUNTS">
</uses-permission>
<uses-permission android:name="android.permission.INTERNET">
</uses-permission>
<uses-permission android:name="android.permission.MANAGE_ACCOUNTS">
</uses-permission>
<uses-permission android:name="android.permission.READ_CONTACTS">
</uses-permission>
<uses-permission android:name="android.permission.READ_PHONE_STATE">
</uses-permission>
<uses-permission android:name="android.permission.USE_CREDENTIALS">
</uses-permission>
<uses-permission android:name="android.permission.VIBRATE">
</uses-permission>
<uses-permission android:name="android.permission.WRITE_SETTINGS">
</uses-permission>
<uses-permission android:name="android.permission.WRITE_EXTERNAL_STORAGE">
</uses-permission>
```

Permissions in the AndroidManifest.xml file

Alternatively, you can also upload the `.apk` file to VirusTotal, a free service that can be used to analyze suspicious files for malware. VirusTotal will scan your file against 55 antivirus engines. It's also important to note that the tool may not identify a valid case if the details are obfuscated in the `.apk` file. Hence, as a forensic investigator, it's important to develop the necessary skills to reverse engineer any suspicious apps and analyze the code to identify malicious behavior.

In some investigations, the nature of the malware that is present on a device may also result in arriving at certain crucial conclusions, which may affect the outcome of the case. For example, consider an internal investigation in a corporation that involves sending abusive messages to other employees. Identifying malware on the device that sends the messages would help solve the case.

Summary

Android app analysis helps a forensic investigator look for valuable data in relevant locations on a device. Reverse engineering Android apps is the process of retrieving source code from an APK file. Using certain tools, such as `dex2jar`, Android apps can be reverse-engineered in order to understand their functionality and data storage, identify malware, and more. In this chapter, we performed analysis on different android applications and we are now able to retrieve data from them. We also learned about different types of Android malware and how to identify them. Tools such as UFED Physical Analyzer come with BitDefender software, which can automatically scan for malware.

The next chapter covers performing forensics on Windows Phone devices.

Section 3: Windows Forensics and Third-Party Apps

This section will cover forensics on Windows phones – right from understanding the Windows Phone OS to data extraction from the device. The last chapter will cover how to perform forensics on some of the most widely used third-party apps, such as Facebook, WhatsApp, and so on. We will look at how data is organized within these apps and some of the techniques that can be readily applied to extract the data within them.

This section consists of the following chapters:

- Chapter 12, Windows Phone Forensics
- Chapter 13, Parsing Third-Party Application Files

Windows Phone Forensics 12

Despite the fact that Windows Phones are not so widely used nowadays, they may still be encountered during forensic investigations. These devices are the most affordable on the market, so understanding how to acquire, analyze, and decode data from Windows Phones is important. Locating and interpreting digital evidence present on these devices requires specialized knowledge of the Windows Phone operating system, and may not always be possible. Commercial forensic and open source tools provide limited support for acquiring user data from Windows devices. As Windows Phones do not occupy much of the mobile market space, most forensic practitioners are unfamiliar with the data formats, embedded databases that are used, and other artifacts that exist on the device. This chapter provides an overview of Windows Phone forensics, describing various methods of acquiring and examining data on Windows mobile devices.

In this chapter, we will cover the following topics:

- Windows Phone OS
- Windows 10 Mobile security model
- Windows Phone filesystem
- Data acquisition
- Commercial forensic tool acquisition methods
- Extracting data without the use of commercial tools
- Key artifacts for examination

Windows Phone OS

Windows Phone is a proprietary mobile operating system developed by Microsoft. It was launched as a successor to Windows Mobile, but it does not provide backward compatibility with the previous platform. Windows Phone was launched in October 2010 with Windows Phone 7. The version history of the Windows Phone operating system then continued with the release of Windows Phone 7.5, Windows Phone 7.8, Windows Phone 8.1, and Windows Phone 10.

Despite the fact that Microsoft claims they have stopped developing this mobile operating system, excluding security patches, you are likely to face it as a mobile forensic examiner.

The following sections will provide more details about Windows Phone, its features, and its underlying security model.

Unlike Android and iOS devices, Windows Phone comes with a new interface, which uses so-called *tiles* for apps instead of icons, as shown in the following image. These tiles can be designed and updated by the user:

The Windows Phone home screen

Similar to other mobile platforms, Windows Phone allows for the installation of third-party apps. These apps can be downloaded from the Windows Phone Marketplace, which is managed by Microsoft. When comparing the number of apps available for iOS and Android devices, Windows Phone pales in comparison. However, applications are available and you should expect to see them on Windows Phone devices.

Windows Phone introduced new features, making it more similar to other smartphones compared to Windows Mobile:

- **Cortana**: This is the personal assistant for the device. It was introduced in Windows 8.1 and is still present on Windows 10 devices. Cortana aids the user by fielding questions using Bing, setting reminders, sending texts, and essentially using all the functionality to provide the user with a better and easier experience. Everything that Cortana does leaves a trace on the device.
- **Wallet**: This stores credit card accounts, boarding passes, tickets, coupons, and more.
- **Geofence and advanced location settings**: These provide the user with additional protection as the phone can detect when it is out of a trusted zone and may lock itself.
- **Additional features**: These are features such as live tiles, enhanced colors, and quiet hours.

Other common applications associated with Windows Phone include OneDrive (formerly SkyDrive), OneNote, and Office 365 synchronization. OneDrive provides the user with access to all of their documents and files from any device. OneNote is essentially the same, but it acts as a notebook or diary. Office 365 provides the user with constant access to their email, calendar, contacts, and more across multiple devices.

The introduction of data synchronization across multiple devices makes our job as forensic examiners difficult. It is our job to determine how the evidence was placed on the device. Is it possible to definitively state how an artifact was placed on a device? To be honest, this depends. Nobody wants to hear this response, but a lot of factors must be considered. What is the app? What OS is running on the device? What is the artifact? For example, let's consider OneDrive. If the device contains documents from OneDrive, the original author should be contained within the metadata. This, together with examining whether or not the content was shared with the device, may provide a glimpse into how the artifact was created. However, when examining a calendar entry when Office 365 is in place, it may be impossible to state whether the user created the entry on their phone, PC, or laptop. The synchronization is instantaneous, and status flags stating where the artifact was created do not always exist. If this artifact is indeed the *smoking gun* of the investigation, you need to apply your skills to uncover other artifacts that support your findings. Digging deeper into the data is required. Now that we are aware of the details of Windows Phone and its features, let's have a look at its security model and see how it keeps the data secure.

Windows 10 Mobile security model

The security model of Windows Phone is designed to make sure that the user data present on the device is safe and secure. The following sections provide a brief explanation of the concepts that Windows Phone security is built on.

Chambers

Windows Phone is heavily built on the principles of least privilege and isolation. This has been consistent since the inception of Windows Phone 7. To achieve this, Windows Phone introduced the concept of **chambers**. Each chamber has an isolation boundary where processes can run. Depending on the security policy of a specific chamber, a process running in this chamber has the privilege of accessing the OS's resources and capabilities (https://www.msec.be/mobcom/ws2013/presentations/david_hernie.pdf). There are four types of security chambers. The following is a brief description of each of them:

- **Trusted Computing Base (TCB)**: The processes here have unrestricted access to most Windows Phone resources. This chamber has privileges to modify policies and enforce the security model. The kernel runs in this chamber.
- **Elevated Rights Chamber (ERC)**: This chamber is less privileged than the TCB chamber. It has privileges to access all resources except the security policy. This chamber is mainly used for services and user-mode drivers, which provide functionality intended for use by other applications on the phone.
- **Standard Rights Chamber (SRC)**: This is the default chamber for preinstalled applications, such as Microsoft Outlook Mobile 2010.
- **Least Privileged Chamber (LPC)**: This is the default chamber for all the applications that are downloaded and installed through the Marketplace Hub (which is also known as the Windows Phone Marketplace).

Next, we will be looking at encryption.

Encryption

Windows Phone 8 introduced BitLocker technology to encrypt all user data that is stored on the device via AES 128-bit encryption. The user can simply flip the switch to enable this feature, and all of their data residing on the internal storage of the device will be encrypted. In addition, the user can encrypt their SD card – assuming the device has one – and set a password or PIN on their device. Should all of these locks and the encryption be enabled, accessing the data on this device may be impossible, unless the password is recovered.

Capability-based model

Capabilities are defined as the resources on the phone (camera, location information, microphone, and more) associated with security, privacy, and cost. The LPC has a minimal set of access rights by default. However, this can be expanded by requesting more capabilities during the installation. Capabilities are granted during the app's installation and cannot be modified or elevated during runtime. For this reason, it is difficult to side-load applications or force custom boot code to the device to gain forensic access, as it is normally rejected prior to bootup.

To install an app on a Windows Phone, you need to sign in to the Marketplace with a Windows Live ID. During installation, apps are required to ask the user for permission before using certain capabilities, an example of which is shown in the following screenshot:

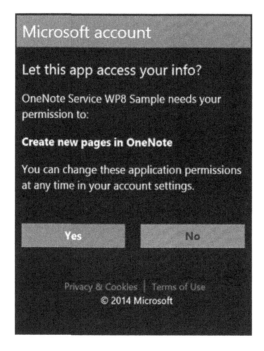

Windows app requesting user permissions (https://i-msdn.sec.s-msft.com/dynimg/IC752370.png)

This is similar to the permission model in Android. This gives the user the freedom to learn about all the capabilities that an application has before installing the application. The list of all capabilities is included in the `WMAppManifest.xml` application manifest file, which can be accessed through Visual Studio or other methods that are defined at `https://docs.microsoft.com/en-us/previous-versions/windows/apps/ff769509(v=vs.105)`.

App sandboxing

Apps in Windows Phone run in a sandboxed environment. This means every application on Windows Phone runs in its own chamber. Applications are isolated from each other and cannot access the data of other applications. If any app needs to save information to the device, it can do so using the isolated storage, which is restricted from access by other applications. Also, the third-party applications installed on Windows Phone cannot run in the background; that is, when the user switches to a different application, the previously used application is shut down (although the application state is preserved). This ensures that the application cannot perform activities such as communicating over the internet when the user is not using the application. These restrictions also make Windows Phone less susceptible to malware, but you should never assume that any device is safe. It is just more challenging for malware to function on these devices.

So far, we have had a look at the four types of security chambers and we now know that Windows Phone 8 uses BitLocker technology for encryption. We have learned about the different capabilities granted during the installation of an application and saw how every application is isolated from each other. Next, we'll look at an important aspect of Windows Phones, which is its filesystem.

Windows Phone filesystem

The Windows Phone filesystem is more or less similar to the filesystems used in Windows 7, Windows 8, and Windows 10. From the root directory, you can reach different files and folders that are available on this device. From a forensic perspective, the following are some of the folders that can yield valuable data. All the listed directories are located in the root directory:

- **Application data**: This directory contains data of applications on the phone, such as Outlook, Maps, and Internet Explorer.
- **Applications**: This directory contains the apps installed by the user. The isolated storage, which is allocated or used by each app, is also located in this folder.
- **My Documents**: This directory holds different Office documents, such as Word, Excel, or PowerPoint files. The directory also includes configuration files and multimedia files, such as music or videos.
- **Windows**: This directory contains files that are related to the Windows Phone operating system.

The acquisition method used here will determine the amount of filesystem access that you have to the device. For example, a physical image may provide access to several partitions that can be recovered from the data dump. A Windows Phone 10 device that contains 27 partitions can be seen in the following screenshot. Partitions **26** (**MainOS**) and **27** (**Data**) contain the relevant data:

```
DPP (1) [8MB]
MODEM_FSG (2) [1MB]
MODEM_FS1 (3) [1MB]
MODEM_FS2 (4) [1MB]
MODEM_FSC (5) [0MB]
DDR (6) [0MB]
SSD (7) [0MB]
UEFI_BS_NV (8) [0MB]
UEFI_RT_NV (9) [0MB]
SBL1 (10) [0MB]
DBI (11) [0MB]
UEFI (12) [2MB]
RPM (13) [0MB]
TZ (14) [0MB]
WINSECAPP (15) [0MB]
TZAPPS (16) [16MB]
BACKUP_SBL1 (17) [0MB]
BACKUP_DBI (18) [0MB]
BACKUP_UEFI (19) [2MB]
BACKUP_RPM (20) [0MB]
BACKUP_TZ (21) [0MB]
BACKUP_WINSECAPP (22) [0MB]
BACKUP_TZAPPS (23) [16MB]
PLAT (24) [8MB]
EFIESP (25) [32MB]
MainOS (26) [1476MB]
Data (27) [5847MB]
```

Windows Phone 10 partitions

While most artifacts will exist in the **Data** partition, it is always best practice to capture and analyze both when possible.

The **MainOS** partition in the preceding screenshot, partition **26**, contains the system data from the Windows Phone. As in all Windows investigations, the system data contains artifacts relevant to investigations.

In this example, partition 27 contains the **User** or **Data** partition. Depending on the device, the partition numbers may vary. In our example, the **Data** partition is shown in the following screenshot as partition **27**. Here, the SMS, email, application data, contacts, call logs, and internet history were recovered using mobile forensic tools. These methods will be discussed later in this chapter:

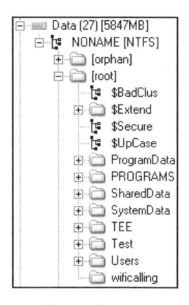

Windows Phone 10 Data partition

Windows Phone also maintains the **Windows registry**, a database that stores environment variables on the operating system. The Windows registry is basically a directory that stores settings and options for the Microsoft operating system. Windows Phone is no different. When examining a Windows Phone, you will expect to see the NTUSER.dat, SAM, SYSTEM, SOFTWARE, SECURITY, and DEFAULT hives. While these hives may be unique to the phone, they can be examined just like traditional Windows registry hives.

A detailed case investigation is included in a paper by Cynthia Murphy. This involves a criminal case of a home invasion and sexual assault and details the efforts of great minds in the forensic community to uncover artifacts that assisted in closing the investigation. Sometimes, the mobile device is the most important artifact pertaining to the case. For more information, please refer to https://www.sans.org/reading-room/whitepapers/forensics/windows-phone-8-forensic-artifacts-35787. Now that we have looked at the file and folder structure, let's learn how to acquire data using this knowledge.

Data acquisition

Acquiring data from a Windows Phone is challenging for forensic examiners, as the physical, filesystem, and logical methods that were defined in previous chapters are not greatly supported. In addition to this, the phone may need to be at a specific battery charge state (%) in order for the commercial tool to recognize and acquire the device. This is often one of the most difficult steps in acquiring Windows Phones.

One of the most common techniques that's implemented by commercial tools attempting data acquisition is to install an application or agent on the device, which enables two-way communication for commands to be sent to the device in order to extract data. This could result in certain changes on the device; nevertheless, this is still forensically sound if the examiner follows standard protocols and has tested the validity of the tool being used. These protocols include proper testing to ensure no user data is changed (and if changed, documenting what occurred), validation of the method on a test device, and documenting all steps taken during the acquisition process. For this acquisition method to work, the app needs to be installed with the privileges of the SRC. This may require you to copy the manufacturer's DLLs, which have higher privileges, into the user app. This allows the app to access methods and resources that are usually limited to native apps. In addition to this, the device must be unlocked, or these methods may not work.

Most examiners rely on forensic tools and methods to acquire mobile devices. Again, these practices are not as supported for Windows Phones. Keep in mind that to deploy and run an app on Windows Phone, both the device and the developer must be registered and unlocked by Microsoft. This restriction can be bypassed by unlocking the device using a public jailbreak for Windows Phone 8 to 10 devices.

For quite a long time, JTAG and chip-off acquisitions were the only options to acquire most Windows Phones. Everything changed in January 2015: Cellebrite implemented an acquisition module that allowed mobile forensic examiners to extract data at the physical level from most Lumia devices.

Later, the Windows Phone Internals project presented a way to unlock the bootloader of some Lumia devices, including 520, 521, 525, 620, 625, 720, 820, 920, 925, 928, 1020, and 1320. This made the physical acquisition of these devices possible. You can learn more about this project at `https://www.wpinternals.net/`. Now, we will look at some of the commercial tools that are used for acquisition methods.

Commercial forensic tool acquisition methods

There are a few commercial tools available that offer support for the acquisition of Windows Phone devices. Cellebrite UFED offers support to acquire Windows Phone devices using the physical, filesystem, and logical methods. To determine whether the device you are examining is supported by the tool, you can download and use the UFED Phone Detective mobile app, which is available for free both in App Store and Google Play:

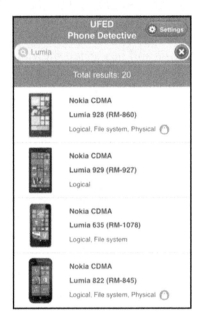

Searching for supported Lumia devices

Some of these acquisition methods are more robust, obtain a full physical dump of the data, and can bypass some lock codes on specific devices. However, some device support includes simply extracting contacts and pictures from the device. It is important for the examiner to realize that specific steps must be taken, as directed by the tool. Acquiring these devices is not easy, and often, you will find that the tool will not be successful.

When the tool seems to fail, attempt to acquire the device using the Smartphone/PDA option offered in UFED. To do this, follow these steps:

1. Launch UFED4PC and select **Mobile Device**.
2. Select **Browse Manually**.

3. Select **Smartphones**.
4. Select the Windows device that you are attempting to acquire.
5. Try all the methods that are offered, starting with physical, filesystem, and logical (in that order, where possible):

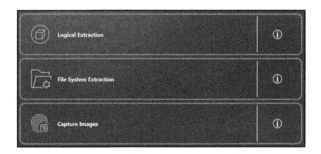

Extraction methods

6. Follow all the remaining steps and try all offered acquisition methods until you're successful.

Cellebrite may alert you that the acquisition is not successful for several reasons. When this occurs, try every option to ensure you have exhausted the commercial options available. An example of an acquisition attempt in UFED4PC is as follows:

1. Launch UFED4PC.
2. Select your Make and Model for the device.
3. Select the **Physical**, **File System**, or **Logical** acquisition method (offerings will vary, depending on the device model).

In this example, only **Logical** acquisition was supported. Two methods are available. The first option uses a cable, while the second uses Bluetooth. In this example, a special UFED cable is required. I selected the UFED cable first, as Bluetooth requires that additional changes are made to the phone during pairing:

UFED4PC Logical extraction options

When attempting to acquire the device with USB cable 100, only multimedia files were accessible.

Then, attempt the same acquisition, but select **Bluetooth**. Follow the instructions given to pair the device with the forensic workstation:

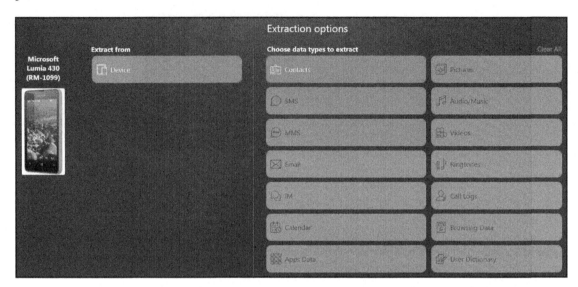

UFED4PC extraction options (Bluetooth)

With this acquisition method, we were able to obtain contacts. Note that there are no methods offered to obtain **SMS**, **MMS**, **Email**, **IM**, **Calendar**, **Call Logs**, **Apps Data**, and others. It is suggested you repeat the generic methods listed in the previous screenshot using the **Smartphone** option in UFED4PC. So far, we have looked at some acquisition methods using commercial tools. Now, let's learn how to extract data without these tools.

Extracting data without the use of commercial tools

In some cases, the physical acquisition of Windows Phone devices is possible only with advance methods, such as JTAG and chip-off. But thanks to the security researcher known as Heathcliff, it became possible to perform physical acquisition on limited phone models and operating system versions with his tool called **WPinternals** (`https://www.wpinternals.net`).

The tool supports the following models of Lumia phones: 520, 521, 525, 620, 625, 720, 820, 920, 925, 928, 1020, and 1320.

As for operating system versions, the following are supported:

- 8.10.12393.890
- 8.10.12397.895
- 8.10.14219.341
- 8.10.14226.359
- 8.10.14234.375
- 8.10.15116.125
- 8.10.15148.160
- 10.0.10512.1000
- 10.0.10536.1004
- 10.0.10549.4
- 10.0.10581.0
- 10.0.10586.11
- 10.0.10586.36

 This method is experimental and can result in bricking the device! Despite the fact that the percentage of bricked devices is relatively low, we recommend that you use it as the last option.

The first step of the acquisition process will be downloading a Windows **Full Flash Update** (**FFU**) file and the emergency files for the phone model you are working with:

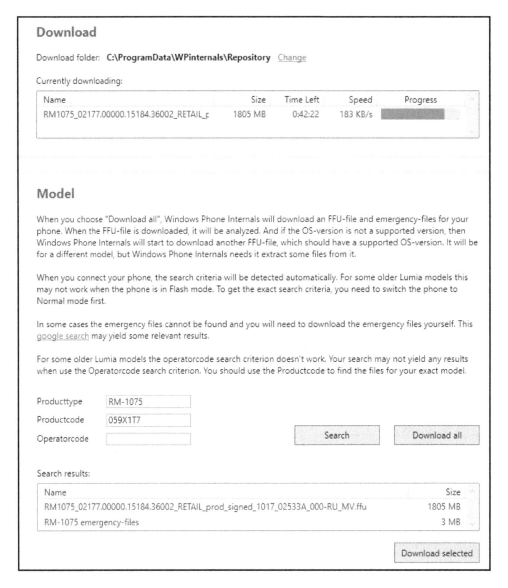

Download

Download folder: **C:\ProgramData\WPinternals\Repository** Change

Currently downloading:

Name	Size	Time Left	Speed	Progress
RM1075_02177.00000.15184.36002_RETAIL_p	1805 MB	0:42:22	183 KB/s	

Model

When you choose "Download all", Windows Phone Internals will download an FFU-file and emergency-files for your phone. When the FFU-file is downloaded, it will be analyzed. And if the OS-version is not a supported version, then Windows Phone Internals will start to download another FFU-file, which should have a supported OS-version. It will be for a different model, but Windows Phone Internals needs it extract some files from it.

When you connect your phone, the search criteria will be detected automatically. For some older Lumia models this may not work when the phone is in Flash mode. To get the exact search criteria, you need to switch the phone to Normal mode first.

In some cases the emergency files cannot be found and you will need to download the emergency files yourself. This google search may yield some relevant results.

For some older Lumia models the operatorcode search criterion doesn't work. Your search may not yield any results when use the Operatorcode search criterion. You should use the Productcode to find the files for your exact model.

Producttype	RM-1075
Productcode	059X1T7
Operatorcode	

Search   Download all

Search results:

Name	Size
RM1075_02177.00000.15184.36002_RETAIL_prod_signed_1017_02533A_000-RU_MV.ffu	1805 MB
RM-1075 emergency-files	3 MB

Download selected

Downloading FFU files

If the downloaded FFU contains an unsupported OS version, then WPinternals will download another FFU to get additional files:

Getting additional files

During the unlocking process, the phone may reboot a couple of times, but this is a normal behavior:

Scanning for flashing profile

Once the profile has been found, the tool flashes the unlocked bootloader:

Flashing unlocked bootloader

If the device has been flashed successfully, it's put into Mass Storage Mode:

You need to manually reset your phone now!

The phone is currently in Mass Storage Mode. To continue the unlock-sequence, the phone needs to be rebooted. Keep the phone connected to the PC. Reboot the phone manually by pressing and holding the power-button of the phone for about 10 seconds until it vibrates. The unlock-sequence will resume automatically.

Mass Storage Mode

Now, the device can be easily imaged, for example, using FTK Imager:

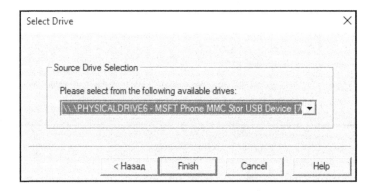

Windows Phone in FTK Imager

Now, we will learn how to extract data from SD cards.

SD card data extraction methods

Windows Phones may contain removable SD cards. These cards may be secured with a key that prevents the SD card from being removed and used, or accessed via other devices (phones, cameras, computers, and more). This is different from the key that is created if the user encrypts the SD card. Brute-force and dictionary attacks can be run on user-encrypted SD cards in an attempt to access the data. When examining a Windows Phone, it is best to research the device to see whether SD card security will be a factor when acquiring data from the device. If so, simply follow the preceding steps and acquire the SD card data through the phone during forensic extraction. Please refer to the following chart.

For devices where the SD card can be removed, you have two scenarios to consider. If the device is on, should you acquire the phone and the SD card as is? If the device is off, should you remove the SD card and acquire the device using FTK Imager? The answer is, it depends. In forensics, we use this statement frequently, but it remains true. If you leave the device on, it must be isolated from the network to ensure that it is not remotely accessed and immediately acquired, or the battery will drain and, ultimately, the device may power down. If the device is off and you remove the SD card, you must ensure that the card remains tied to the device itself and is acquired both externally and internally to ensure all data is captured. In a normal situation, the following chart suggests the recommended steps to handle SD cards that are found in Windows Phones:

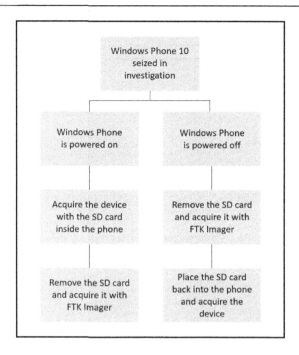

Most commercial forensic tools will offer to extract data from SD cards. Often, the phone extraction process will only extract data residing on the SD card. This is often the case when there is no support for a specific Windows Phone. If the SD card is not recognized by the tool and the data is not extracted, it is likely that the SD card has been encrypted by the user, and the password for the device is different from the password for the SD card. When this occurs, try to crack the passcode and reacquire the device. Note that cracking a passcode on an SD card may not always be possible, but it's worth a shot trying brute-force and dictionary attacks as you would on a standard hard drive or external device.

When acquiring an SD that has been removed from a Windows Phone, FTK Imager is a free and reliable option to create a forensically sound image that can be examined in a variety of tools. To create an SD card image, follow these steps:

1. Remove the SD card from the device and make sure to document all identifiers on the card and the phone to ensure that they are not permanently separated.
2. Insert the SD card into a *write blocker* and insert this into your forensic workstation.
3. Launch FTK Imager.
4. Select **File** and then **Create Disk Image**.

5. Select **Physical Drive**:

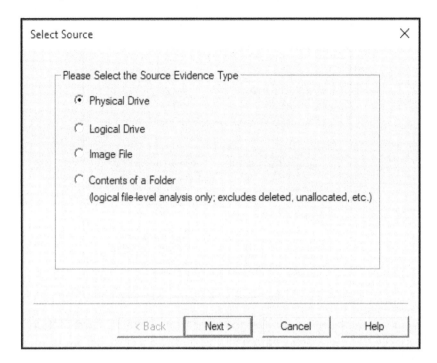

FTK Imager – creating a disk image

6. Use the drop-down list to select the correct device.

Look at the make and size to ensure that you are acquiring the correct device.

7. Select **Finish**.

8. Click on **Add** and select the image type. For this example, **Raw (dd)** is going to be used as it is supported by most commercial and open source methods for analysis:

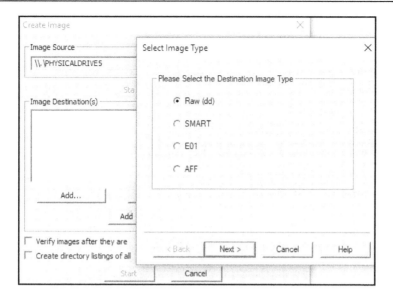

FTK Imager – selecting the image type

9. Enter the relevant case information and select **Next**. This can be skipped.
10. Select the image destination:

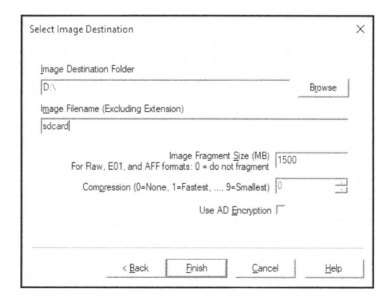

FTK Imager – saving your image file

11. Select **Finish** and then select **Start**. It is recommended that you verify images after they are created.

Once complete, your results will be displayed. We will cover analyzing the SD card data in the following sections.

Key artifacts for examination

In this section, we are going to introduce you to the location of some of the most common Windows Phone forensic artifacts, including contacts, SMS, and call and internet history.

Extracting contacts and SMS

All the contacts and incoming and outgoing short messages (SMS) in Windows Phone 7–10 are stored in the file named `store.vol`, which is present under the `\Application Data\Microsoft\Outlook\Stores\DeviceStore` (Windows 7) and `Users\WPCOMMSERVICES\APPDATA\Local\Unistore` (Windows 8-10) directories. An example of a Windows 10 `store.vol` file can be seen in the following screenshot:

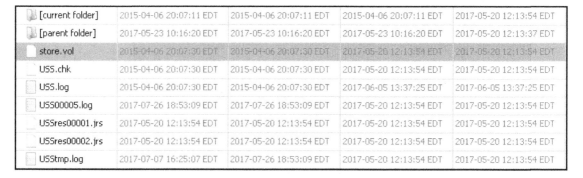

[current folder]	2015-04-06 20:07:11 EDT	2015-04-06 20:07:11 EDT	2015-04-06 20:07:11 EDT	2017-05-20 12:13:54 EDT
[parent folder]	2017-05-23 10:16:20 EDT	2017-05-23 10:16:20 EDT	2017-05-23 10:16:20 EDT	2017-05-20 12:13:37 EDT
store.vol	2015-04-06 20:07:30 EDT	2015-04-06 20:07:30 EDT	2017-05-20 12:13:54 EDT	2017-05-20 12:13:54 EDT
USS.chk	2015-04-06 20:07:30 EDT	2015-04-06 20:07:30 EDT	2017-05-20 12:13:54 EDT	2017-05-20 12:13:54 EDT
USS.log	2015-04-06 20:07:30 EDT	2015-04-06 20:07:30 EDT	2017-06-05 13:37:25 EDT	2017-06-05 13:37:25 EDT
USS00005.log	2017-07-26 18:53:09 EDT	2017-07-26 18:53:09 EDT	2017-05-20 12:13:54 EDT	2017-05-20 12:13:54 EDT
USSres00001.jrs	2017-05-20 12:13:54 EDT	2017-05-20 12:13:54 EDT	2017-05-20 12:13:54 EDT	2017-05-20 12:13:54 EDT
USSres00002.jrs	2017-05-20 12:13:54 EDT	2017-05-20 12:13:54 EDT	2017-05-20 12:13:54 EDT	2017-05-20 12:13:54 EDT
USStmp.log	2017-07-07 16:25:07 EDT	2017-07-26 18:53:09 EDT	2017-05-20 12:13:54 EDT	2017-05-20 12:13:54 EDT

The store.vol file in a Windows Phone

Now, let's learn how to extract the call history.

Extracting call history

Call history data can currently be extracted from the `Phone` file. It's important to note that the file doesn't have an extension and is located at `\Users\WPCOMMSERVICES\APPDATA\Local\UserData\`. Here is an example of a Windows 10 `Phone` file:

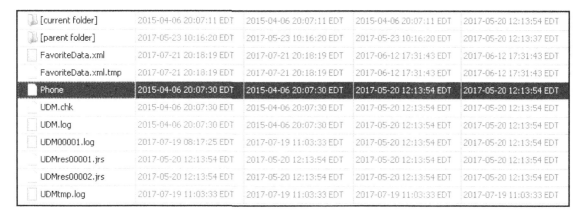

The Phone file in a Windows Phone

In a similar manner, we will be extracting internet history in the following section.

Extracting internet history

Internet history can be extracted from the `WebCacheV01.dat` file located at `\Users\DefApps\APPDATA\Local\Microsoft\Windows\WebCache\`. Here is an example of a Windows 10 `WebCacheV01.dat` file:

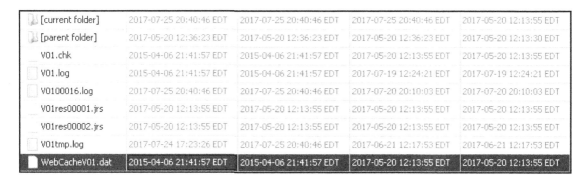

The WebCacheV01.dat file in a Windows Phone

These files can be examined manually, for example, with a hex viewer, or can be parsed automatically with mobile forensic tools. Here is the `WebCacheV01.dat` file being parsed with Magnet AXIOM:

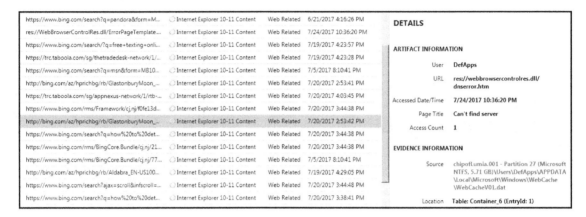

WebCacheV01.dat file parsed with Magnet AXIOM

With this, we've covered how to extract SMS, contacts, call, and internet history from a Windows Phone.

Summary

Acquiring data from Windows Phone devices is challenging since they are secure, and commercial forensic tools and open source methods do not provide easy solutions for forensic examiners like you. Multiple tools, chip-off, JTAG, and the methods we defined in this book are some of the methods that provide access to user data on Windows Phone devices. Often, you will find that Windows Phone devices require multiple extraction methods to acquire accessible data. The biggest challenge is getting access to the device to acquire the data. Once the data is available, all the extracted information can be analyzed by you.

In this chapter, we covered the interface, important features, and the security model of the Windows Phone device. Then, we had a look at the different partitions and folder structure within the Windows filesystem. The Windows Phone registry is similar to the registry in the Microsoft operating system. We saw how to extract data with and without using commercial tools and looked at some common Windows Phone forensic artifacts. With this knowledge, you can now extract user data from a Windows Phone using multiple extraction methods.

The next chapter will walk you through parsing third-party application files.

Parsing Third-Party Application Files

13

Third-party applications have taken the smartphone community by storm. Most smartphone owners have more than one app on their device that they rely on to chat, game, get directions, or share pictures. According to `https://www.statista.com/statistics/276623/number-of-apps-available-in-leading-app-stores/`, there are almost 5 million apps worldwide for various smartphones. Apple's App Store offers approximately 1.8 million apps, Google Play offers 2.47 million, Amazon offers 600,000, and Windows offers 670,000. This number is expected to grow exponentially through 2020.

The goal of this chapter is to introduce you to the various applications seen on Android, iOS devices, and Windows Phones. Each application will vary due to versions and devices, but their underlying structures are similar. We will look at how the data is stored and why preference files are important to your investigation.

We will cover the following topics in detail in this chapter:

- Different third-party applications
- How applications are stored on iOS devices
- How applications are stored on Android devices
- Windows Phone application storage
- How to use both commercial and open source solutions to parse application data

Introduction to third-party applications

Third-party applications are an integral part of mobile device investigations; often, the key artifacts seem to exist within an application. This requires you to understand where application data is stored on the device, how application data is saved for that platform, and which tool best helps to uncover the evidence. Manual parsing is often a key factor when examining third-party applications on any smartphone. While some commercial tools, such as Belkasoft Evidence Center or Magnet AXIOM, are known for application parsing support, no tool is perfect and it's virtually impossible for tools to keep up with the frequent updates that are released for each application.

Most often, you'll find that the commercial tools available parse the most popular applications on the market. For example, when Facebook purchased WhatsApp, Belkasoft, Cellebrite, Magnet Forensics, and Oxygen Forensics started supporting this application. Facebook is extremely popular, but data isn't always extracted or parsed, due to security features that are built into the app—this is where all apps differ. Our best advice is to test, test, and test! You can download an app, populate data, and examine the results to see how your view of the evidence compares to your actual evidence. This practice will enable you to understand how updates change the artifacts, how evidence locations change, and how to manually extract artifacts that your tools are missing. Additionally, reverse-engineering an app and analyzing its code will help you to identify where the data is stored and how it is stored.

Most applications do not require a data plan for use; they can fully function via a Wi-Fi network, which means that apps can still function if a person travels to a region in which their device would not usually work. For example, when I travel, I rely on Skype, Viber, and WhatsApp to call and text family and friends. To use these apps, all that is required is that my smartphone is connected to Wi-Fi.

We have already addressed some third-party application extraction and analysis tips in this book. In addition to this, we discussed the files that need to be examined to understand and analyze application data in Chapter 5, *iOS Data Analysis and Recovery*; Chapter 10, *Android Data Analysis and Recovery*; Chapter 11, *Android App Analysis, Malware, and Reverse Engineering*; and Chapter 12, *Windows Phone Forensics*. This chapter will dive deeper into the applications and relevant files and will prepare you for the analysis of these artifacts. Each application has a purpose. Most tools provide support for the most popular application in each category. The rest is up to you. A quick look at the applications presented by the Oxygen Forensic Detective tool is shown in the following screenshot. As expected, these are not all of the applications that are present on the device; rather, these are just the ones that the tool knows how to parse:

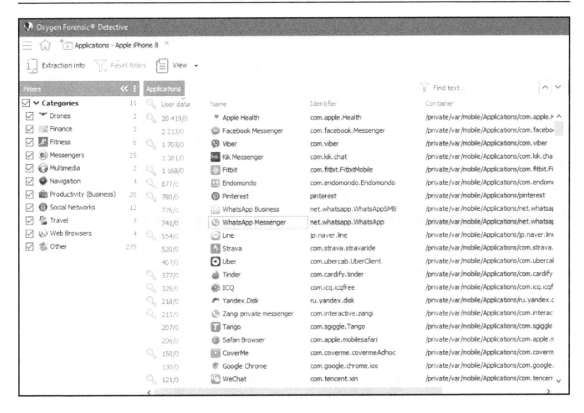

Example of applications parsed by Oxygen Forensic Detective on an Apple device

In the next section, we will analyze some of the widely used chat applications.

Chat applications

Chat applications are among the most common applications on the market. These applications provide users with the ability to chat or call outside the standard services offered by the network service provider. These apps may often be more secure compared to other apps. By secure, we mean that the apps may offer encryption, private profiles, private group chats, and more. Additionally, these apps enable the user to message or call others without the need for a data plan, as Wi-Fi provides all of the access that they need. Facebook Messenger, WhatsApp, Skype, Tango, and Snapchat are some of the more popular applications.

Parsing artifacts from chat applications is not always simple. Often, multiple tools and methods will be required to extract all of the data within them. Commercial tools may only parse a portion of the data, forcing you to learn how to examine and recover all data or miss evidence. In the following screenshot, Oxygen Forensic Detective is being used to parse chat messages from Tango on an Android device. Note that the message does not show the image in the table. However, this image can be *pieced* back into the message (notice the screenshot that is shown with an arrow pointing to the message to which it belongs), to provide an overall picture of what was being shared in a conversation. This was a manual process and was not performed by the tool:

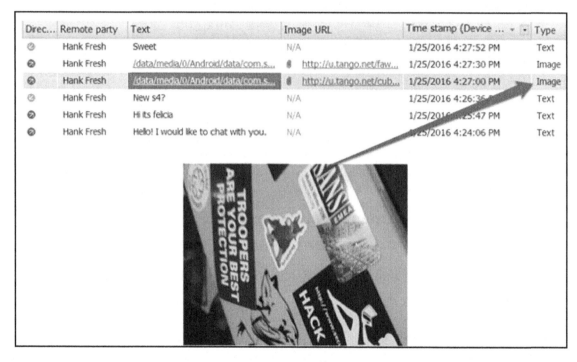

An example of piecing application chat logs back together

Next, we will take a look at GPS apps.

GPS applications

Most users branch out from their standard phone apps for GPS support. This includes getting directions to locations and obtaining maps for areas of interest. Common GPS applications include Waze and Google Maps. Waze goes beyond just providing directions, as it also alerts the user to road hazards, traffic, and police officers that are to be found along the route they are driving:

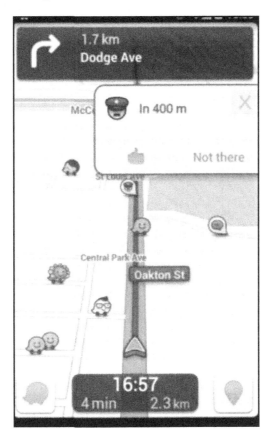

The Waze application

Other applications that store location information include Twitter, Instagram, Facebook, and Foursquare. These applications enable a user to alert friends and followers to their location when they create a post or share an image or video. All of these transactions are tracked within the app. Understanding this is key to uncovering additional artifacts that are not reported by your forensic tool.

When examining location information from GPS applications, it is best to assume that you need to manually examine the databases and preference files that are associated with that application. We recommend using your forensic tool to triage the data on the device and then dive deeply into the artifacts, which will be discussed later in this chapter. An example of Waze being parsed by UFED Physical Analyzer can be found in the following screenshot. Here, we can see that the user had 5 favorite locations, 74 mapped locations, and 70 recent directions. All of this information must be manually verified if it pertains to the investigation. This is because the tool cannot determine whether the user typed the address, whether it was suggested, or whether the user even traveled to that location. Proper skills are required by you to tie a user to a specific location, and this takes more than a forensic tool:

The Waze application in UFED Physical Analyzer

We will now analyze some of the popular secure messaging apps.

Secure applications

If data is secure and self-destructing, did it ever even exist? Ignore the claims of data retention and hunt for that data, as these apps often make claims that are simply untrue. Although applications are designed with security in mind, updates are released quickly and quality assurance checks may not be strong enough to catch everything. On occasion, you will find an app with an encrypted or non-existent database, but the file includes a journal, write-ahead logs, or shared memory files that contain portions of chats that were supposed to be encrypted. In addition to this, the user can save media files that are shared, take screenshots of conversations, and do much more. Often, you may uncover the images, audio, and video files that were shared and supposed to be encrypted.

Some popular secure messaging applications include Telegram, Wickr, and Signal. Some of these are encrypted, where nothing is recoverable. However, this all depends on the device, the OS running on the smartphone, and the version of the app. The security level of these apps is publicly advertised, but again, take this with a grain of salt. You should always assume that there could be a vulnerability in the app that may provide you with access forensically. Dig for this evidence!

Financial applications

Applications that utilize financial information, such as credit card information and personal banking, are required to be encrypted and secure. iOS devices will not acquire these apps without an Apple ID and password. Even if you have the user's Apple ID and password, the data extracted should still be encrypted. Some examples of financial applications include Google Pay, Microsoft Wallet, PayPal, Apple Pay, and in-app purchases. When you examine a device, you may see that the app was installed with the associated application metadata, but account information and transactions will not be accessible.

Social networking applications

Commercial support for social networking applications is strong as they are the most popular apps downloaded from app stores. These applications allow users to make posts, share locations, chat publicly and privately, and essentially catalog their lives. Common social networking applications include Facebook, Twitter, and Instagram. Often, users will enable one app, such as Instagram, to have access to Facebook and Twitter so that posting is seamless. Hence, when examining devices, the user may find multiple copies of the same file or conversation due to the sharing that takes place between apps.

When examining these apps with commercial tools, it is common for chats and contacts to be parsed, meaning that other data may be overlooked. Again, this means you must look at the data dump to ensure that nothing is missed. As an example, we are going to take a look at Twitter. This application stores a lot of information that may require more than one tool to parse. Additionally, the user may have to manually examine the database files to ensure that all artifacts have been recovered.

Let's take a look at what the tool was able to extract. As stated several times in this book, start with what the tool is telling you is installed, and then formulate keywords and methods to dig deep into the filesystem. We can see the user account information for Twitter, as well as the file path where this data is being extracted, in the following screenshot:

ARTIFACT INFORMATION

User ID	767674047173918720
User Name	**oskulkin**
Profile Created Date/Time	**8/22/2016 10:45:30 AM** ⏱
Description	**#DFIR professional. #ThreatIntel enthusiast. Opinions are my own.I [tab]MJjDFIRXXIXMJ j ThreatIntelXXI XXIM**
Web URL	**https://t.co/jhNd2msB3f**
Followers	**658**
Friends	**207**
Statuses	**309**
Image URL	**https://pbs.twimg.com/ profile_images/1218460619764064257/ BaefFcqO_normal.jpg**
Friend Metadata Updated Date/Time	**1/19/2020 11:07:23 AM** ⏱
Header URL	**https://pbs.twimg.com/ profile_banners/767674047173918720/1 579338626**

EVIDENCE INFORMATION

Source	**samsung SM-J710F Full Image - MMCBLK0.raw - Partition 24 (EXT-family, 11.24 GB)\data\com.twitter.android \databases\767674047173918720-58.db**
Recovery Method	**Parsing**
Deleted source	
Location	**Table: users(_id: 1)**
Evidence number	**samsung SM-J710F Full Image - MMCBLK0.raw**

Twitter as parsed by Magnet AXIOM

The next logical step is to view what the tool can tell you about the application and how it was used. Magnet AXIOM provided the following information for Twitter account usage. Note that both public tweets and private messages (DMs) are recovered:

Twitter Direct Messages	137
Twitter Tweets	179
Twitter Users	1,256

Twitter usage by Magnet AXIOM

After examining what was parsed by the tool, the database files should be examined to ensure that nothing was missed. This is not always simple, as each account and function may have a unique database. By function, we mean that contacts may be stored in one database while chats and account information are stored in another. Once you become more familiar with common applications, you will know where to look first.

In the following screenshot, we can see all of the databases that are associated with Twitter. Again, start with what you know and dig deeper:

0-scribe.db	File	.db	16,384	1/19/2020 9:29:43 AM	1/19/2020 9:29:43 AM	1/19/2020 3:34:39 PM
0-scribe.db-journal	File	.db-journal	16,928	1/19/2020 9:29:43 AM	1/19/2020 9:29:43 AM	1/19/2020 9:32:27 AM
global.db	File	.db	368,640	1/19/2020 9:29:44 AM	1/19/2020 9:29:44 AM	1/19/2020 11:07:17 AM
global.db-journal	File	.db-journal	12,824	1/19/2020 9:29:44 AM	1/19/2020 9:29:44 AM	1/19/2020 9:32:00 AM
0-58.db	File	.db	454,656	1/19/2020 9:29:44 AM	1/19/2020 9:29:44 AM	1/19/2020 9:29:45 AM
0-58.db-journal	File	.db-journal	8,720	1/19/2020 9:29:44 AM	1/19/2020 9:29:44 AM	1/19/2020 9:29:45 AM
767674047173918720-lru_key_value.db	File	.db	28,672	1/19/2020 9:31:59 AM	1/19/2020 9:31:59 AM	1/20/2020 6:43:51 AM
767674047173918720-lru_key_value.db-journal	File	.db-journal	21,032	1/19/2020 9:31:59 AM	1/19/2020 9:31:59 AM	1/19/2020 11:07:10 AM
767674047173918720-scribe.db	File	.db	24,576	1/19/2020 9:31:59 AM	1/19/2020 9:31:59 AM	1/20/2020 7:35:38 AM
767674047173918720-scribe.db-journal	File	.db-journal	53,864	1/19/2020 9:31:59 AM	1/19/2020 9:31:59 AM	1/20/2020 7:35:38 AM
767674047173918720-58.db	File	.db	1,814,528	1/19/2020 9:31:59 AM	1/19/2020 9:31:59 AM	1/20/2020 4:13:07 AM
767674047173918720-58.db-journal	File	.db-journal	185,192	1/19/2020 9:31:59 AM	1/19/2020 9:31:59 AM	1/19/2020 11:07:23 AM
767674047173918720-drafts.db	File	.db	28,672	1/19/2020 9:32:00 AM	1/19/2020 9:32:00 AM	1/19/2020 9:32:00 AM
767674047173918720-drafts.db-journal	File	.db-journal	8,720	1/19/2020 9:32:00 AM	1/19/2020 9:32:00 AM	1/19/2020 9:32:00 AM
767674047173918720-dm.db	File	.db	20,480	1/19/2020 9:32:03 AM	1/19/2020 9:32:03 AM	1/19/2020 9:32:03 AM
767674047173918720-dm.db-journal	File	.db-journal	12,824	1/19/2020 9:32:03 AM	1/19/2020 9:32:03 AM	1/19/2020 9:32:03 AM

Twitter databases containing user activity

Each database may contain unique data that can be parsed for additional artifacts. These applications also contain unique `user_id` values, which can be used as keywords to search for other devices with traces of communication within an investigation.

Custom queries can be written to parse Twitter databases of interest. A good example of how to do this is shown as follows. This query is specific to parsing Twitter contacts:

```
SELECT _id AS "Index",
user_id AS "User ID",
username AS "Username",
name AS "Name",
datetime (profile_created/1000,'UNIXEPOCH','localtime') AS "Profile
Created",
description AS "Twitter Description",
web_url AS "Website URL",
location AS "Location",
followers AS "Followers",
friends AS "Following",
users.statuses AS "Number of Tweets",
image_url AS "Profile Image URL",
datetime (updated/1000,'UNIXEPOCH','localtime') AS "Profile Updated"
FROM users
```

So far, we have looked at various kinds of third-party apps and how tools can aid an investigator in extracting the data. We will now look at some of the fundamental concepts that will help an investigator while analyzing the data.

Encoding versus encryption

The terms *encoding* and *encryption* are used so frequently when discussing applications and smartphone data that they are often confused. Encoding is essentially the process of obfuscating a message or piece of information to appear as raw code. In some cases, the goal of encoding is to make the data unrecognizable to the computer or the user. In reality, the primary goal of encoding is to transform the input into a different format using a publicly available scheme. In other words, anyone can easily decode an encoded value. Encryption, however, transforms the data using a key to keep its content confidential. So, encrypted text can only be reversed if you have the key.

Most applications claim that they encrypt data or that the data is never saved to disk. While this is true for some, most are simply encoded. Encoding options can vary, but the most common option for smartphone data is Base64. Messaging apps often rely on Base64 encoding to make the data appear to be hidden or *safe*. A common artifact of Base64 is the padding of the data with = when the encoded bytes are not divisible by three.

A few years ago, Oxygen Forensics and Autopsy were two of the few tools that supported the decoding of Base64 payloads from applications derived from smartphones. For these tools to parse the data, they must support the application containing the encoding. Currently, MSAB, UFED Physical Analyzer, and Magnet IEF provide Base64 decoding support.

An example of Base64-encoded messages is shown in the following screenshot. This data is from the Tango chat application:

Base64-encoded Tango messages

Encryption is a bit more difficult as the app itself may not even provide access to the encrypted data. For example, you may find that the database directory or the cells containing the encrypted data are simply empty. Occasionally, you will have access to the encrypted blobs within the databases, but this data cannot always be decrypted. Again, when you face encrypted data, look elsewhere. Have you examined the journal and write-ahead logs? Have you examined the cache and media directories? Have you examined the SD card? These are common questions you will often have to ask yourself to ensure that you are not relying on your forensic tools too much and that you are covering your bases to ensure nothing is overlooked. As we've explained, start with what you know. We know that the cache and database directories store user data, so this is a great place to start your manual examination, as you can see in the following screenshot:

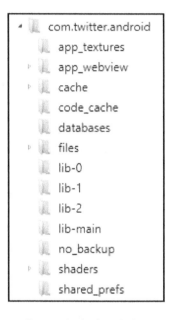

Data storage locations for applications

In the following sections, we will cover how applications store their data within the device and the significance of various types of storage options.

iOS, Android, and Windows Phone application data storage

Almost all applications rely on SQLite for data storage. These databases can be stored internally on the device or the SD card for relevant phones. When SQLite is used, temporary memory files are commonly associated with each database to make SQLite more efficient. These files are **rollback journals (JOURNAL)**, **Write-Ahead Logs (WAL)** and **Shared Memory (SHM)** files. These files may contain data that is not present in the SQLite database. We can see several WAL and SHM files associated with various WhatsApp database files in the following screenshot:

An SHM file and WAL example

In addition to SQLite databases, other devices rely on Plist, XML, JSON, and DAT files for application data storage, account data storage, purchase information, and user preferences. These files will be discussed in the Android, iOS, and Windows Phone sections of this chapter.

iOS applications

Apple relies on SQLite and Plist as common locations for application data storage. On occasion, JSON files will be used for application data. Examining applications recovered from an iOS device can be overwhelming. We suggest you start with what you know and what your tool is telling you. Examine the **Installed Applications** listed by your tool of choice. From here, go directly to the applications directory and ensure that nothing is being overlooked. When a user deletes an app, the databases often remain and the link to the installed application is simply broken. Examining all areas of the iOS device will prevent you from missing data:

Installed applications on an iPhone

After examining the installed applications, search the `Library` and `Documents` directories for any relevant Plist files that may contain application artifacts. Finally, examine the `Media` directory on the iPhone as well as the one associated with the app to recover additional artifacts, such as shared photos, videos, audio files, and profile pictures. In the following screenshot, we are examining the `Media` directory associated with the WhatsApp application:

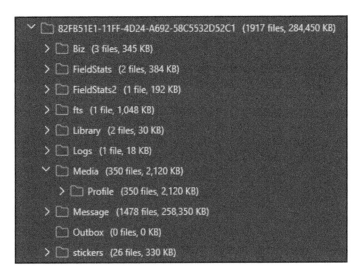

Application data on an iPhone

We will now take a look at data storage in Android applications.

Android applications

Android devices rely heavily on SQLite for application storage. The preference files for each application are often in the DAT or XML file formats. More so than an iOS device, examining applications on an Android device may be one of the most tedious tasks. This is due to the various locations where data may be stored. The best place to start is with a tool that will provide a listing of what is installed on the device. Next, go to the subdirectories off of the `/Root` directory. Remember, these applications may possess unique names and may be difficult to locate.

You may have to research the application to gain a better understanding of the filenames that are associated with each of them. The following screenshot is an example of application directories on an Android device:

Application data on an Android device

Each of these application directories will contain a lot of data to examine. We recommend starting with the Databases and Cache directories and then expanding your analysis to other locations on the device. The next locations to examine include the Media and Cache partitions. If the data appears to be missing or is claimed to have been deleted, do not forget to examine the Downloads directory on the device and SD card.

Application data can exist in several locations in the Media directories. Using a tool, such as UFED Physical Analyzer, which provides keyword-searching capabilities spanning beyond parsed items, will really help to locate artifacts pertaining to specific applications. We are looking at the large amount of data stored in the Media directory on an Android device in the following screenshot. This data is unique from what is stored in the application directories that were discussed previously. Each location needs to be thoroughly examined to ensure that nothing is missed. It is important that you take what you learned in previous chapters to analyze Android application data:

Unique application data in the Media directory

We will now look at apps installed on Windows Phone and their acquisition.

Windows Phone applications

Applications found on Windows Phones are no different from those found on iOS and Android devices. SQLite is the most common format used for data storage. However, not all devices allow for SQLite files to be stored internally on the phone. For these devices, all application data will be found on the SD card. Some may view this as lucky because it saves us from having to examine several locations on the device, but the SD card and the applications themselves may be encrypted.

Where possible, it is best to remove the SD card and acquire it using a forensic tool. When this is not possible, the next best method would be to try to acquire the SD card through the phone using a forensic tool. Again, this will often result in missed data. By the way of a final effort, live analysis can be completed by mounting the device and using Windows Explorer to view the applications stored on the device and SD card, as discussed in `Chapter 12`, *Windows Phone Forensics*.

Forensic methods used to extract third-party application data

Almost all commercial tools will attempt to support the extraction of third-party applications. We recommend that you test your tools thoroughly and often, if you rely on tool output for your investigative results. This is because the apps are updated so frequently that it is nearly impossible for the tools not to miss something. You must learn about the applications, how they work, and how the devices store data for each app. We strongly recommend that you use your tool to triage the case and then dive into the data to manually extract anything that the tools miss. Make sure that you only include factual data in your forensic report and not everything that the tools parse, as the tools cannot decipher the difference between a device and human creation. Only a trained examiner can do this with confidence.

Commercial tools

As you have seen in this book, there are many tools that can handle the job of smartphone forensics. However, there are a few that really shine when it comes to parsing application data. Magnet AXIOM, Oxygen Forensic Detective, and UFED Physical Analyzer are a few that do a good job of recovering data from the application categories discussed in this chapter. We will take a quick look at how to leverage each of these tools to parse application data. Keep in mind that these tools will not find every application and will not parse all data for applications.

Oxygen Forensic Detective

Oxygen Forensic Detective can be used to examine application data. For this example, we are assuming that acquisition is complete and we are simply attempting to analyze the data. Note that Oxygen is capable of acquiring and analyzing smartphones. In this example, we acquired the device with Cellebrite UFED and analyzed it with Oxygen. To load a data dump of a device and examine its application artifacts, perform the following steps:

1. Launch Oxygen Forensic Detective.
2. Select the **Import File** option and choose your image. Multiple image formats are supported for ingestion into Oxygen.
3. After parsing is complete, start examining the parsed applications:

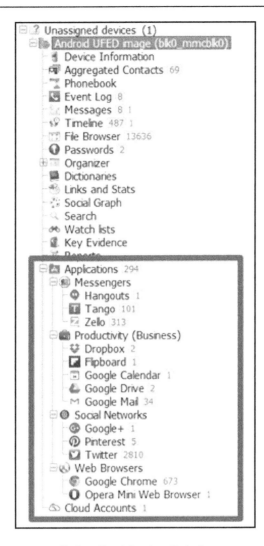

The Oxygen Forensic Detective application view

4. Next, start examining applications of interest by clicking on the application and examining all of the associated files.

5. Once you select the application, you will be presented with the data that was parsed and the full file path from where the data was extracted. Use this path to manually verify the findings. We are looking at the Pinterest application in the following screenshot. Note how the container, file, and table of interest are provided and hyperlinked for the user. The tool is even encouraging you to dig deeper and verify the findings:

Oxygen Detective Pinterest example

Oxygen Detective has built-in features for keyword searching, bookmarking, and reporting. In addition, the SQLite Database and Plist Viewer will provide you with a method for examining relevant application data

6. Report all account information, chats, messages, locations, and any other data of interest, as this provides relevance to your investigation.

The next tool that we will be looking at is Magnet AXIOM.

Magnet AXIOM

Magnet AXIOM has been known as one of the leaders in internet and application parsing for digital media. It is just as strong with mobile devices. Again, one tool cannot do the job, but AXIOM has proven to be the strongest and parses the most applications from Android, iOS, and Windows Phones. To use AXIOM to examine application artifacts, perform the following steps:

1. Launch AXIOM, create a new case, and then select **MOBILE** (note that if **MOBILE** is grayed out, you need to obtain a license that provides mobile support from Magnet Forensics):

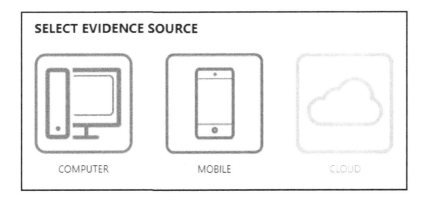

Selecting the evidence source

2. Select **LOAD EVIDENCE** and navigate to your image file. More than one image can be loaded and parsed at the same time.

3. Select **GO TO ARTIFACT DETAILS** and determine what you want to parse. We recommend selecting all of the apps:

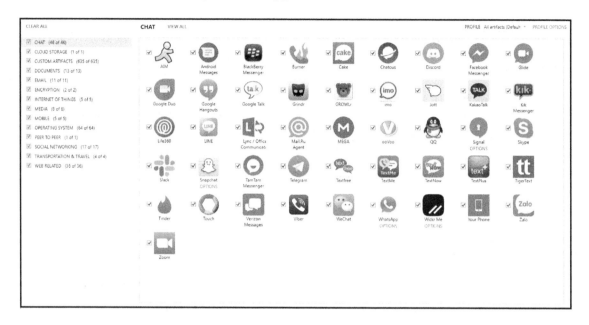

Magnet AXIOM supported artifacts

4. Select **ANALYZE EVIDENCE**.

5. Once complete, you can use Artifacts:

WEB RELATED	26,890
CHAT	**129,310**
Facebook Messenger Groups	2
Facebook Messenger Messages	1
iOS iMessage/SMS/MMS	16,222
iOS Telegram Channel Chats	224
iOS Telegram Chats	210
iOS Telegram Messages	95,738
iOS Telegram Users	8,780
iOS WhatsApp Chats	176
iOS WhatsApp Contacts	405
iOS WhatsApp Groups	10
iOS WhatsApp Messages	7,426
Textfree Attachments	112
Textfree Messages / Calls	4
SOCIAL NETWORKING	**3,295**
MEDIA	**43,947**

Application Artifacts in Magnet AXIOM

The first step in the examination is to review what has been parsed by AXIOM. In the preceding screenshot, we can see that Telegram was parsed. Start your examination in the most relevant location. For example, if you are looking for **Telegram Chats**, go right to that location and start examining the artifacts. Note that **Messages** and **Chats** are pulled into two different categories. This is common when private messaging is used. All relevant application containers should be examined. Additionally, AXIOM provides the full file path from which the data was recovered. Use another tool to navigate to this file for verification and manual examination.

AXIOM also provides logical keyword search (it will search what it can parse and nothing else), bookmarking, and reporting. Make sure that you only report factual application artifacts and incorporate these into your final forensic report.

UFED Physical Analyzer

Physical Analyzer is one of the most well-known mobile forensic tools on the market. This tool is one of the best platforms to manually conduct an examination in addition to leveraging the data parsed by the tool. For application analysis, Physical Analyzer is good at parsing chats and contacts for each supported application. For data that is not parsed, Physical Analyzer provides an analytical platform that enables the user to browse the filesystem to uncover additional artifacts. Keyword searching is robust in this tool and is capable of searching raw hex as well as parsed data. In addition, a SQLite viewer is included.

To conduct a forensic examination of application data in Physical Analyzer, perform the following steps to get started:

1. Launch Physical Analyzer by double-clicking on the UFED shortcut image file or by double-clicking the tool icon.
2. Load the image file and wait until parsing completes.
3. Examine the parsed artifacts, as shown in the following screenshot:

Data parsed by Physical Analyzer

We recommend examining what is parsed and referring to the hyperlink of where the data is being extracted. Navigate to this path and then examine the entire application directory.

To find the application directory, leverage built-in keyword searching capabilities to aid in the investigation. Remember, you may have to conduct research to determine the filenames associated with the app if this is not apparent.

Open source/free tools

For those on a budget, it is possible to examine application data from smartphones using open source solutions and cheap tools. These solutions are more difficult to use, and they are often not the answer for those new to forensics who need the assistance of a tool in data extraction and analysis. Examining application data is tedious, and if you do not know where to look, you will likely need to spend some money to get a head start. Tools such as Andriller can be purchased for around $500. While this is not free, it's also not $10,000, which is what some of the other commercial tools cost. In the following section, we will cover a few of our favorite tools that are useful in parsing application data from smartphones.

Working with Autopsy

Autopsy is one of the best tools for filesystem examinations. Unfortunately, iOS parsing is not provided in Autopsy, but it still may be useful for filesystem images. Autopsy can be downloaded from `http://sleuthkit.org/autopsy/`. When using Autopsy, the Android Analyzer module will parse some application data from the device. Let's look at how to use Autopsy for Android image analysis.

To use Autopsy, download the software and install it on a Windows machine and follow these instructions. Make sure that you are always using the latest version:

1. Launch Autopsy.
2. Create a new case:

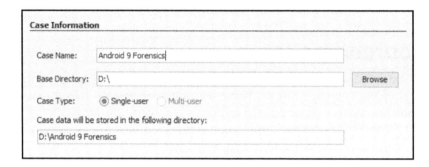

Autopsy case creation

3. Select **Next** and then click on **Finish**.
4. Navigate to your image file and select **Next**.
5. Select the modules that you wish to run. **Keyword Search** and **Android Analyzer** will be the most fruitful for an Android device:

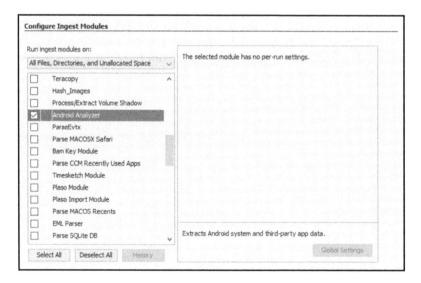

Autopsy module selection

Ingest Modules are tools built into Autopsy that can be run when the case has started or at any point afterward. The default modules in this version of Autopsy are as follows:

- **Recent Activity**: This extracts recent user activity such as web browsing, recently used documents, and installed programs.
- **Hash Lookup**: This identifies known and notable files using supplied hash databases, such as a standard NSRL database. It also allows importing custom hash databases.
- **File Type Identification**: This matches file types based on binary signatures.
- **Archive Extractor**: This extracts archive files (`.zip`, `.rar`, `.arj`, `.7z`, `.gzip`, `.bzip2`, and `.tar`). It automatically extracts these file types and puts their contents into the directory tree.
- **EXIF Parser**: This ingests JPEG files and retrieves their EXIF metadata.
- **Keyword Search**: This performs file indexing and periodic search using keywords and regular expressions in lists. It allows the loading of custom keywords/lists.
- **Email Parser**: This module detects and parses `mbox` and `pst/ost` files and populates email artifacts in the blackboard.
- **Extension Mismatch Detector**: These are flag files that have a non-standard extension based on their file types.
- **E01 Verifier**: This validates the integrity of E01 files.
- **Android Analyzer**: This extracts Android system and third-party app data.
- **Interesting Files Identifier**: This identifies interesting items, as defined.

Also, you can install third-party modules for Autopsy. Some of them are really useful for Android forensics. A good example is Parse SQLite DB by Mark McKinnon. This module parses any SQLite database it finds and imports it into the extracted content. This and other modules can be downloaded from this GitHub: `https://github.com/markmckinnon/Autopsy-Plugins`

Autopsy provides access to filesystem data faster than any commercial or open source tool available. Knowing where to go from there is the hard part. So, again, start with anything that is in the extracted content and then dive into the filesystem to examine the files discussed in this book and any relevant application data, as shown in the following screenshot:

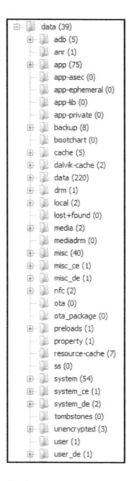

Browsing the filesystem with Autopsy

Once you have identified applications of interest, start with what is parsed and then examine the relevant database, cache, and preference files. Autopsy includes basic SQLite Viewer that can be used for triage purposes. If you need to run queries, we recommend using DB Browser for SQLite or browsers included in commercial products, for example, Belkasoft Evidence Center, especially if you want to analyze data from free lists and unallocated space.

Android Analyzer can decode some artifacts automatically, for example, contacts, calls, and SMS. The following screenshot shows the results of the decoded SMS messages:

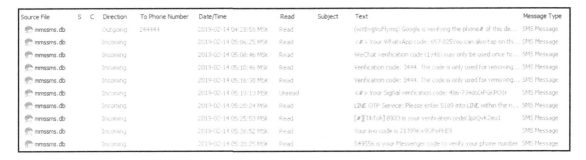

Source File	S	C	Direction	To Phone Number	Date/Time	Read	Subject	Text	Message Type
mmssms.db			Outgoing	244444	2019-02-14 04:28:59 MSK	Read		(wYBvgVoFlymq) Google is verifying the phone# of this de...	SMS Message
mmssms.db			Incoming		2019-02-14 05:06:25 MSK	Read		<#> Your WhatsApp code: 657-82SYou can also tap on thi...	SMS Message
mmssms.db			Incoming		2019-02-14 05:08:46 MSK	Read		WeChat verification code (1948) may only be used once to...	SMS Message
mmssms.db			Incoming		2019-02-14 05:10:46 MSK	Read		Verification code: 3444. The code is only used for removing...	SMS Message
mmssms.db			Incoming		2019-02-14 05:16:38 MSK	Read		Verification code: 3444. The code is only used for removing...	SMS Message
mmssms.db			Incoming		2019-02-14 05:19:13 MSK	Unread		<#> Your Signal verification code: 486-734doDiFGtPO1r	SMS Message
mmssms.db			Incoming		2019-02-14 05:20:24 MSK	Read		LINE OTP Service: Please enter 5189 into LINE within the n...	SMS Message
mmssms.db			Incoming		2019-02-14 05:25:53 MSK	Read		[#][TikTok] 8933 is your verification code/JpzQvk2eu1	SMS Message
mmssms.db			Incoming		2019-02-14 05:26:52 MSK	Read		Your imo code is 21399k+90FePKE9	SMS Message
mmssms.db			Incoming		2019-02-14 05:33:25 MSK	Read		549556 is your Messenger code to verify your phone number	SMS Message

SMS messages decoded by Autopsy

Now, we will be looking at some more methods of extracting data.

Other methods of extracting application data

One of the easiest ways to parse application data is to create custom SQLite queries and Python scripts to parse data of interest. We have discussed several suggestions and examples of queries and scripts throughout this book. Python is one of the best solutions because it is free and we have full access to its libraries. One thing to keep in mind is that our scripts have to be updated frequently to keep up with application updates. Also, make sure that your encoding schemas are correct to prevent application artifacts from being missed or not interpreted correctly.

In addition to Python scripts, free parsers that support application extraction already exist. WhatsApp Extract is a free tool for both Android and iOS that will extract WhatsApp application data from devices. Often, this free tool will extract more data than the commercial solutions, depending on the permissions the user allocated during installation. Others, such as Mari DeGrazia (`http://az4n6.blogspot.in/p/downloads.html`), Adrian Leong (`https://github.com/cheeky4n6monkey/4n6-scripts`), Sarah Edwards (`https://github.com/mac4n6`), and Alexis Brignoni (`https://github.com/abrignoni`) have developed scripts to parse applications, recover deleted data from SQLite free pages, decode `Base64`, and more. We recommend using what is already available before developing your own.

Summary

In this chapter, we learned about how to successfully parse and extract data from popular third-party apps. Many apps are not what they claim to be. Never trust what you read about apps, as quality assurance testing across apps is not consistent, and we have determined several vulnerabilities and security flaws over the years that provide us with methods of piecing application data back together. Also, application updates will change the way we need to look at the data found. Understanding each smartphone and how it stores application data is the first step toward successfully examining applications on smartphones. Knowing that updates may change data locations, encoding, and encryption, as well as how your tool functions, is one of the hardest concepts for examiners to grasp. It is your job to learn the capabilities of the application to uncover the most data from the mobile device.

Understanding how an application works is hard enough without having to consider how to extract artifacts. As you have read in this book, there are many ways to parse data from smartphones. One tool is never enough, and the reality is that mobile forensics can be expensive. We hope that we have provided you with a practical guide that teaches you how to acquire and analyze artifacts that are recovered from smartphones. Take what you've learned and apply it immediately to your methods to conduct mobile forensics or use it to make you more prepared in your next job. Remember that practice, testing, and training will make you better at your job and will help you to perfect the art of mobile forensics.

Other Books You May Enjoy

If you enjoyed this book, you may be interested in these other books by Packt:

Digital Forensics and Incident Response
Gerard Johansen

ISBN: 978-1-78728-868-3

- Create and deploy incident response capabilities within your organization
- Build a solid foundation for acquiring and handling suitable evidence for later analysis
- Analyze collected evidence and determine the root cause of a security incident
- Learn to integrate digital forensic techniques and procedures into the overall incident response process
- Integrate threat intelligence in digital evidence analysis
- Prepare written documentation for use internally or with external parties such as regulators or law enforcement agencies

Learning Python for Forensics
Preston Miller, Chapin Bryce

ISBN: 978-1-78328-523-5

- Discover how to perform Python script development
- Update yourself by learning the best practices in forensic programming
- Build scripts through an iterative design
- Explore the rapid development of specialized scripts
- Understand how to leverage forensic libraries developed by the community
- Design flexibly to accommodate present and future hurdles
- Conduct effective and efficient investigations through programmatic pre-analysis
- Discover how to transform raw data into customized reports and visualizations

Leave a review - let other readers know what you think

Please share your thoughts on this book with others by leaving a review on the site that you bought it from. If you purchased the book from Amazon, please leave us an honest review on this book's Amazon page. This is vital so that other potential readers can see and use your unbiased opinion to make purchasing decisions, we can understand what our customers think about our products, and our authors can see your feedback on the title that they have worked with Packt to create. It will only take a few minutes of your time, but is valuable to other potential customers, our authors, and Packt. Thank you!

Index

reliable 28

S

Made in the USA
Las Vegas, NV
07 October 2021